*It should prove a cherished visitor in every home where sorrow knocks, and where does it not?
— Dr. Robert Gordis
Adjunct Professor of Religion
Columbia University

A Treasury of Comfort
by Sidney Greenberg

This volume is designed primarily to meet the needs of those who find themselves in the valley of the shadow. It should prove a trustworthy companion which offers the consolation and guidance of psalmist and prophet, poet and philosopher, sage and scientist, and even the humble folk whose only claim to a hearing is their own heroic encounter with grief.

It brings together the distilled wisdom of the Jewish heritage as it speaks in prose and verse through its texts and representatives. Because the influence of Judaism has been diffused throughout western culture and thought, its basic attitudes and teachings have found expression in the lives and writings of non-Jews as well. All selections have been chosen with a view to their power to inspire and instruct.

The time to develop a mature philosophy toward death is before, not after, it strikes. It is therefore of crucial significance that we develop an intelligent understanding of death, a courageous acceptance of life, a triumphant faith by which to live with dignity.

ABOUT THE EDITOR

Sidney Greenberg, editor of A Treasury of Comfort, has edited and authored several books, each of which was designed to help people live more abundantly, more creatively, more heroically.

A Treasury of Comfort, his first anthology, is perhaps his best known. His other anthologies include A Modern Treasury of Jewish Thoughts, A Treasury of the Art of Living, and The Bar Mitzvah Companion. He has authored two volumes of sermons — Adding Life to our Years and Finding Ourselves. In addition, his sermons have been published in annual collections of best Jewish sermons. He has also contributed articles to a variety of periodicals and he has served on the editorial boards of several magazines.

Born in New York City, Sidney Greenberg received his A.B. degree at Yeshiva University and he was ordained at the Jewish Theological Seminary in 1942. The Seminary also awarded him the Degree of Doctor of Hebrew Literature in 1947.

Since his ordination he has served continuously as the Rabbi of Temple Sinai in Philadelphia. During this period he took a leave of absence to serve as chaplain with the United States Air Force.

A Treasury of Comfort has enjoyed wide acclaim among people of every creed because of its universal message in the face of a universal problem — how to confront the inevitability of death with fortitude and with faith.

A
TREASURY
OF
COMFORT

EDITED BY

SIDNEY GREENBERG

W *Published by*
Melvin Powers
ILSHIRE BOOK COMPANY
12015 Sherman Road
No. Hollywood, California 91605
Telephone: (213) 875-1711 / (818) 983-1105

The Editor wishes to make acknowledgment to the following for permission to quote the designated items (number before hyphen indicates page, after hyphen, position on page) :

Abingdon-Cokesbury, 75-2, from *Sunset to Dawn* by Leslie R. Smith, copyright 1944 by Whitmore and Stone; 78-1, *The Glory of God* by Georgia Harkness, copyright 1943 by Whitmore and Stone; Abingdon-Cokesbury Press and The Pilgrim Press, 257-2; Rabbi Morris Adler, Detroit, Mich., 44-3, 133-2, 202-3; Brandt and Brandt, 35-2, from *Collected Poems* pub. by Oxford Univ. Press, copyright 1916 by Conrad Aiken; The American Ethical Union, 248-2; Association Press, 215-2; Atlantic Monthly, 14-5, 39-1; Reuben Avinoam, 82-1; Francis H. Bangs, 4-3; Behrman's Jewish Book House, 156-1, from *Anthology of Modern Jewish Poetry;* Rabbi Louis Beinstock, Temple Sholom, Chicago, Ill., 127-2, 133-1, 126-1; Ernest Benn, Ltd., 244-3; Bloch Pub. Co., 25-1, from *A Book of Jewish Thoughts;* Bobbs Merrill, 166-1, 247-2; Rabbi Ben Zion Bokser, Forest Hills, N. Y., 185-2; Margaret E. Bruner and Kaleidograph Press, 72-3, 72-4, 9-3, 23-1; Margaret E. Bruner and Indianapolis Sunday Star, 10-4, 14-3; Central Conference of American Rabbis, 100-3, 209-4, 238-3; Chicago Sun-Times, 152-2, from *God Called Him* by James J. Metcalfe; Thomas Curtis Clark, 261-4, 271-2; Rabbi Beryl D. Cohon, Brookline, Mass., 13-2, 227-3, 229-1; Bob Considine, 232-1; Thomas Y. Crowell Co., 192-1; Dept. for the Commemoration of the Fallen, Ministry of Defense, Israel, 30-3, 170-2, 230-1; Detroit News, 62-1, from Verses I Like by Winnie Lynch Rockett; Doubleday & Co., 42-4, from *We Bereaved* by Helen Keller, 80-2, 125-2, 161-1, 162-1, 207-1, 255-1, from *When Sorrow Comes* by Grace Perkins Oursler and April Armstrong, 130-2, 136-1, 142-1, 201-2, from *Modern Parables* by Fulton Oursler; E. P. Dutton & Co., 113-1, from *The Wall of Weeping* by Edmund Fleg, 9-1, 172-2, from *The Light of the World* by Phillips Brooks, 23-3, from *Harp of My Heart* by Hugh Robert Orr, 29-2, from *Death and General Putnam* by Arthur Guiterman, 112-1, 175-4, from *The Best-Loved Poems of the American People* by Hazel Felleman, 98-1, from *An Airman's Letter to His Mother;* Evangelical Pub., 101-3; Farrar, Strauss & Young, 145-1 from *Victory in My Hands* by Harold Russell; Forward Movement Pub., 63-2, 107-2; Free Thought Press Assoc., 157-1; Funk & Wagnalls Co., 172-1, from *Inspiration and Ideals* by Grenville Kleiser; Rabbi R. B. Gittlesohn, Temple Israel, Boston, Mass., 233-1; Harcourt, Brace & Co., 250-2, from *Basic Judaism* by Milton Steinberg, copyright 1950; Harper & Bros., 208-2, from *The Secret of Victorious Living* by H. E. Fosdick, 71-3, 150-1, 181-1, from *Death Be Not Proud* by John Gunther, 54-1, 62-3, 189-1, 249-2, from *Masterpieces of Religious Verse* by J. D. Morrison, 105-4, from *The Funeral Encyclopedia* by Charles L. Wallis, 160-1; Sarah Henderson Hay, 260-3; Houghton, Mifflin & Co., 254-3; Jewish Agency for Palestine, 194-3; The Jewish Publication Society, 47-5, from *The Spirit Returneth* by Selma Stern, 115-2, from *Mesillat Yesharim* by Moses Luzatto, 94-5, from *Kiddush Ha-Shem* by Sholem

To

HILDA

and our three daughters

SHIRA BETH, REENA KEREN

AND ADENA JOY

IN APPRECIATION

Elsewhere are listed the names of those publishers, authors and individuals whose generosity made this book possible, and who placed me deeply in their debt. In addition, I am intensely grateful to my dear wife and helpmate upon whose counsel and sympathetic understanding I depended heavily and often. Her gracious assumption of the added duties, domestic and communal, occasioned by my preoccupation with this work in the midst of an already crowded rabbinate, made it possible for me to devote the necessary energies to the completion of this work.

Dr. Simon Greenberg, provost of the Jewish Theological Seminary of America, and Rabbi Morris Adler of Detroit, Michigan, were exceedingly kind to read the manuscript and to make many valuable suggestions. The book is a better one for their attention.

My very good friend, Mr. Marty Josephs, cannot be thanked too warmly. It was his persistent urging which encouraged me to undertake the work and kept me from abandoning it in moments when my own enthusiasm waned. His enormous experience in the field of publishing was unselfishly placed at my disposal and guided me through the complex machinery of book-making.

Only one who has compiled or written a book of this size can gauge adequately the staggering amount of typing and mechanical work involved. Almost all of the work in this instance was done voluntarily by Mrs. Albert Wanicur, whose kindness was matched only by her competence. This expression of warmest appreciation is meager recompense indeed for countless hours of cheerful labor.

Mrs. Herman Leff, the uncommonly efficient secretary of our congregation, was helpful in many ways—big and small. Her availability at all times for discussion and suggestions lightened my task considerably. My genuine gratitude is also extended to Mrs. William Eisenberg who was ever willing to contribute her effort to the book.

Lastly, I pay affectionate tribute to the good men and women of Temple Sinai whose grief spurred me on in this venture in the fervent hope that I could create some literary medium which would soften the shock of bereavement and offer the courage and the faith to carry on.

CONTENTS

INTRODUCTION

THE twentieth century enjoys many significant claims to distinction. Among these, none is more noteworthy than the impressive gains scored in the direction of lengthening the human life-span. Spectacular scientific discoveries in preventive as well as curative medicine, improved living conditions, the shortening of the working day and week—these are some of the more important factors which have added decades to the life expectancy of our generation. Optimistic forecasts for the future anticipate an even longer life-span for our children.

Notwithstanding these dramatic forward strides, death will not be denied. It will only be deferred. Each of us has an appointment with sorrow, "a rendezvous with death." None can hope for exemption from death's inexorable laws nor from the poignant sadness of parting from loved ones.

Despite its inevitability, the death of a dear one is often a deeply disturbing emotional experience. We are rarely, if ever, quite prepared for it. We read daily of the death of strangers, from time to time we hear of the passing of acquaintances. Our passion for life, however, is so strong that we cannot truly assimilate the thought that those we love are also heir to the common fate which awaits all with severe impartiality.

This is especially true when death comes to a child or to a young parent. The impact of such tragedy always finds us in a state of total emotional unpreparedness. The shock is compounded by its maddening untimeliness, by the bitter realization that there were so many unlived years of love and laughter, adventure and hope. We who live during these turbulent days of international strife must reckon seriously with the grievous prospect of countless young lives prematurely cut down by "man's inhumanity to man."

To be sure, sorrow does not strike all with equal intensity. The impact will vary according to the circumstances surrounding the death, the age of the departed, the intimacy of the relationship that prevailed and the inner resources of the survivor.

As a rabbi who is called upon quite regularly to minister to people in their bereavement, I have long felt the need for a volume which can bring strength and solace to the mourners. Well-meaning friends help by their very presence during the initial days of mourning but beyond that they usually are able to contribute little. Most believe that avoiding the subject of the grief is the healthiest procedure. Actually, the very reverse is true. Where sorrow is concerned, not repression but expression is the wholesome discipline. The emotional catharsis afforded by an opportunity to speak of the departed should be welcomed not shunned, yet one rarely hears any real therapeutic conversation in a home touched by sorrow. After the first few days immediately following the death, the flow of friends to the mourner's home usually subsides and soon stops altogether. The members of the family who were brought together by sorrow return to their respective homes. Now the full impact of the loneliness and the loss begins to be felt. How genuine is the need for help at this time! How numerous are the parasitic weeds that may now begin to flourish in the soil of sorrow!

This volume is designed primarily to meet the needs of those who find themselves in the valley of the shadow. It should prove a trustworthy companion which offers the consolation and guidance of psalmist and prophet, poet and philosopher, sage and scientist, and even the humble folk whose only claim to a hearing is their own heroic encounter with grief. It brings together the distilled wisdom of the Jewish heritage as it speaks through its texts and representatives. Because the influence of Judaism has been diffused throughout western culture and thought, its basic attitudes and teachings have found expression in the lives of writings of non-Jews as well. The editor has therefore not hesitated to include selections of non-Jewish authors where he felt that the views were in harmony with Jewish insight and doctrine. All selections have been chosen with a view to their power to inspire and instruct. It is the sincere hope of the editor that this volume may serve as a tunnel dug through the mountain of grief which opens into the green fields of revived hope and renewed faith in life's creative possibilities.

While the book is aimed especially at the mourner, its value is not restricted to the hour of bereavement. Realistically speaking, we are all potential mourners. The time to develop a mature philosophy toward death is before, not after, it strikes, just as one should learn to swim before one gets shipwrecked, not after. The analogy suffers in only one respect. Most of us will never be shipwrecked but the need for a sustaining outlook upon death and a reasonable knowledge of how to handle our grief is one which we shall all almost certainly experience. Moreover, we are frequently involved in the sorrows of others, and our own spiritual resources and insights can be of distinct service. It is therefore of crucial significance that we develop a mature understanding of death, a courageous acceptance of life, a triumphant faith by which to live with dignity and die without fear. If this book contributes however slightly to the achievement of such an outlook, the labors that went into its creation will have been very amply rewarded.

SIDNEY GREENBERG

Temple Sinai

Philadelphia, Pa.

August, 1954; Elul 5714

TIME—THE GENTLE HEALER

In the hour of bereavement we feel most acutely what Swift called "the sting of perishable things." At the moment of deep hurt it appears indeed that there is no balm for our gaping wounds. We tend to despair of ever regaining our emotional equilibrium.

At such a time we are scarcely amenable to solace. Words of comfort ring hollow in the dark night of sorrow. That is why an ancient sage counseled wisely: "Do not comfort thy friend when his deceased is still lying before him." Premature comfort can often be more harmful than no comfort because it seems to mock the hurt, to make light of our torment.

It is never too soon, however, to accept the reassuring thought that pain, no less than pleasure, is transient. A simple farmer was asked by a visitor from the city during a severe rainstorm whether he thought it would stop raining. He answered drily: "It usually does."

Nature rushes benevolently to our assistance when we have been hurt, whether in body or in spirit. If we do not despair, the healing process does restore us as it has healed other mourners from the beginning of time. To be sure, the scar may very well continue to throb sensitively when we experience emotional bad weather. The sense of loss may always remain with us; but the sharp pain subsides and we discover the way to a healthy readjustment to our new circumstances. The Psalmist wisely spoke of walking "through the valley of the shadow." No road of life can detour around the valley. By the same token, however, the valley is open on both sides. Having entered into it, we need not make of it our permanent dwelling place. After we have lingered there for a while, we can walk through it and out. With the Psalmist we can then affirm

1

gratefully out of the depths of our own experience: "Though weep-
ing tarries in the night, joy comes in the morning."

ISAIAH

Thy sun shall no more go down,
Neither shall thy moon withdraw itself;
For the Lord shall be thine everlasting light,
And the days of thy mourning shall be ended.

ANGEL OF PATIENCE
John Greenleaf Whittier

To weary hearts, to mourning homes,
God's meekest Angel gently comes:
No power has he to banish pain,
Or give us back our lost again;
And yet in tenderest love, our dear
And Heavenly Father sends him here.

There's quiet in that Angel's glance,
There's rest in his still countenance!
He mocks no grief with idle cheer,
Nor wounds with words the mourner's ear;
But ills and woes he may not cure
He kindly trains us to endure.

Angel of Patience! sent to calm
Our feverish brows with cooling palm;
To lay the storms of hope and fear,
And reconcile life's smile and tear;
The throbs of wounded pride to still,
And make our own our Father's will!

O thou who mournest on thy way,
With longings for the close of day;
He walks with thee, that Angel kind,

And gently whispers, "Be resigned;
Bear up, bear on, the end shall tell
The dear Lord ordereth all things well!"

IN THE NIGHT GOD SPEAKS
Moses Ibn Ezra (Translated by Emma Lazarus)

He speaks: "My son, yea, I will send thee aid,
Bend thou thy steps to me, be not afraid.
No nearer friend than I am, hast thou made,
Possess thy soul in patience one more night."

A PEAR TREE
Rachel (Translated from the Hebrew by the editor)

This is the conspiracy of Spring. . . .
A man awakens from sleep
and sees a pear tree flowering before his window.
Suddenly, the mountain of sorrow that lay upon
his heart
is shattered and is gone.

You understand: he could not persist
in grieving for his one blossom withered by
angry autumn's blast—
Since smiling Spring was bringing for his solace
a giant garland of flowers
To his very window.

William Makepeace Thackeray
To endure is greater than to dare.

WE SHOULD LEARN NOT TO GROW IMPATIENT
Joshua Loth Liebman

We should learn not to grow impatient with the slow healing
process of time. We should discipline ourselves to recognize that

there are many steps to be taken along the highway leading from sorrow to renewed serenity and that it is folly to attempt prematurely to telescope and compress these successive stages of recuperation into a miraculous cure. We should not demand of ourselves more than nature herself will permit. We should anticipate these stages in our emotional convalescence: unbearable pain, poignant grief, empty days, resistance to consolation, disinterestedness in life, gradually giving way under the healing sunlight of love, friendship, social challenge, to the new weaving of a pattern of action and the acceptance of the irresistible challenge of life.

PSALMS

Resign thyself unto the Lord, and wait patiently for Him. . . .

PATIENCE
Emma Lazarus

The passion of despair is quelled at last;
The cruel sense of undeserved wrong,
The wild self-pity, these are also past;
She knows not what may come, but she is strong;
She feels she hath not aught to lose nor gain,
Her patience is the essence of all pain. . . .

There is a deeper pathos in the mild
And settled sorrow of the quiet eyes.
Than in the tumults of the anguish wild,
That made her curse all things beneath the skies;
No question, no reproaches, no complaint,
Hers is the holy calm of some meek saint.

I NEVER KNEW A NIGHT SO BLACK
John Kendrick Bangs

I never knew a night so black
Light failed to follow on its track.
I never knew a storm so gray
It failed to have its clearing day.

I never knew such bleak despair
That there was not a rift, somewhere.
I never knew an hour so drear
Love could not fill it full of cheer!

ACCEPT THE JUDGMENT

Rachel (Translated from the Hebrew by the editor)

Accept the judgment, O humbled heart,
Accept the judgment this time, too,
Without struggle, without wrath.

High in the north, snow-covered fields
Conceal the grain ripening
Secretly, silently.

O humbled heart, bear your wintry fate
And be like those seeds
That wait for summer.

FROM "AUTUMN SONNETS #4"

Robert Nathan

It would be wiser, since we live in fear,
To use our sorrows to correct our ways.
If winter be the color of our days,
Then learn of winter to be still and clear.
The greener spring, the new and happy year
Is not for us but for the birds to praise;
It is the snow that over autumn lays
Its quiet hand that is our teacher here.
For see, it has its lesson for the soul:
Look how the tree with piety keeps fast
The bud and blossom hidden in the bole.
So bear the winter with its frosty blast,
And seek, beneath the season of our grief,
The spring unending and the waiting leaf.

SERVIUS SUPLICIUS

There is no grief which time does not lessen.

Elizabeth Barrett Browning

Thank God, bless God, all ye who suffer not
More grief than ye can weep for; . . . those tears will run
Soon in long rivers down the lifted face,
And leave the vision clear for stars and sun.

PSALMS

Who healeth the broken in heart,
And bindeth up their wounds.

Jeremiah

I will change their grief to gladness
I will console and cheer them after their sorrow.

FROM "TRANSIENCE"

Sarojini Naidu

Nay, do not grieve tho' life be full of sadness,
Dawn will not veil her splendor for your grief,
Nor spring deny their bright, appointed beauty
To lotus blossom and ashoka leaf.

Nay, do not pine, tho' life be dark with trouble,
Time will not pause or tarry on his way;
Today that seems so long, so strange, so bitter,
Will soon be some forgotten yesterday.

Nay, do not weep; new hopes, new dreams, new faces,
The unspent joy of all the unborn years,
Will prove your heart a traitor to its sorrow,
And make your eyes unfaithful to their tears.

Talmud

God says to man: "With thy very wounds I will heal thee."

PLINY THE YOUNGER

As a fresh wound shrinks from the hand of the surgeon, then gradually submits to and even calls for it; so a mind under the first impression of a misfortune shuns and rejects all comfort, but at length, if touched with tenderness, calmly and willingly resigns itself.

John Henry Newman

There are wounds of the spirit which never close, and are intended in God's mercy to bring us nearer to Him, and to prevent us leaving Him, by their very perpetuity. Such wounds, then, may almost be taken as a pledge, or at least as a ground for the humble trust, that God will give us the great gift of perseverance to the end. . . . This is how I comfort myself in my own great bereavements.

ENDURANCE

Elizabeth Akers Allen

How much the heart may bear and yet not break!
How much the flesh may suffer and not die!
I question much if any pain or ache
Of soul or body brings our end more nigh:
Death chooses his own time; till that is sworn,
All evil may be borne.
   Behold, we live through all things—famine, thirst,
Bereavement, pain, all grief and misery,
All woe and sorrow; life inflicts its worst,
On soul and body—but we cannot die,
Though we be sick, and tired, and worn—
Lo, all things can be borne!

Job

It is good that a man should quietly wait, till my relief should come.

Forbes Robinson

God knows how much you can bear, and He will not, if you will only persevere, allow you to be utterly confounded.

SORROW SHALL PASS

Leland Foster Wood

Times of sorrow come in all families, yet there is always hope of better things. After cold and barrenness come seasons of life and fruitfulness.

An old, old voice
Deeper than sorrow and pain
Speaks in the inner ear
Like the rhythmic beat of rain.

As the rain wets the trees
And feeds the roots of the grass
And refreshes the waiting world,
So also sorrow shall pass;

Shall pass like a drifting cloud
That moves across the sky;
For every cloud moves on,
And the sun comes out by and by.

And as fresh flowers come
Where the earth was bare and cold
So the seeds of joy shall grow
Though long they lie in the mold.

GRIEF MUST SEE THE END
Phillips Brooks

I beg you, if God sends you grief, to take it largely by letting it first of all show you how short life is, and then prophesy eternity. Such is the grief of which the poet sings so nobly:

> Grief should be
> Like joy, majestic, equable, sedate;
> Confirming, cleansing, raising, making free,
> Strong to consume small troubles, to command
> Great thoughts, grave thoughts, thoughts lasting
>   to the end.

But grief, to be all that, must see the end; must bring and forever keep with its pain such a sense of the shortness of life that the pain shall seem but a temporary accident, and all that is to stay forever after the pain has ceased, the exaltation, the unselfishness, the mystery, the nearness of God, shall seem to be the substance of the sorrow.

Job

Behold, happy is the man whom God correcteth; therefore despise not thou the chastening of the Almighty. For He maketh sore and bindeth up; He woundeth, and His hands make whole.

TIME'S HEALING SNOWS
Margaret E. Bruner

> I would not dwell too long upon my grief,
> But let it lie much like the fallen leaf;
> Then hallowed by time's many healing snows,
> Its residue may blossom in a rose.

ISAIAH

And in that day thou shalt say: I will give thanks unto
    Thee, O Lord;

For though Thou wast angry with me
Thine anger is turned away and Thou comfortedst
  me.
Behold, God is my salvation;
I will trust and not be afraid
For God the Lord is my strength and song
And He has become my salvation.

Cicero

No grief is so acute but time ameliorates it.

PSALMS

They that sow in tears
Shall reap in joy.

Ralph Waldo Emerson

Patience and fortitude conquer all things.

FOR ONE LATELY BEREFT
Margaret E. Bruner

Though now you are bereft and ways seem black,
  With emptiness and gloom on every hand;
Some day Time's healing touch will lead you back,
  And gradually your heart will understand
That what you bore must come to one and all,
  And Peace, the clean white flower born of pain,
Will slowly, surely, rise from sorrow's pall,
  And happiness will come to you again.

ISAIAH

For a small moment have I forsaken thee;
But with great compassion will I gather thee.

In a little wrath I hid My face from thee for a moment;
But with everlasting kindness will I have compassion on thee,
Saith the Lord thy Redeemer.

LAMENTATIONS

For the Lord will not cast off forever: but though He cause grief, yet will He have compassion according to the multitude of His mercies. For He doth not afflict willingly nor grieve the children of men.

THE HEALING POWER OF NATURE

James Gordon Gilkey

Some years ago one of the giant Sequoia trees in California was cut down, and scientists were given the opportunity to make a detailed examination of it. They counted the rings in the wood, determined the age and the history of the tree, and then published this interesting statement: "This Sequoia was a seedling in 271 B.C. Five hundred and sixteen years later, it was severely damaged by a forest fire. But Nature immediately set to work to repair the damage, and began to fold successive layers of living tissue over the gigantic scar left by the flames. This effort continued for more than a century, and by the year 350, the wounds had been completely healed. In later centuries two other fires damaged the tree badly. But when the tree was finally cut down, the scar left by the first of these fires had been completely obliterated, and the scar left by the second was in process of being covered. That last scar was a gigantic wound eighteen feet wide and thirty feet high, but had Nature been given a chance even that wound would have been entirely healed."

You and I are not living in a world which injures us, and then does nothing to aid us. Ours is a world which brings pain and hardship, suffering and disaster, but then sets in motion ingenious agencies which quietly but steadily repair the damage. "The healing power of Nature"—how familiar and how beneficent it is! What help it brings, to men as well as to trees!

AND THOU SHALT CHOOSE LIFE

An Associated Press story carrying the date-line June 19, 1954, conveyed a reassuring lesson to those who have been pulled to the abyss of despair by the heavy hand of grief.

The incident unfolded when a Mr. Donald Robertson in Herkimer, N.Y., received an unsigned letter of appreciation from a woman whom he had met briefly nine years previous aboard an eastbound train from California. He was returning from the Pacific theatre where he had flown 69 missions in his B-25. She was a young widow of a serviceman killed in action. When they met in the vestibule of the car he did not even remotely suspect that he had interrupted her attempt to commit suicide by jumping off the speeding train. Her letter made all that quite plain now.

February 1, 1945, that was the date nine years ago. The Battle of the Bulge had ended and the telegrams were being delivered. Mine came in the morning. "The War Department regrets to inform you that your husband—." Those words will be engraved in my mind forever.

February 1, 1945, that night I was on the train speeding on a journey that seemed endless. You were on the train, too, speeding to the wife you hadn't seen since the war began. I doubt if you remember me now. The girl in the black dress, sad and lonely, sitting across the aisle.

If you hadn't come into the vestibule when you did, I'd have opened the door and jumped out. Did I thank you for that, and for all the kind things you did for me . . . ?

Two years later I married again. I have a fine husband, two wonderful children and a lovely home. To think that I am so happy now and owe it all to a stranger on the train who helped me through my darkest hours. . . .

Tonight I think I'll look at the moon—I'll say, "Hi, Mr. Robertson. Thanks for saving my life." I'm truly grateful.

The letter was signed only, "Sincerely . . ."

Our anonymous widow was on the verge of a desperate irrevocable act because she had seen no possibility of ever finding happiness or even meaning in life. But after the grim, dark hours had passed, the dawn of revived hope broke, and with it came new opportunities for creative, zestful living. Such is the reward of those who hold on tenaciously and do not surrender, those who respond heroically to the challenging Biblical summons: "And thou shalt choose life."

GOD'S PLEDGE TO YOU

Anonymous

Not cloudless days;
Not rose-strewn ways;
Not care-free years,
Devoid of sorrow's tears—
But—strength to bear
Your load of human care,
And grace to live aright
And keep your raiment white,
And love to see you through;
That is God's pledge to you.

THE HIDDEN AND THE REVEALED

Beryl D. Cohon

Some of us . . . do not give nature a chance to rebuild its landscape within our own minds and hearts. . . .

We know that God in His wisdom has given us the power to regain vision after whatever blow strikes us. The power to regain vision and regain balance, to muster our energies anew, is a capacity that goes with the healthy personality.

In front of our Temple is a bush. I hope you noticed it this morning as you passed by it. It is straightening itself out; it is showing signs of green. Soon it will be a glorious bush—thriving, bursting with color. But last January it was crushed to earth. I feared it would never come up again. Snow drifts burdened it to the ground. Snow slides from the roof of the Temple buried it all the more. On top of that, the snow plow heaped added burdens of snow on it. It was completely buried. But now, a glorious miracle!

Nature rebuilds its landscape. It will rebuild the landscapes of our lives if we give it a chance. . . .

Hosea

For He hath torn, and He will heal us,
He hath smitten, and He will bind us up.

Job

Thou shalt forget thy misery, and remember it as waters that pass
away.

TIME'S HAND IS KIND

Margaret E. Bruner

For those who place their blooms on new-made graves
And feel that life holds nought but emptiness,
Know that time's hand in kindness ever saves
The heart from too much sorrow and distress.
Yet all deep wounds heal slowly, it would seem,
But gradually the yearning pain will cease . . .
Thus will your grief become a hallowed dream
And, in its stead, will come a strange new peace.

TIME GILDS WITH GOLD

Ella Wheeler Wilcox

From "This, Too, Shall Pass Away"

Has some misfortune fallen to your lot?
This, too, will pass away; absorb the thought,
And wait—your waiting will not be in vain,
Time gilds with gold the iron links of pain.
The dark today leads into light tomorrow;
There is no endless joy, no endless sorrow.

ANTIDOTES FOR ADVERSITY

M. Beatrice Blankenship

A few years ago I was facing one of the most difficult complications
of a never-too-simple existence. Every path I tried seemed to be un-

mistakably marked "No Exit." Driving home from the city late one afternoon with my small children, I was wearily pondering my problems once more, going over and over what could be done. Suicide had more than once occurred to me, but I could not reconcile it with my responsibility toward the children. Suddenly it flashed in my mind that I could take them, too, thereby saving them the weariness and futility of which life seemed to be composed.

Just ahead of us lay a curve in the road where four people had recently been killed. I only needed to step a little harder on the accelerator and keep my hand steady on the wheel, and before any of us had time to be afraid, we should all have escaped from living. There was a black flash before my eyes, I stepped on the brake instead of the accelerator, and came around the curve at my usual cautious speed. . . .

In less than three months the complications had resolved themselves and were succeeded by two of the happiest years of my life. Though things have a way of turning difficult every once in a while, and though I have not as much strength to encounter them as I used to have, I have not again considered suicide as a way out. . . .

I think I was held back, first, by consideration for my family, coupled with a doubt whether, no matter what my own feelings about life, I had the right to deprive the children of theirs although I had given it to them. As a secondary but still powerful consideration, there was even then reluctance to acknowledge once and for all that I was defeated. And while I was confusedly thinking these things, we rounded the curve and came out facing the somber beauty of the afterglow over a purple winter sea.

I have always especially loved the time when the sky burns dark orange on the horizon, the ocean shades from ice-green to darkest purple and the little waves near the shore are for the moment as rigid as if carved out of lapis lazuli, but the utter beauty and peace of that evening sea brought tears to my eyes. I realized then, and at intervals I have ever since, that no matter what life does to you, there is still a refuge from which you cannot be torn. The "sweet things" are still free, and there is no one of us, no matter how lonely and poor, who cannot have his share by just looking around him. . . .

If there is one merciful thing about life, it is that things do change. If joy goes and sorrow comes, why, sorrow goes and peace comes, if we will let it—and peace is a sweeter thing than joy, and more lasting. If we will only give ourselves time, and if we will live each hour, each moment, as it comes,—not trying to face in one instant's comprehension the entire future stripped of all we may have cherished, or of everything that to us makes life worth living, and before we know it months have rolled by, and the particular burden which made our life intolerable is softened on the horizon of memory, or else has changed and modified so that, even if it still exists, we can almost forget it.

Bret Harte

Never a tear bedims the eye
That time and patience will not dry.

HOLD ON! HOLD FAST!

David Polish

A survivor of a concentration camp tells of one ghastly night when he thought that no one in the camp could endure any longer. After a day of satanic torture, all the inmates were routed out in the dead of night and compelled to go through fiendishly conceived drills and exercises. In the numbing cold, men fell and were shot or beaten. Toward dawn, they were all lined up, the stronger ones holding up the dying and the maimed. There they stood at rigid and grotesque attention, freezing and bleeding. From somewhere, no one knows where, a single word ran like an electric current down the lines: *"Aushalten—*hold on, hold fast!" They clung to each other, but unseen hands supported them. That hour of endurance was fraught with cosmic meaning. And for us, too, a call goes out to stand and to endure, for God and for the ages.

"Weeping may tarry for the night, but joy will surely come in the morning."

FROM "THE HARDEST TIME OF ALL"

Sarah Doudney

There are days of silent sorrow
    In the seasons of our life,
There are wild, despairing moments,
    There are hours of mental strife;

There are times of stony anguish,
  When the tears refuse to fall;
But the waiting time, my brothers,
  Is the hardest time of all.

But at last we learn the lesson
  That God knoweth what is best;
For with wisdom cometh patience,
  And with patience cometh rest.
Yea, a golden thread a-shining
  Through the tangled woof of fate;
And our hearts shall thank Him meekly,
  That He taught us how to wait.

LAST YEAR'S GRIEF

Robert Nathan

Here's last year's grief
In the green leaf
And all he knows is
That Time will take
All heartbreak,
And turn it to roses.

Shakespeare

How poor are they who have not patience!
What wound did ever heal, but by degrees?

Leigh Hunt

It is a part of the benignity of Nature that pain does not survive like pleasure, at any time, much less where the cause of it is an innocent one. The smile will remain reflected by memory, as the moon reflects the light upon us when the sun has gone into heaven. . . .

LEARN TO WAIT
Author unknown

Learn to wait—life's hardest lesson
Conned, perchance, through blinding tears;
While the heart throbs sadly echo
To the tread of passing years.
Learn to wait—hope's slow fruition;
Faint not, though the way seems long;
There is joy in each condition;
Hearts through suffering may grow strong.
Thus a soul untouched by sorrow
Aims not at a higher state;
Joy seeks not a brighter morrow;
Only sad hearts learn to wait.

FOUR THINGS
Author unknown

These things are beautiful beyond belief:
The pleasant weakness that comes after pain,
The radiant greenness that comes after rain,
The deepened faith that follows after grief,
And the awakening to love again.

To live in hearts we leave behind
Is not to die.

—Thomas Campbell

MEMORY—LIFE'S AFTERGLOW

In Maeterlinck's beautiful play The Blue Bird, *the children Tyltyl and Mytil are about to set out in search of the fabled blue bird of happiness. The Fairy tells them that on their journey they will come to the land of memory where upon turning the magic diamond in Tyltyl's hat they will see all their departed loved ones—their grandparents, brothers and sisters. "But how can we see them when they are dead?" asks Tyltyl in amazement. To which the Fairy answers gently: "How can they be dead, when they live in your memory?"*

This power of memory to confer immortality upon those we love has been gratefully acknowledged by mourners of all times. Death cannot rob us of our past. The days and years we shared, the common adventures and hopes, the "little nameless, unremembered acts of kindness and of love"—all these are part of the ineradicable human record. Death has no dominion where memory rules. This thought received eloquent affirmation by Whittier who prayerfully asked: "Grant but memory to us and we can lose nothing by death." Centuries before him a Talmudic sage declared: "The righteous are considered alive even in death."

Strangely, these very memories which ultimately help us to cheat death are likely to be quite painful while the anguish of parting is still fresh.

A husband of my acquaintance whose wife died after a brief illness refused to return from the funeral to the home they had shared. For some time he also sought to avoid meeting any persons they had known or visiting any places which would tend to evoke reminiscences of the past. He was thus expressing in a rather extreme way a feeling many mourners experience. "The leaves of memory" do seem "to make a mournful rustling in the dark" when the darkness has just fallen.

Time, however, that most faithful ally of the mourner serves him loyally here, too. With its benign alchemy it gradually draws the sting out of memory and converts it into a source of comfort and often, if the departed has lived well, inspiration. Those who have witnessed a western sunset know that the most enchanting time of day is often around evening. After the hot summer sun sets, while nature breathlessly waits for the light to be rolled away before the darkness, the sky is suddenly clad in the spectacular brilliance of multicolored light. These indescribably gorgeous colors are the day's afterglow.

Wordsworth said that infants who come into the world come "trailing clouds of glory." It is equally true to observe that many depart from the world trailed by "clouds of glory." Memory perpetuates these and does not let them die. "God gave us memory so that we might have roses in December."

MEMORY

Percy Bysshe Shelley

Music, when soft voices die,
Vibrates in the memory—
Odors, when sweet violets sicken,
Live within the sense they quicken.

Rose leaves, when the rose is dead,
Are heaped for the beloved's bed;
And so thy thoughts, when thou art gone,
Love itself shall slumber on.

IMMORTALITY

Edwin Hatch

For me—to have made one soul
The better for my birth;
To have added but one flower
To the garden of the earth;
To have struck one blow for truth

In the daily fight with lies;
To have done one deed of right
In the face of calumnies;
To have sown in the souls of men
One thought that will not die—
To have been a link in the chain of life
Shall be immortality.

FROM "THE EXCURSION"
William Wordsworth

And, when the stream
Which overflowed the soul was passed away,
A consciousness remained that it had left,
Deposited upon the silent shore
Of memory, images and precious thoughts
That shall not die, and cannot be destroyed.

BLESSING HANDS OVER OUR LIVES
Hans Zinsser

At times the dead are closer to us than the living, and the wisdom
and affection of the past stretch blessing hands over our lives, pro-
jecting a guardian care out of the shadows and helping us over
hard places. For there are certain kinds of love that few but the
very wise fully understand until they have become memories.

THEY NEVER QUITE LEAVE US
Margaret E. Sangster

They never quite leave us, our friends who have passed
    Through the shadows of death to the sunlight above;
A thousand sweet memories are holding them fast
    To the places they blessed with their presence and love.
The work which they left and the books which they read
    Speak mutely, though still with an eloquence rare,
And the songs that they sang, the words that they said,
    Yet linger and sigh on the desolate air.

And oft when alone, and oft in the throng,
  Or when evil allures us, or sin draweth nigh,
A whisper comes gently, "Nay, do not the wrong,"
  And we feel that our weakness is pitied on high.

Jerusalem Talmud

Monuments need not be erected for the righteous; their deeds are their memorials.

Maccabees

And thus this man died, leaving his death for an example of a noble courage, and a memorial of virtue, not only unto young men, but unto all his nation.

LOVE WHICH SURVIVES THE TOMB
Washington Irving

The sorrow for the dead is the only sorrow from which we refuse to be divorced. Every other wound we seek to heal—every other affliction to forget; but this wound we consider it a duty to keep open—this affliction we cherish and brood over in solitude. Where is the mother who would willingly forget the infant that perished like a blossom from her arms, though every recollection is a pang? Where is the child that would willingly forget the most tender of parents, though to remember be but to lament? Who, even in the hour of agony, would forget the friend over whom he mourns? Who, even when the tomb is closing upon the remains of her he most loved; when he feels his heart, as it were, crushed in the closing of its portal, would accept of consolation that must be bought by forgetfulness?

No, the love which survives the tomb is one of the noblest attributes of the soul. If it has its woes, it has likewise its delights; and when the overwhelming burst of grief is calmed into the gentle tear of recollection; when the sudden anguish and the convulsive agony over the present ruins of all that we most loved is softened away into pensive meditation on all that it was in the days of its loveliness—who would root out such a sorrow from the heart? Though it may sometimes throw a passing cloud over the bright hour of gaiety, or spread a deeper sadness over the hour of gloom, yet who would exchange it, even for the song of pleasure or the burst of revelry? No, there is a voice from the tomb sweeter than song. There is a remembrance of the dead to which we turn even from the charms of the living.

REMEMBERING
Margaret E. Bruner

Once when a silence fell upon the heart,
The world at hand grew dim—almost unreal;
And wrapped in thought it seemed that I could feel
Your presence near, though we were far apart;
There was no need of any conjurer's art—
I saw your face in questioning appeal,
As if some message you would thus reveal,
Trusting I, too, would turn to memory's chart.

And in this mood the years were brushed aside—
We walked together down a woodsy hill;
We stood upon the ledge and viewed the wide
Fields where the river glided by, until
There was no other world . . . our spirits met
Briefly to say that neither would forget.

DEATH CANNOT KILL WHAT NEVER DIES
William Penn

They that love beyond the world cannot be separated. Death cannot kill what never dies. Nor can Spirits ever be divided that love and live in the same Divine Principle; the Root and Record of their Friendship. Death is but crossing the world, as Friends do the Seas; they live in one another still.

FROM "THEY SOFTLY WALK"
Hugh Robert Orr

They are not dead who live
In hearts they leave behind.

In those whom they have blessed
They live a life again,
And shall live through the years
Eternal life, and grow
Each day more beautiful
As time declares their good,
Forgets the rest, and proves
Their immortality.

FROM "JOYCE LIEBERMAN, A TRIBUTE OF FAREWELL"
Milton Steinberg

Not often in my lifetime have I come upon a spirit so loving and lovable, so gentle, sensitive and truly innocent as Joyce Lieberman. . . . as long as I knew Joyce—and it was for well over half of her brief life span—she was first a very sick child, then an invalided and foredoomed young woman. Yet in her presence, even at her bedside, one was rarely, if ever, aware of illness, so gay, so eager, so vital and alive in spirit was she. . . .

She did no one ill because she wished no one ill. She practiced no guile because she was incapable of it. . . . Under the extremest of provocations she remained altogether sweet, gentle, kindly, a wisher-well to all the world.

Indeed, in her case illness seems to have been, as it were, a crucible, in which her spirit was progressively refined and purified until nothing base or ignoble was left in it.

Always affectionate, she became ever more affectionate as her numbered days slipped by, steadily more devoted to her friends, among whom I was and am proud to be counted; ever more loving to her so much-loved mother, father and brother.

From earliest childhood she was responsive and poetic, wide awake to beauty in nature, to goodness in men, to grace in art and literature, to nobility in religion and moral aspiration. This sensitivity, too, broadened and deepened with time. At the end it included almost everything good and lovely—from trees budding in the spring, to Beethoven Quartets, the Jewish tradition and the American democratic dream. Some of this sensitivity found an outlet in the poetry she composed. But most of it went into the ardor with which she appreciated life, her wide-eyed, breathless wonder and love of it. . . .

This, it seems to me, is the crowning paradox of her being—that she who had so slight reason to love life loved it so well; that she who had so little ground for happiness was a fundamentally happy person. . . .

And so, Joyce, the loving and lovable, the gentle, sensitive, innocent child, is gone from us. And yet not altogether and entirely.

Long, long ago, a wise man said that he who touches pitch must be defiled with it. But if that be so, then it is also true that he who touches what is warm and luminous must carry away with him something of warmth and light.

On the hearts and minds of all who knew and loved Joyce, something of her soft, quiet sweetness will remain forever. All of us are, I am sure, somehow better, gentler, truer people for having had the privilege of her companionship, so brief yet so lovely.

KINDLING THE SABBATH LIGHT
Philip M. Raskin

From memory's spring flows a vision tonight,
My mother is kindling and blessing the light;

The light of Queen Sabbath, the heavenly flame,
That one day in seven quells hunger and shame.

My mother is playing and screening her face,
Too bashful to gaze at the Sabbath light's grace.

She murmurs devoutly, "Almighty, be blessed,
For sending Thy angel of joy and of rest.

"And may as the candles of Sabbath divine
The eyes of my son in Thy Law ever shine."

Of childhood, fair childhood, the years are long fled:
Youth's candles are quenched, and my mother is dead.

And yet ev'ry Friday, when twilight arrives,
The face of my mother within me revives;

A prayer on her lips, "O Almighty, be blessed,
For sending us Sabbath, the angel of rest."

And some hidden feeling I cannot control
A Sabbath light kindles deep, deep in my soul.

Talmud

The righteous are called living even when they are dead, and the wicked are called dead even when they are living.

REMEMBERING ADDS RICHNESS
Zelda Popkin

In the spiritual gifts of a marriage, the giving and receiving of life, lie the strengths from which many a new life is built. One lives with all of one's past. Nothing and no one ever completely dies. It is not necessary or desirable to forget. Remembering adds richness to all our remaining days.

Years of being together have left their impact, a heritage intangible yet rich, made out of gestures and words, experiences shared, the casual warmths of daily contacts. There lies man's true immortality. He lives on in every person whose life touched his.

Going on means opening the little passageways, sealed off in the first weeks of grief because they held memories too poignant, opening the doors, letting the richness of shared experiences come through, saying, "I'd like to go there—I remember what fun we had in that place," not, "I can't bear to go. Our happy times there are over now."

OUR DEAD
Robert Nichols

From "Ardours and Endurance"

They have not gone from us. O no! they are
The inmost essence of each thing that is
Perfect for us; they flame in every star;
The trees are emerald with their presences.
They are not gone from us; they do not roam
The flaw and turmoil of the lower deep,
But have now made the whole wide world their home,
And in its loveliness themselves they steep.

They fail not ever; theirs is the diurn
Splendour of sunny hill and forest grave;
In every rainbow's glittering drop they burn;
They dazzle in the massed clouds' architrave;
They chant on every wind, and they return
In the long roll of any deep blue wave.

MOTHER WILL HUSH YOU AND HEAL YOU

A condolence letter to a friend upon the death of his aged mother after a period of illness.

Dear Bill: I was truly saddened to learn of the passing of your mother and I am writing to add my expression of sympathy to the outpouring of condolences which must be reaching you from countless friends.

Mother's death was neither shocking nor tragic. Perhaps as you contrasted her fading powers with the vigorous personality you had drawn upon so heavily, her end might even have brought with it a measure of relief. Yet the coming of nightfall is always accompanied by poignant sorrow even when the day has been long, the sun bright and the twilight difficult.

At a time like this, we usually find a real measure of comfort in contemplating the imperishable role our departed have played in our lives. The pulsating memories, the sustaining influence, the invisible roots entwined around the very essence of our being—all these we know cannot be erased by the hand of death from the blackboard of our lives.

In your own case I strongly feel that your solace must have another dimension. You can derive comfort not only from the thought of what your mother meant to you, but also from the realization of what you meant to her. Your extraordinary success as a human being and as a friend to so many was a profound source of joy to her. How she basked in your reflected glory! In addition, the extreme kindness and thoughtfulness you and Rose always showed her were her favorite topic of discussion. Directly and indirectly you discharged well your filial duties.

In one of her poems, Sara Teasdale says: "Places I know come back to me like music—Hush me and heal me when I am very tired." In the time to come, I know, your mother will come back to hush you and heal you.

Sincerely,
Sidney Greenberg

SORROWS HUMANIZE OUR RACE
Jean Ingelow

Sorrows humanize our race;
Tears are the showers that fertilize this world
And memory of things precious keepeth warm
The heart that once did hold them.

They are poor that have lost nothing: they are poorer far
Who losing, have forgotten: they most poor
Of all, who lose and wish they might forget;
For life is one, and in its warp and woof
There runs a thread of gold that glitters fair,
And sometimes in the pattern shows more sweet
Where there are sombre colors. It is true
That we have wept. But O, this thread of gold,
We would not have it tarnish; let us turn
Oft and look back upon the wondrous web,
That memory is possession.

William Wordsworth

The thought of our past years in me doth breed Perpetual benediction.

LIFE WATERED BY STREAMS OF MEMORY
Jacob P. Rudin

The exact circumstances surrounding the death of the poet Ibn
Gabirol are unknown. According to one legend, however, a certain
Mohammedan, jealous of Ibn Gabirol's genius, killed him and
buried his body beneath a tree. Some time after, people began to
notice that a fig tree in the garden of the Mohammedan was bearing
a particularly large and luscious fruit, like none that grew elsewhere. Curiosity was aroused, and the tree was dug up in order to
discover the secret of its remarkable fertility. Then it was discovered that Ibn Gabirol was buried there.

All life grows riper and fuller when rooted in the lives of upright
men and women; when its soil is enriched by deeds of loving kind-

ness and mercy. All life becomes lovelier when it is watered by streams of memory and fed by the cool springs of recollection and remembrance.

IN MEMORIAM
Joseph Auslander

They are not dead, our sons who fell in glory,
Who gave their lives for Freedom and for Truth.
We shall grow old, but never their great story,
Never their gallant youth.
In a perpetual springtime set apart,
Their memory forever green shall grow,
In some bright secret meadow of the heart
Where never falls the snow.

FOR ALL WHO MOURN
Arthur Guiterman

That he was dear to you so many a year
    But darkens your distress.
Would you he were less worthy and less dear
    That you might grieve the less?

He was a golden font that freely poured
    What goldenly endures,
And though that font be gone, its bounty, stored
    And treasured, still is yours.

The Past is deathless. Souls are wells too deep
    To spend their purest gains.
All that he gave to you is yours to keep
    While memory remains.

Who never had and lost, forlorn are they
    Far more than you and I
Who had and have. Grudge not the price we pay
    For love that cannot die.

Psalms

The righteous shall be had in everlasting remembrance.

FOR YOU I SHALL CONTINUE TO LIVE

Avraham Kreizman
(Translated from the Hebrew by Eliezer Whartman)

One of the most poignant letters to come to light was that written by Chicago-born Avraham Kreizman, who came to Palestine as a child in 1921. Avraham fell in the War of Independence, alone, hurling hand grenades to protect the withdrawal of his friends. He left a wife and two young daughters. Here, three days before the end, he writes to his wife:

I know: When I die, for you I shall continue to live. No one will take me from your faithful and tender heart. But if you meet a comrade who will understand your sorrow, and you love him a bit and your love brings forth a new life and a son is born to you—give him and let him carry my name and let him be my continuation.

And if it comes to pass that he does not understand—leave him without pain and let the child be our son alone. . . .

And when it comes to pass that a new settlement is built here, come and plant poppies in this place: they grow so beautifully here and thrive so well! And let this be the place of my grave. . . .

And perhaps you will err and your flowers will not be planted on my grave but on that of one of my comrades nearby. Well . . . another wife will think of her husband as she plants flowers on mine.

No one will be overlooked. Because we lay close to each other in this spot and there is no space here to divide a man and his friends. . . .

WHEN THE DAY COMES

Avraham Kreizman (Translated from the Hebrew by the editor)

And if I will not be with you
When the day comes
To hold you and support you,
To look into your eyes

And whisper silently: Be strong!
Please, dear,
Remember the last glance
In the night of parting. . . .

And if I will not be with you
When they bring him for the first time,
To feed him, warm him, fondle him
And whisper words of love to him,
Please, dear,
Remember the rock, the ocean
And the whisper of the waves. . . .

And if I will not be with you
The first to kiss you and him
And to call you "Mother" and him
"My child, my precious child" . . .
Please, dear,
Remember a moonlit night
And a bridge by the side of the road. . . .

And if I will not be with you
I, your husband,
Whom you chose for a companion
To believe, to love,
To be a father to your child,
And to bring
Two flowers to your bed,
Please, dear,
Remember the field of flowers
And we picking in it. . . .

And if I will not be with you
When you return to the nest,
When you see my reflection in his eyes
Or when his mouth will remind you of mine,
And for a moment you will forget
That I am no longer,
Please, dear,
Remember that I am with you,
With you always, always. . . .

TRANSFIGURATION

Louisa May Alcott

Mysterious death! who in a single hou
    Life's gold can so refine,
    And by thy art divine
Change mortal weakness to immortal power!
How can we mourn like those who are bereft,
    When every pang of grief
    Finds balm for its relief
In counting up the treasures she has left?
Faith that withstood the shocks of toil and time;
    Hope that defied despair;
    Patience that conquered care;
And loyalty whose courage was sublime;
The great deep heart that was a home for all,
    Just, eloquent and strong
    In protest against wrong;
Wise charity, that knew no sin, no fall;
The Spartan spirit that made life so grand,
    Mating poor daily needs
    With high, heroic deeds
That wrested happiness from Fate's hard hand.
We thought to weep, but sing for joy instead,
    Full of the grateful peace
    That follows her release;
For nothing but the weary dust lies dead.
Oh, noble woman! never more a queen
    Than in the laying down
    Of scepter and of crown
To win a greater kingdom, yet unseen.
Teaching us how to seek the highest goal,
    To earn the true success—
    To live, to love, to bless—
And make death proud to take a royal soul.

FROM "SNOW-BOUND"
John Greenleaf Whittier

And yet, dear heart! remembering thee,
Am I not richer than of old?
Safe in thy immortality,
What change can reach the wealth I hold?
What chance can mar the pearl and gold
Thy love hath left in trust for me?
And while in life's long afternoon,
Where cool and long the shadows grow,
I walk to meet the night that soon
Shall shape and shadow overflow,
I cannot feel that thou art far,
Since near at need the angels are;
And when the sunset gates unbar,
Shall I not see thee waiting stand,
And, white against the evening star,
The welcome of thy beckoning hand?

NO FUNERAL GLOOM
William Allingham

No funeral gloom, my dears, when I am gone,
Corpse-gazings, tears, black raiment, graveyard grimness;
Think of me as withdrawn into the dimness,
Yours still, you mine; remember all the best
Of our past moments, and forget the rest;
And so, to where I wait, come gently on.

MADE DEARER BY MEMORIES
Morris Joseph

The balm, according to the Rabbinical idea, is created before the wound . . . with the sorrow, comes the remedy for it; for it is enfolded in the sorrow. We are taught by our trouble, uplifted by it, consoled by it. . . . We take the ruins of the old happiness and build upon them a fairer and more durable edifice. We let our beloved go, but we receive him back, made dearer, more living, by sanctified and inspiring memories. . . .

IMMORTAL

Florence Earle Coates

How living are the dead!
Enshrined, but not apart,
How safe within the heart
We hold them still—our dead,
Whatever else be fled!

Our constancy is deep
Toward those who lie asleep
Forgetful of the strain and mortal strife
That are so large a part of this, our earthly life.
They are our very own—
From them—from them alone
Nothing can us estrange,
Nor blight autumnal, no, nor wintry change.

The midnight moments keep a place for them,
And though we wake to weep
They are beside us still in joy, in pain,
In every crucial hour, they come again
Angelic from above—
Bearing the gifts of blessing and of love
Until the shadowy path they lonely trod
Becomes for us a bridge,
That upwards leads to God.

Hannah Senesh

There are stars whose light reaches the earth only after they themselves have disintegrated and are no more. And there are men whose scintillating memory lights the world after they have passed from it. These lights which shine in the darkest night are those which illumine for us the path. . . .

EVEN NOW NOAM STANDS BEFORE ME
(Translated from the Hebrew by the editor)

Noam Grossman was killed in Israel's War of Independence at the age of twenty-one.

To my esteemed friends, the Grossmans:

I know that it would be futile to try to comfort you. Ordinary words and customary phrases cannot help carry the burden—so sacred and heavy a burden. If only I could help you ever so slightly. . . .

Noam was very dear to us. He was strong and good and brave and the possessor of rare beauty of soul. How we loved him! We admired the serenity that flowed from his eyes and his modesty.

High school, guard duty, university, Haganah—stages along the road. We were friends. And today, when so many of our friends fall en route to our goal, those with whom we learned, dreamed, fought and sweated, comrades in jest and in deadly earnest, they come back to us. Among them the noble figure of our Noam stands out. His winning smile floats in upon us like the gentle evening breeze. And it is possible . . . that those we love, who dwell deep in our hearts, these do not die for us. They will visit us often, they will stand by us at all times. In difficult moments they will sustain us with counsel, with vision and with a smile. For us they live and nothing is taken away from them, nothing. . . .

Even now Noam stands before me. . . . He assures all of us that the ideals for which he died remain firm and abide and that we shall be privileged to witness their fulfilment—and he shall be with us. . . !

Respectfully yours,
Baruch Amon

FROM "DISCORDANTS"
Conrad Aiken

Music I heard with you was more than music,
And bread I broke with you was more than bread.
Now that I am without you, all is desolate,
All that was once so beautiful is dead.

Your hands once touched this table and this silver,
And I have seen your fingers hold this glass.
These things do not remember you, beloved:
And yet your touch upon them will not pass.

For it was in my heart you moved among them,
And blessed them with your hands and with your eyes.
And in my heart they will remember always:
They knew you once, O! Beautiful and wise!

REQUIEM

Lucia Trent

When I have died
Let there be no recalling
Of the procession of broken days;
Autumn must come,
And in her wake the falling
Of tired leaves on old and hardened ways.

When I have died
Let there be but rejoicing
For all the sunlit beauties I have known;
Remembrance of friendship,
And the voicing
Of each new joy in radiant overtone!

Let there be but the memory
Of my dreaming,
Of star-domed vistas down the unborn years;
The memory of a faith
I have kept gleaming,
The broken benediction of my tears!

FROM "VOICES OF THE PAST"

Adelaide Ann Procter

O there are Voices of the Past
Links of a broken chain,
Wings that can bear me back to Times

Which cannot come again;
Yet God forbid that I should lose
The echoes that remain!

THE DEAD

Mathilde Blind

The dead abide with us. Though stark and cold,
Earth seems to grip them, they are with us still:
They have forged our chains of being for good or ill,
And their invisible hands these hands yet hold.

THE KADDISH

L. Kompert

Its origin is mysterious; angels are said to have brought it down from heaven and taught it to men. About this prayer the tenderest threads of filial feeling and human recollection are entwined; for it is the prayer of the orphans! When the father or mother dies, the surviving sons are to recite it thrice daily, morning and evening, throughout the year of mourning, and then also on each recurring anniversary of the death—on the Yahrzeit.

It possesses wonderful power. Truly, if there is any bond strong and indissoluble enough to chain heaven to earth, it is this prayer. It keeps the living together, and forms the bridge to the mysterious realm of the dead. One might almost say that this prayer is the watchman and the guardian of the people by whom alone it is uttered; therein lies the warrant of its continuance. Can a people disappear and be annihilated so long as a child remembers its parents? It may sound strange: in the midst of the wildest dissipation has this prayer recalled to his better self a dissolute character, so that he has bethought himself and for a time at least purified himself by honoring the memory of his parents.

Because this prayer is a resurrection in the spirit of the perishable in man, because it does not acknowledge death, because it permits the blossom, which, withered, has fallen from the tree of mankind, to flower and develop again in the human heart, therefore it possesses sanctifying power. To know that when thou diest, the earth falling on thy head will not cover thee entirely; to know that there remain behind, those who, wherever they may be on this wide earth, whether they may be poor or rich, will send this prayer after thee; to know that thou leavest them no house, no estate, no field by which they must remember thee, and that yet they will cherish thy memory as their dearest inheritance—what more satisfying knowledge canst thou ever hope for? And such is the knowledge bequeathed to us all by the Kaddish.

Cicero

The life of the dead is placed in the memory of the living.

MY HEREAFTER

Juniata De Long

Do not come when I am dead
To sit beside a low green mound,
Or bring the first gay daffodils
Because I love them so,
For I shall not be there.
You cannot find me there.

I will look up at you from the eyes
Of little children;
I will bend to meet you in the swaying boughs
Of bud-thrilled trees,
And caress you with the passionate sweep
Of storm-filled winds;
I will give you strength in your upward tread
Of everlasting hills;
I will cool your tired body in the flow
Of the limpid river;
I will warm your work-glorified hands through the glow
Of the winter fire;
I will soothe you into forgetfulness to the drop, drop
Of the rain on the roof;
I will speak to you out of the rhymes
Of the Masters;
I will dance with you in the lilt
Of the violin,
And make your heart leap with the bursting cadence

Of the organ;
I will flood your soul with the flaming radiance
Of the sunrise,
And bring you peace in the tender rose and gold
Of the after-sunset.

All these have made me happy:
They are a part of me;
I shall become a part of them.

TESTAMENT

Anne Morrow Lindbergh

But how can I live without you?—she cried.
I left all world to you when I died:
Beauty of earth and air and sea;
Leap of a swallow or a tree;
Kiss of rain and wind's embrace;
Passion of storm and winter's face;
Touch of feather, flower and stone;
Chiseled line of branch or bone;
Flight of stars, night's caravan;
Song of crickets—and of man—
All these I put in my testament,
All these I bequeathed you when I went.

But how can I see them without your eyes
Or touch them without your hand?
How can I hear them without your ear,
Without your heart, understand?

These, too, these, too
I leave to you!

"IN MY EYES ALL ARE EQUAL"

*It was a period of profound crisis for Samaria, the capital of the
northern kingdom of ancient Israel. The King of Aram and his
armies had besieged the city and its inhabitants were being starved
to death. So intense had the hunger become, that mothers began
to devour their young. When this news reached the King of Israel,
the Bible tells us, "he rent his clothes . . . and the people looked
and behold he had sackcloth within upon his flesh."*

*What a shock that sight must have been to the people! Each
citizen knew of his personal troubles and tragedies. But how amazed
they all must have been to see that beneath his royal robe, even
the king was wearing sackcloth—the symbol of personal sorrow and
misfortune.*

*A deep truth speaks out to us from this incident—one that we
ought to keep steadily before us especially in time of grief. "Why
did this happen to me?" we frequently ask amidst sorrow, as though
we alone were singled out by a malicious destiny.*

*In the bitter mood of the Book of Lamentations we complain:
"Behold and see if there be any sorrow like unto my sorrow . . .
wherewith the Lord hath afflicted me in the day of fierce anger."
We rarely stop to realize that even kings wear sackcloth.*

*The better we get to know people, the more impressed do we
become with this one fact. Rare indeed is the individual without
a sackcloth. Some of us wear a sackcloth of a deep frustration—a
career to which we aspired but did not attain, a heart we sought
but failed to win. Some of us wear the sackcloth of a haunting
sense of inadequacy, or a deeply bruised conscience. Blasted hopes,*

unrealized dreams, anguish and grief—is any life unfamiliar with them? Has anyone ever been granted an exemption from sorrow or made a truce with death? Is not the sackcloth the common garment of all men?

If we would learn to wear life's sackcloths properly, we must cover them with the robe of understanding. We must realize that, as the Bible puts it, "Man is born to trouble." Trouble far from being a gate-crasher in life's arena actually has a reserved seat there. Human life is attended at its beginning by the piercing cries of the infant and at its end by the agonized wailing of the bereaved. In between, there are sadness, heartbreak, disease. For that reason, the great tragedians of literature have not wanted for themes. All they had to do was to observe life carefully and report it faithfully, and the tragedy spelled itself out. "Yet, though men bolt and bar their house from thee, To every door, O Pain, thou hast a key."

In our own hour of sorrow our human oneness is most poignantly underscored. We are indeed knit to one another in a common brotherhood of pain. This kinship should evoke our most compassionate regard for one another. In our hour of tribulation we can become more keenly attuned to "the still sad music of humanity," we can become more sensitive to the needs and hurts of others. Out of such moments there can be born, too, the firm resolve to unite with our fellowmen to delay death and to soften some of the ravages it leaves in its wake. Our common destiny can spur us on to uncommon achievement.

VISION

Elizabeth N. Hauer

There have been times when I have looked at life
From out the eyes of sorrow, and have felt
The utter loneliness of black night vigils.
There have been times when I have wept hot tears
And tasted of their salt
And drunk the dregs of sadness to the end.

There have been times—and then another's heartaches,
So deep and rending as to mock my own,

Has cut, flamelike, across my blurring vision,
Dwarfing my paltry tragedies to nought.

FROM "RESIGNATION"

Henry Wadsworth Longfellow

There is no flock, however watched and tended,
  But one dead lamb is there!
There is no fireside, howsoe'er defended,
  But has one vacant chair!

The air is full of farewells to the dying,
  And mournings for the dead;
The heart of Rachel for her children crying,
  Will not be comforted!

George Crabbe

Grief is to man as certain as the grave:
Tempests and storms in life's whole progress rise,
And hope shines dimly through o'er-clouded skies;
Some drops of comfort on the favour'd fall,
But showers of sorrow are the lot of all.

Metastasio

If inward griefs were written on the brow, how many would be
pitied who are now envied!

THE BEREAVED—THE LARGEST COMPANY IN THE WORLD

Helen Keller

We bereaved are not alone. We belong to the largest company
in all the world—the company of those who have known suffering.
When it seems that our sorrow is too great to be borne, let us think
of the great family of the heavy-hearted into which our grief has

given us entrance and, inevitably, we will feel about us their arms, their sympathy, their understanding.

Believe, when you are most unhappy, that there is something for you to do in the world. So long as you can sweeten another's pain, life is not in vain. . . .

Robbed of joy, of courage, of the very desire to live, the newly bereaved frequently avoids companionship, feeling himself so limp with misery and so empty of vitality that he is ill-suited for human contacts. And yet no one is so bereaved, so miserable, that he cannot find someone else to succor, someone who needs friendship, understanding, and courage more than he. The unselfish effort to bring cheer to others will be the beginning of a happier life for ourselves. . . .

Often when the heart is torn with sorrow, spiritually we wander like a traveler lost in a deep wood. We grow frightened, lose all sense of direction, batter ourselves against trees and rocks in our attempt to find a path. All the while there is a path—a path of Faith—that leads straight out of the dense tangle of our difficulties into the open road we are seeking. Let us not weep for those who have gone away when their lives were at full bloom and beauty. Who are we that we should mourn them and wish them back? Life at its every stage is good, but who shall say whether those who die in the splendor of their prime are not fortunate to have known no abatement, no dulling of the flame by ash, no slow fading of life's perfect flower?

Wisdom of Ben Sira

Fear not the sentence of death;
Remember them that have been before thee, and that
   come after:
This is the sentence from the Lord over all flesh.

Susan Coolidge

Men die, but sorrow never dies;
The crowding years divide in vain,
And the wide world is knit with ties
Of common brotherhood in pain.

OUR KINSHIP WITH ALL HUMANITY
Zelda Popkin

Many reach out for and feel for the first time their kinship with all humanity. "At first, when my husband died," a woman told me some time ago, "I felt it was a special punishment visited just upon me. My friends had their families. My world had collapsed. Then one day I read in the papers of a plane crash. It was carrying important people. All were lost.

"It hit me like a flash of revelation. I said to myself: 'The wives of those men are traveling the same road I am. All over the world there are women like me.' I stopped feeling sorry for myself. I felt sorry for them, instead."

Chateaubriand

It is with sorrows, as with countries, each man has his own.

THE UNIVERSAL HERITAGE
Morris Adler

Sorrow is the obverse side of love. To ask for immunity from sorrow is to ask for more than a special dispensation granted no other. It is to ask that we love not, gain no friends or devotedly serve any cause. To enter into any relationship of deep meaning is to run the risk of sorrow. When we become parents, or link our life to another's, or find a friend who is closer than brother, w inevitably expose ourselves to the pangs of separation or the grief of injury or illness or death. But let us for a moment consider the alternative. One meets people whom life has wounded deeply. Fate dealt them a harsh blow. A dear one died, or a friend betrayed a trust. A hope failed of fulfillment or a kindness was repaid with ingratitude. They decide never again to give hostages to life. Life is not going to find an exposed flank in their case. They will not open their hearts in trust; they will not permit acquaintance to ripen into friendship; they are prepared to forego love, family, children. They are resolved that no human being will become so dear to them that his passing will bring grief. They protect themselves against sorrow. But they also shut out the possibilities of joy, companionship, the richest and most vital satisfactions of life. Charles Dickens' *Great Expectations* tells of a woman whose groom disappeared on their wedding day. She wears her wedding gown through the years and compels her life to stop still and deathlike at the hour of her great sorrow.

But such surrender does not necessarily indicate deepest feeling. There are people whose self-pity is greater than their grief and who in mourning replace the object of their sorrow with their own hurt.

We shall be helped in maintaining our balance during life's trials if we remember that sadness is the universal heritage of mankind. The contingency of pain is the only condition on which love, friendship and happiness are ever offered to us. This recognition is the hallmark of maturity.

Daniel Webster

One may live as a conqueror, a king or a magistrate; but he must die as a man.

DEPART SATISFIED
Marcus Aurelius

Man, thou hast been a citizen in this great state (the world): what difference does it make to thee whether for five years (or three)? for that which is conformable to the laws is just for all. Where is the hardship then, if no tyrant nor yet an unjust judge sends thee away from the state, but nature who brought thee into it? the same as if a praetor who has employed an actor dismisses him from the stage. "But I have not finished the five acts, but only three of them."

—Thou sayest well, but in life the three acts are the whole drama; for what shall be a complete drama is determined by him who was once the cause of its composition, and now of its dissolution: but thou art the cause of neither. Depart then satisfied, for he also who releases thee is satisfied.

Shakespeare

. . . all that live must die,
Passing through nature to eternity.

John Gay

The prince, who kept the world in awe,
The judge, whose dictate fix'd the law,
The rich, the poor, the great, the small,
Are level'd: death confounds 'em all.

THE COMMON DATE WITH ADVERSITY
Morris Adler

Who among men has not at one time or another known the sharp pain of grief, the poignant hurt of loss? Who has been able to insulate himself against the slings and arrows of outrageous fortune, or escape the disappointment and melancholy to which human flesh is heir? Is there anyone here to whom sadness is strange or anguish alien? Is there an individual from whom life has not wrung tears or whose lips have never uttered a sigh? Every mortal has a date with adversity, loss and death. . . .

If there is one experience that is common to all men, then, it is sorrow. An old and familiar story illustrates the universality of sadness. A patient came to a physician in the city of Naples. He complained of melancholia. He could not rid himself of a deep feeling of sadness. The physician said, "I advise you to visit the theatre where the incomparable Carlini is appearing. This great comedian daily convulses large crowds with laughter. By all means go to see Carlini. His amusing antics will drive away your melancholy."

At these words, the patient burst into tears and sobbed, "But, doctor, I am Carlini." . . . This awareness that sorrow is man's common lot will not restore a lost one, or heal an ailment. It should, however, save us from an outpouring of that self-pity to which we would succumb were we to feel that none has ever suffered as we.

Job

There the wicked cease from troubling;
And there the weary are at rest.
There the prisoners are at ease together;
They hear not the voice of the taskmaster.

> The small and great are there alike;
> And the servant is free from his master.

First Chronicles

For we are strangers before Thee, and sojourners, as all our fathers were: our days on the earth are as a shadow, and there is no abiding.

Joseph Jefferson

Inscription on Joseph Jefferson's monument at Sandwich, Cape Cod, Mass.

We are but tenants, and . . . shortly the great Landlord will give us notice that our lease has expired.

Psalms

What man is he that liveth and shall not see death, that shall deliver his soul from the power of the grave?

Horace

Pale death enters with impartial step the cottages of the poor and the palaces of the rich.

THE MOTHER OF THE GREAT KING

In *The Spirit Returneth,* by Selma Stern, Deborah asks her grandmother how she managed to recover after a family sorrow. Others in the family, according to Grandmother, never got over it, their hearts turning to stone within them.

"How did it come about, Grandmother, that you yourself grew to be so different?" Deborah asked.

The old woman smiled. "It was a little song that caused me to change."

"A little song?" Deborah asked wonderingly.

"Yes, it was a song which a minstrel sang many years ago in our dance house. It is a sad song, but it is also a very consoling song, and all who think that they have suffered more ill than any of their fellows ever have should hear it and take it to heart. For it tells how Alexander of Macedon consoled his own mother. When he knew that his death was near, he wrote her a letter. 'My mother, remember that all earthly things are transitory and that your son was not a small king but a great king. Wherefore you are not to bear yourself like the mother of a little king, but like the mother of a great king. And so after my death command a great hall to be built and command furthermore that on a given day all the princes of the empire shall come thither and be merry and be of good cheer. And cause it to be proclaimed that none is to come who has suffered any ill, for the joy at that feast shall be a pure and perfect joy and shall not be darkened by the thoughts of any concerning any sorrow that has come upon him.'

"When now the time had come that her son was dead, she acted exactly according to his will. She caused a magnificent hall to be built; she named the day on which the princes were to come to the feast. When the appointed day came, on which the feast was to take place, she was prepared for many, many people. And not a single soul came. She asked the people in her court: 'What is the meaning of this thing? Why do not the guests come to this great hall which I have caused to be built?' The answer she received was this: 'Dear Queen, you issued the command that none should come who has suffered any grief or any ill. But there is no such human being in the whole world, and therefore there is no guest who could come.' And this consoled the mother of the great king."

Henry Wadsworth Longfellow

Believe me, every man has his secret sorrows, which the world knows not; and oftentimes we call a man cold when he is only sad.

HEARTBREAK ROAD

Helen Gray Cone

As I went up by Heartbreak Road
    Before the break of day,
The cold mist was all about,
    And the wet world was gray;
It seemed that never another soul
    Had walked that weary way.

But when I came to Heartbreak Hill,
  Silver touched the sea;
I knew that many and many a soul
  Was climbing close to me;
I knew I walked that weary way
  In a great company.

TO LEARN HOW TO DIE
Montaigne

The profit of life consists not in the space, but rather in the use. Some man hath lived long, that hath a short life, Follow it whilst you have time. It consists not in number of years, but in your will, that you have lived long enough. Did you think you should never come to the place, where you were still going? There is no way but hath an end. And if company may solace you, doth not the whole world walk the same path?

Thomas Southerne

Sooner or later, all things pass away,
And are no more: The beggar and the king,
With equal steps, tread forward to their end.

THE EMPEROR EXITS LIKE THE BEGGAR
Richard C. Trench

I remember an Eastern legend which I have always thought furnished a remarkable though unconscious commentary on the words of the Psalmist. Alexander the Great, we are there told, being upon his deathbed, commanded that when he was carried forth to the grave his hands should not be wrapped as was usual in the cere-cloths, but should be left outside the bier, so that all might see them, and might see that they were empty, that there was nothing in them; that he, born to one empire, and the conqueror of another, the possessor while he lived of two worlds—of the East and of the West—and of the treasures of both, yet now when he was dead could retain no smallest portion of these treasures; that in this matter the poorest beggar and he were at length upon equal terms.

Joshua

And, behold, this day I am going the way of all the earth.

THE RAINY DAY
Henry Wadsworth Longfellow

The day is cold, and dark, and dreary;
It rains, and the wind is never weary;
The vine still clings to the mouldering wall,
But at every gust the dead leaves fall,
    And the day is dark and dreary.

My life is cold, and dark, and dreary;
It rains, and the wind is never weary;
My thoughts still cling to the mouldering past,
But the hopes of youth fall thick in the blast,
    And the days are dark and dreary.

Be still, sad heart! and cease repining;
Behind the clouds is the sun still shining;
Thy fate is the common fate of all,
Into each life some rain must fall
    Some days must be dark and dreary.

Socrates

If all the misfortunes of mankind were cast into a public stock, in order to be equally distributed among the whole species, those who now think themselves the most unhappy would prefer the share they are already possessed of, before that which would fall to them by such a division.

DEATH THE LEVELER

James Shirley

The glories of our blood and state
  Are shadows, not substantial things;
There is no armor against Fate;
  Death lays his icy hand on kings:
    Sceptre and Crown
    Must tumble down,
And in the dust be equal made
With the poor crooked scythe and spade.
Some men with swords may reap the field,
  And plant fresh laurels where they kill:
  But their strong nerves at last must yield;
  They tame but one another still:
    Early or late
    They stoop to fate,
And must give up their murmuring breath
When they, pale captives, creep to death.
The garlands wither on your brow;
  Then boast no more your mighty deeds!
Upon Death's purple altar now
See where the victor-victim bleeds.
    Your heads must come
    To the cold tomb:
Only the actions of the just
Smell sweet and blossom in their dust.

Death stands above me, whispering low
I know not what into my ear;
Of his strange language all I know
Is, there is not a word of fear.

—Walter Savage Landor

FEAR NOT DEATH

The emotion grief is actually a composite of many different feelings. Added to the pain of parting, there may be loneliness, remorse or even a harrowing sense of guilt. Not infrequently grief also contains a burdensome ingredient of fear—the fear of death.

However one looks upon death, it is certainly a venture into the unknown, and man usually experiences deep anxiety in the presence of the unfamiliar. Little wonder then that the thought of death has so often evoked dread. William Randolph Hearst had so powerful a fear of death that the very mention of the word in his presence was strictly prohibited. Even in his newspapers, the subject had to be handled with utmost delicacy.

Yet it is possible to face death without dread. Many have so faced it. When the father of Robert Browning lay on his deathbed his cheerfulness so surprised his physician that he asked the patient's daughter in a low voice: "Does the old gentleman know he is dying?" The patient overheard the question and answered: "Death is no enemy in my eyes."

In Jewish history there have been tens of thousands of men and women who in times of persecution deliberately chose death rather than live with dishonor. These acts of Kiddush Hashem, "sanctification of the Name of God," are a powerful tribute to the loyalty and the heroism of the martyrs. In a sense, they also reveal the equanimity with which these pious souls faced death.

Perhaps the most famous of Jewish martyrs in Talmudic times was Rabbi Akiba. As he was being put to death by the Romans for the capital offense of teaching Judaism, he said to his weeping disciples: "All my life I was disturbed over the verse 'And Thou shalt love the Lord thy God with all thy heart, with all thy soul and with all thy might.' The phrase 'with all thy soul' has been interpreted to mean that we must serve God even at the peril of our soul. And I was agitated over my inability to fulfil this verse. At last the opportunity has presented itself to me to love God 'with all my soul.' Now I am at peace."

Strangely, it is not the exceptional person who faces death serenely. While so many live with a fear of death, they actually seem to die in a spirit of calm acceptance. Such at least, is the overwhelming testimony of those who see people die.

Dr. Frank Adair is only one of many prominent physicians who bear witness to the courage and calm ninety-nine per cent of dying patients exhibit. Dr. Adair said: "The haunting fear which the average person carries all through life is dissipated by the approach of death."

If we can succeed in accepting the inexorable fact of our own death with equanimity, perhaps it will mitigate our sorrow over the death of our loved one. We can even learn to regard death not as an enemy but as a friend, who at the appointed hour leads us like Longfellow's little child at bedtime "half willing half reluctant to be led." Sancho Panza in "Don Quixote" spends a desperate night clinging to a window ledge, afraid of falling. When day breaks, he discovers that all the while his feet had been only an inch from the ground. Our fear of death may be as groundless as Sancho's fear of falling. Death may be but the threshhold over which we pass from time to eternity; from the realm of the perishable to the realm of the indestructible. And if we come to terms with death, who would dare to set a limit on what we could extract from life?

It is a real hour of triumph when a man can banish the fear of death from his heart and honestly say with the poet Sarah Williams "Though my Soul may set in darkness, it will rise in perfect light,

I have loved the stars too fondly to be fearful of the night."

YE WHO FEAR DEATH, REMEMBER APRIL

John Richard Moreland

Ye who fear death, remember April
With swords of jade on a thousand hills
And the warm, south wind that whispers
Of cornel and of purple squills.
Ye who fear death, remember April,
With moon-white trees, the new-turned sod,
And the bare brown branch that quickens
Like a sudden thought of God.
Ye who fear death, remember April,
Earth holds the seed until that hour
Of miracle when out of clay
Comes forth at last the flamelike flower!

William Penn

For Death is no more than a Turning of us over from Time to Eternity.

SLEEP IN THE QUIET NURSERY OF NATURE

Joshua Loth Liebman

I often feel that death is not the enemy of life, but its friend, for it is the knowledge that our years are limited which makes them so precious. It is the truth that time is but lent to us which makes us, at our best, look upon our years as a trust handed into our temporary keeping. We are like children privileged to spend a day in a great park, a park filled with many gardens and playgrounds and azure-tinted lakes with white boats sailing upon the tranquil waves. True, the day allotted to each one of us is not the same in length, in light, in beauty. Some children of earth are privileged to spend a long and sunlit day in the garden of the earth. For others the day is shorter, cloudier, and dusk descends more quickly as in a winter's tale. But whether our life is a long summery day or a shorter wintry afternoon, we know that inevitably there are storms and squalls which overcast even the bluest heaven and there are sunlit rays which pierce the darkest autumn sky. The day that we are privileged to spend in the great park of life is not the same for all human beings, but there is enough beauty and joy and gaiety in the hours if we will but treasure them. Then for each one of us the moment comes when the great nurse, death, takes man, the child, by the hand and quietly says, "It is time to go home. Night is coming. It is your bedtime, child of earth. Come; you're tired. Lie down at last in the quiet nursery of nature and sleep. Sleep well. The day is gone. Stars shine in the canopy of eternity."

Charles Lewis Slattery

Death, then, is still a great mystery. But it is not a mystery shrouded in darkness. Its mystery is of the light. It is a profound part of life, capable of displaying, in those who face it with courage, a richness and a beauty which no other part of life can equal.

ON HIS SEVENTY-FIFTH BIRTHDAY
Walter Savage Landor

I strove with none; for none was worth my strife,
    Nature I loved, and next to Nature, Art;
I warmed both hands before the fire of Life,
    It sinks and I am ready to depart.

Robert Montgomery

There's nothing terrible in death;
'Tis but to cast our robes away,
And sleep at night, without a breath
To break repose till dawn of day.

IT IS A CURSE NEVER TO DIE
Epictetus

If heads of grain had feeling, ought they to pray that they should not be harvested? I would have you know that it is a curse never to die. The ship goes down. What, then, am I to do? Whatever I can. I drown without fear, neither shrinking nor crying out against God, but recognizing that what is born must also perish. For I am part of the whole, as an hour is part of a day. I must come on as the hour, and like an hour, pass away. Regard yourself as but a single thread of all that go to make up the garment. Seek not that the things which happen to you should be as you wish, but wish the things that happen to you to be as they are, and you will find tranquillity.

Author unknown

Death is terrible, but still more terrible is the feeling that you might live forever and never die.

A VISION WITH NO TERRORS
Dr. H. D. Van Fleet

I have sat with dying men of every race and creed—Hindus, Shintoists, Catholics, Protestants, Jews, Mohammedans. They died in peace. And I have found that the sweetness of death is intensified in all men by a childlike faith in their own religion. Except for their own interpretation of religion, what men cling to is the same throughout the world.

Thus the occasional temporary apprehension about death stems, I believe, from the fact that an individual may not have prepared to meet it. His goals in life may have been too high; he isn't satisfied with what he has done; he may never have felt close to God. These anxieties can make the idea of dying untenable to him for the moment, until—consciously or unconsciously—he goes back to the religious beliefs that he learned as a child. . . .

As a doctor who has seen many people expire after a protracted illness, I know that it is often sweet to die. Frequently I have seen a change of expression as the moment of death approached, almost a smile, before the last breath was taken.

Science cannot explain this, as science cannot explain the dynamic power which controls life. What a man may see at the point of death will probably remain an eternal mystery. But it should remain, too, a vision with no terrors for any of us.

Epictetus

Not death or pain is to be feared, but the fear of death or pain. Well said the poet therefore: "Death has no terror; only a death of shame!"

HE HAD NO FEAR

Dr. Walter C. Alvarez

. . . I have seen any number who were conscious and clear-headed up to the last few moments of life. They didn't seem to be too much concerned with what was happening to them. Others, of course, are told of their fate honestly.

I remember in particular a man with a hopeless cancer who listened to the results of my examination and then said: "Doctor, answer me this: If you had this thing and you had a brilliant boy in his junior year in medical school, would you expend your savings on an operation which might prolong your life for a few months or do nothing?"

"I'd leave the money for the boy," I answered.

"That's what I hoped you'd say," he replied. "That's what I'm going to do."

That man's wife told me that he had not the remotest idea what was the matter with him, that he'd kill himself if he learned the truth. Little did she know her husband. He knew perfectly well what was wrong with him before I told him. And his only thought was for his son.

That man's courage was typical of men and women I have seen with fatal illnesses. He not only was brave, he had no fear.

REQUIEM

Robert Louis Stevenson

Under the wide and starry sky,
Dig the grave and let me die.
Glad did I live and gladly die,
    And I laid me down with a will.

This be the verse you grave for me:
Here he lies where he longed to be;
Home is the sailor, home from the sea,
And the hunter home from the hill.

Robert Louis Stevenson

Robert Louis Stevenson, on his death-bed wrote to a friend about an old woman who had frightened some primitive natives with her ventriloquism:

All the old women in the world might talk with their mouths shut and not frighten you or me, but there are plenty of other things that frighten us badly. And if we only knew about them, perhaps we should find them no more worthy to be feared than an old woman talking with her mouth shut. And the names of some of these things are Death and Pain and Sorrow.

Epictetus

Reflect that the chief source of all evils to man, and of baseness and cowardice, is not death, but the fear of death.

SERENELY TO ACCEPT WHAT HAPPENS
Joshua Loth Liebman

Judaism encourages us . . . to recognize that it (death) is as natural an aspect of human life as birth. When man has established a confidence in life and the God of life, he is prepared serenely to accept what happens after death even as he does not worry about what took place before birth. When we become morbidly and obsessively preoccupied with the thought of the end of life, we show that we have fallen in love with ourselves to such an extent that we cannot tolerate the idea of a possible final sleep. Yet the fear of death is a deceiver. We think that we are frightened of death, when actually beneath the surface we are frightened of many things that life has inflicted upon us—some forgotten rejection in childhood, some imprisonment in a dark and foreboding closet as a punishment for a childish prank or tantrum, some identification with an annihilationist mother or a punishing father. It should come as a liberation to recognize that it is not death that is to be feared, but many of the scares of life which are to be removed, understood, discarded.

As mature people we must learn not to love ourselves excessively nor to mistrust the universe morbidly. The truth is that we change and die every day a little. Yes, we die every day a little bit without fear. Our skins change. The cells in our hands and in our brains perish and are reborn. Our whole life is strewn with the bones of hopes discarded, dreams outgrown, loves broken, friendships embraced. We change and die every dawn and every sunset, yes, without fear. Let us recognize that we are part of nature, both in life and in death. The atoms composing us are arranged differently in the moment of our conception, at the time of birth as we grow and clothe our skeleton with the flesh and muscles, the tendons and the veins of maturity, and then when the curtain is drawn over our earthly frame, the atoms of our being are rearranged and enter once again the treasury of nature and we are at rest. The shock of corn has fallen upon the soil from which it sprang and we are once more in the bosom of the Divine.

Marcus Aurelius

Think not disdainfully of death, but look on it with favor, for nature wills it like all else. . . . Look for the hour when the soul shall emerge from this its sheath, as now thou awaitest the moment when the child she carries shall come forth from the wife's womb.

IF THE GENERATIONS DID NOT
COME AND GO

Joshua Loth Liebman

Judaism . . . teaches us to understand death as part of the Divine pattern of the universe. Actually we could not have our sensitivity without fragility. Mortality is the tax that we pay for the privilege of love, thought, creative work—the toll on the bridge of being from which clods of earth and snow-peaked mountain summits are exempt. Just because we are human, we are prisoners of the years, yet that very prison is the room of discipline in which we, driven by the urgency of time, create.

We can face death without dread when we learn that the Angel of Death plays a very vital role in life's economy. Actually there could be no growth, no progress, if generations did not come and go. There also would be very little meaning to existence if the years were not marked off in the calendar of time by childhood, adolescence, youth, and age. There is a time to run gaily with all the intense excitement of a boy with flushed cheeks racing on a summer's day towards the winding river of sport and adventure; there is also the time when that boy, transformed by the alchemy of the years into an old man, no longer seeks to run but is quite content to sit and browse even unto the twilight.

THE VALIANT TASTE DEATH BUT ONCE

Shakespeare

Cowards die many times before their deaths;
The valiant never taste of death but once.
Of all the wonders that I yet have heard,
It seems to me most strange that men should fear;
Seeing that death, a necessary end,
Will come when it will come.

NOTHING IN HIS LIFE

Shakespeare

Nothing in his life
Became him like the leaving it; he died
As one that had been studied in his death
To throw away the dearest thing he owed,
As 'twere a careless trifle.

DO NOT DESPISE DEATH

Marcus Aurelius

Do not despise death, but be well content with it, since this, too, is one of those things which nature wills. For such as it is to be young and to grow old, and to increase and to reach maturity, and to have teeth and beard and gray hairs, and to beget, and to be pregnant, and to bring forth, and all the other natural operations which the seasons of thy life bring, such also is dissolution. This, then, is consistent with the character of a reflecting man, to be neither careless nor impatient nor contemptuous with respect to death, but to wait for it as one of the operations of nature.

DEATH

William Croswell Doane

We are too stupid about death. We will not learn
How it is wages paid to those who earn,
How it is the gift for which on earth we yearn,
To be set free from bondage to the flesh;
How it is turning seed-corn into grain,
How it is winning Heaven's eternal gain,
How it means freedom evermore from pain,
How it untangles every mortal mesh.

ACCEPTING DEATH

Dorothy Thompson

The mother of a friend of mine died the other day. My friend's eleven-year-old daughter was sent away until after the funeral. She must be spared a knowledge of death. Is this not characteristic of our society? We treat death as if it were an aberration. Age approaches but beauticians, masseur and gland specialists cooperate to keep alive the illusion that we are not really growing older. Anything that reminds us of the inescapable fact that we are to die seems morbid to us. Yet without the serene acceptance of death as inexorable we lose all the magic and wonder of life and live in constant unconscious fear. For only when one is no longer afraid to die is one no longer afraid at all. And only when we are no longer afraid do we begin to live in every experience, painful or joyous; to live in gratitude for every moment, to live abundantly.

DEATH IS A FRIEND

Montaigne

Nature herself gives us courage. . . . Death is not to be feared. It is a friend. No man dies before his hour. The time you leave behind was no more yours than that which was before your birth and concerneth you no more. Make room for others as others have done for you. Like a full-fed guest, depart to rest. . . . The profit of life consists not in the space, but in the use. Some man hath lived long that has had a short life. . . .

Depart then without fear out of this world even as you came into it. The same way you came from death to life, return from life to death. Yield your torch to others as in a race. Your death is but a piece of the world's order, but a parcel of the world's life.

HIS TENDER HANDS

Winnie Lynch Rockett

His tender hands have fashioned tiny things:
The wee blue petals of forget-me-nots;
A drop of mist; an insect's tissue wings;
A poppy seed; a caterpillar's spots;
The sensitive antennae of a bee;
Each amber globule of the desert sands—
Then shall I fear, when He has said to me,
"Thy days, my little one, are in my hands?"

THE FAITH OF THE POET

Victor Hugo

You say, "Where goest thou?" I cannot tell,
And still go on. If but the way be straight,
It cannot go amiss! Before me lies
Dawn and the Day; the Night behind me; that
Suffices me; I break the bonds; I see,
And nothing more; believe, and nothing less.
My future is not one of my concerns.

MY SOUL AND I

Charles Buxton Going

As treading some long corridor,
    My soul and I together go;

Each day unlocks another door
   To a new room we did not know.
And every night the darkness hides
   My soul from me awhile—but then
No fear nor loneliness abides:
   Hand clasped in hand, we wake again.
So when my soul and I at last
   Shall find but one dim portal more,
Shall we, remembering all the past,
   Yet fear to try that other door?

APOLOGY OF SOCRATES

Plato

Let us reflect in another way, and we shall see that there is great reason to hope that death is a good, for one of two things: either death is a state of nothingness and utter unconsciousness, or, as men say, there is a change and migration of the soul from this world to another. Now if you suppose that there is no consciousness, but a sleep like the sleep of him who is undisturbed even by the sight of dreams, death will be an unspeakable gain. For if a person were to select the night in which his sleep was undisturbed even by dreams, and were to compare with the other days and nights of his life, and then were to tell us how many days and nights he had passed in the course of his life better and more pleasantly than this one, I think that any man, I will not say a private man, but even the great king, will not find many such days or nights, when compared with the others. Now if death is like this, I say that to die, is gain: for eternity is then only a single night. But if death is the journey to another place, and there, as men say, all the dead are, what good, O my friends and judges, can be greater than this?

DEATH IS NOT THE ENEMY OF LIFE

Anonymous

From "Forward Movement"

Much of our horror of death comes from the feeling (even though it may never be expressed) that it is the enemy of life. We love life; therefore it is natural to dread death. But death is no more the enemy of life than sleep is the enemy of work and play. Sleep makes it possible for us to work and play the next day. Death makes it possible for us to live on. It has therefore a real contribution to make to life in the large, being the gateway through which we slip from the lower life into the higher, from the briefer into that which is eternal.

THE BIRTHDAY OF ETERNITY
Seneca

As the mother's womb holds us for ten months, making us ready, not for the womb itself, but for life, just so, through our lives we are making ourselves ready for another birth. . . . Therefore look forward without fear to that appointed hour—the last hour of the body, but not of the soul. . . . That day, which you fear as being the end of all things, is the birthday of your eternity.

Lucan

None but those shadowed by death's approach are suffered to know that death is a blessing; the gods conceal this from those who have life before them, in order that they may go on living.

Henry Wadsworth Longfellow

Good-night! good-night! as we so oft have said,
    Beneath this roof at midnight, in the days
    That are no more, and shall no more return.
Thou hast but taken up thy lamp and gone to bed;
    I stay a little longer, as one stays
    To cover up the embers that still burn.

DEATH IS AN AFFIRMATIVE EXPERIENCE
Zelda Popkin

There is no human experience which man fears more and understands less, and this very dread largely prevents him from understanding it. He pushes it back in his mind, as though by refusing to acknowledge the possibility, he may avert it. Yet death is a major experience of life. It is an affirmative experience, since through it, the living grow in depth.

DEATH IS NOT A THING TO BE FEARED
Cicero

What a poor dotard must he be who has not learnt in the course of so long a life that death is not a thing to be feared? Death, that is either to be totally disregarded, if it entirely extinguishes the soul, or is even to be desired, if it brings him where he is to exist forever. A third alternative, at any rate, cannot possibly be discovered. Why then should I be afraid if I am destined either not to be miserable after death or even to be happy?

TERMINATION OF ACTIVITY IS NO EVIL
Marcus Aurelius

Termination of activity, cessation from movement and opinion, and in a sense their death, is no evil. Turn thy thoughts now to the consideration of thy life, thy life as a child, as a youth, thy manhood, thy old age, for in these also every change was a death. Is this anything to fear? Turn thy thoughts now to thy life under thy grandfather, then to thy life under thy mother, then to thy life under thy father; and as thou findest many other differences and changes and terminations, ask thyself, Is this anything to fear? In like manner, then, neither are the termination and cessation and change of thy whole life a thing to be afraid of.

CONQUER THE FEAR OF DEATH
Leo Tolstoy

Man is a being beyond time and beyond space who is conscious of himself in the conditions of space and time. One should conquer the fear of death; and when you cease to fear it, you cease to serve yourself, a mortal, and you will serve an immortal God, from whom you came and to whom you are going.

Not long ago I experienced a feeling, not exactly a reasoning, but a feeling, that everything that is material and I myself, with my own body, is only my own imagination, is the creation of my spirit, and that only my soul exists. It was a very joyous feeling.

Mrs. Thomas Henry Huxley
Lines on the gravestone of Thomas Henry Huxley

And if there be not meeting past the grave,
If all is darkness, silence, yet 'tis rest.
Be not afraid, ye waiting hearts that weep,
For still he giveth His beloved sleep,
And if an endless sleep He wills, 'tis best.

WE NEED NOT DIE WHILE WE ARE LIVING
Henry Ward Beecher

What if the leaves were to fall a-weeping, and say, "It will be so painful for us to be pulled from our stalks when autumn comes?" The glory of death is upon the leaves; and the gentlest breeze that blows takes them softly and silently from the bough, and they float slowly down like fiery sparks upon the moss. It is hard to die when the time is not ripe. When it is, it will be easy. We need not die while we are living.

Isaiah

Say to them that are of fearful heart, be strong, fear not.

MEDITATIONS
Solomon Ibn Gabirol (Translated by Emma Lazarus)

Forget thine anguish,
Vexed heart, again.
Why shouldst thou languish,
With earthly pain?
The husk shall slumber,
Bedded in clay
Silent and sombre,
Oblivion's prey!

But, Spirit immortal,
Thou at Death's portal,
Tremblest with fear.
If he caress thee,
Curse thee or bless thee,
Thou must draw near,
From him the worth of thy works to hear.

Why full of terror,
Compassed with error,
Trouble thy heart,
For thy mortal part?
The soul flies home—
The corpse is dumb.
Of all thou didst have,
Follows naught to the grave.
Thou fliest thy nest,
Swift as a bird to thy place of rest.

Wisdom of Ben Sira

Make little weeping for the dead, for he is at rest.

FROM "THE SLEEP"
Elizabeth Barrett Browning

Of all the thoughts of God that are
Borne inward unto souls afar,
Along the Psalmist's music deep,
Now tell me if that any is,
For gift or grace, surpassing this—
"He giveth His beloved sleep"?

What would we give to our beloved?
The hero's heart, to be unmoved,
The poet's star-tuned harp, to sweep,
The patriot's voice, to teach and rouse,
The monarch's crown, to light the brows?
He giveth His beloved sleep.

What do we give to our beloved?
A little faith all undisproved,
A little dust to overweep,
And bitter memories to make
The whole earth blasted for our sake:
He giveth His beloved sleep.

"Sleep soft, beloved!" we sometimes say,
But have no tune to charm away
Sad dreams that through the eyelids creep.
But never doleful dream again
Shall break the happy slumber when
He giveth His beloved sleep.

And, friends, dear friends, when it shall be
That this low breath is gone from me,
And round my bier ye come to weep,
Let One, most loving of you all,
Say, "Not a tear must o'er her fall!
He giveth His beloved sleep."

WHEN THOU PASSEST THROUGH THE WATERS

Cecil

My first convictions on the subject of religion were confirmed by observing that really religious persons had some solid happiness among them, which I felt the vanities of the world could not give. I shall never forget standing by the bedside of my sick mother. "Are you not afraid to die?" I asked. "No." "No? Why does the uncertainty of another state give you no concern?" "Because God has said, 'Fear not; when thou passest through the waters, I will be with thee; and through the rivers, they shall not overflow thee.' Let me die the death of the righteous."

Wisdom of Solomon

The souls of the righteous are in the hand of God,
And no torment shall touch them.
In the eyes of the foolish they seemed to have died:

And their departure was accounted to be their hurt,
And their journeying away from us to be their ruin:
But they are in peace.

WHAT IS DEATH?

Author unknown

What is death? A little broadening of a ripple
Upon the eternal shore.
A little loosening of the bands that cripple—
This and nothing more.
What's death? A parting of the cloud above us
Which hides the sun,
A gold vision of the souls that love us
And labor done.
What's death? The opening of a perfect flower;
No watcher sees
The silent spirit, who at twilight hour
The bondman frees.
What's death? God's mercy strange
Uncomprehended;
The undiscovered goal;
The land of promise when the toil
Is ended—
The day-dawn of the soul.

Psalms

The Lord is my shepherd; I shall not want.
He maketh me to lie down in green pastures;
He leadeth me beside the still waters.
He restoreth my soul;
He guideth me in straight paths for His name's sake.
Yea, though I walk through the valley of the shadow of death,
I will fear no evil,
For Thou art with me;
Thy rod and Thy staff, they comfort me.

T. C. Williams

Death is an angel with two faces:
To us he turns
A face of terror, blighting all things fair;
The other burns
With glory of the stars, and love is there.

Ella Wheeler Wilcox

I think of death as some delightful journey
That I shall take when all my tasks are done.

Cato

He who fears death has already lost the life he covets.

PROSPICE

Robert Browning

Fear death?—to feel the fog in my throat,
    The mist in my face,
When the snows begin, and the blasts denote
    I am nearing the place,
The power of the night, the press of the storm,
    The post of the foe;
Where he stands, the Arch Fear in a visible form,
    Yet the strong man must go;
For the journey is done and the summit attained,
    And the barriers fall,
Though a battle's to fight ere the guerdon be gained,
    The reward of it all.
I was ever a fighter, so—one fight more,
    The best and the last!
I would hate that death bandaged my eyes, and forbore,
    And bade me creep past.
No! let me taste the whole of it, fare like my peers
    The heroes of old,

Bear the brunt, in a minute pay glad life's arrears
    Of pain, darkness, and cold.
For sudden the worst turns the best to the brave,
    The black minute's at end,
And the elements' rage, the fiend-voices that rave,
    Shall dwindle, shall blend,
Shall change, shall become first a peace out of pain,
    Then a light, then thy breast,
O thou soul of my soul! I shall clasp thee again,
    And with God be the rest!

Wisdom of Ben Sira

Fear not the sentence of death; why dost thou refuse when it is the good pleasure of the Most High?

Plutarch

What can they suffer that do not fear to die?

FRIENDSHIP WITH DEATH AS WITH LIFE
John Gunther

No fear of death or any hereafter. During our last summer at Madison, I would write in my diary when I couldn't sleep. "Look Death in the face. To look Death in the face, and not be afraid. To be friendly to Death as to Life. Death as a part of Life, like Birth. Not the final part. I have no sense of finality about Death. Only the final scene in a single act of a play that goes on forever. Look Death in the face: it's a friendly face, a kindly face, sad, reluctant, knowing it is not welcome but having to play its part when its cue is called, perhaps trying to say, "Come, it won't be too bad, don't be afraid, I understand how you feel, but come—there may be other miracles!" No fear of Death, no fight against Death, no enmity toward Death, friendship with Death as with Life.

THE LANDSMAN
Robert Nathan

Oh, troubled heart, the fall with colder breath
Blows in the tassel as the farmers reap;
So in the autumn comes the landsman, death,
His step is quiet, and his house is sleep.

Richard Baxter

Richard Baxter, when on his deathbed suffering great pain, was asked how he felt, and replied, "Almost well." At length the final hour arrived, and he became, in his own language, "Entirely well."

SELFISHNESS
Margaret E. Bruner

Death takes our loved ones—
We are bowed in grief. For whom?
Are we not selfish?
A mourner weeps for himself,
The dead know not of sorrow.

THERE IS NO SADNESS
Margaret E. Bruner

Oh, you who mourn that autumn's loveliness
Must pass—her gold and crimson glory fade—
Earth's music for a space must have an end,
These last high notes conclude her serenade.

For like the climax of a perfect song,
The singer's ardor dies and he must rest;
So must the shriveled leaf and withered flower
Sink to oblivion on earth's deep breast.

And pity not the trees whose boughs are bare,
They knew creation's pangs—its joy and grief;
They meet with eagerness the icy wind—
There is no sadness in the falling leaf.

Deuteronomy

And the Lord, He it is that doth go before thee
He will be with thee, He will not fail thee,
Neither forsake thee: fear not, neither be dismayed.

David Weinberg

He who fears death is really afraid of life.

THE CARRIAGE IS DISMISSED
John Bigelow

Sleep and death—they differ in duration rather than in quality. Perhaps both are sojourns in the spiritual, the real world. In one case our carriage waits nightly to take us back from the entrance of slumber, while in the other, having arrived at our destination and with no further use for the carriage, it is dismissed.

Rabbi Bunam

When Rabbi Bunam was lying on his deathbed, he said to his wife who wept bitterly, "Why dost thou weep? All my life has been given to me merely that I might learn to die."

A NURSE BOTH AFFECTIONATE AND STERN
From H. G. Wells

On his seventieth birthday, H. G. Wells was honored by a group of English authors. When he arose to acknowledge their tributes, he said that he was reminded of his feelings as a child when his nurse would say to him: "Master Henry, it's your bedtime." He would protest, of course, as all children do at bedtime, even though he knew in his heart that sleep would bring him much welcome rest. "Death," continued Wells, "is a nurse both affectionate and stern; when the time comes, she says to us: 'Master Henry, it's your bedtime.' We protest a little, but we know quite well that the time for rest has come and that in our hearts we are longing for it."

Jonathan Swift

It is impossible that anything so natural, so necessary, and so universal as death should ever have been designed as an evil to mankind.

Samuel Coleridge

Death came with friendly care, the opening bud to heaven conveyed, and bade it blossom there.

Francis Bacon

Men fear Death as children fear to go in the dark; and as that natural fear in children is increased with tales so is the other. . . . It is as natural to die as to be born; and to a little infant perhaps the one is as painful as the other.

Henry Wadsworth Longfellow

And as she looked around, she saw how Death the consoler,
Laying his hand upon many a heart, had healed it forever.

NATURE
Henry Wadsworth Longfellow

As a fond mother, when the day is o'er,
    Leads by the hand her little child to bed,
    Half willing, half reluctant to be led,
    And leave his broken playthings on the floor,

Still gazing at them through the open door
  Nor wholly reassured and comforted
  By promises of others in their stead,
  Which though more splendid, may not
    please him more;
So Nature deals with us, and takes away our
  Playthings one by one, and by the hand
  Leads us to rest so gently, that we go
Scarce knowing if we wish to go or stay,
  Being too full of sleep to understand
  How far the unknown transcends
    what we know.

WHY SHOULD WE FEAR?
Sir Philip Sidney

Since Nature's works be good, and death doth serve
As Nature's work, why should we fear to die?
Since fear is vain, but when it may preserve,
Why should we fear that which we cannot fly?

THE LESSON OF THE STARS
Leslie R. Smith

A small child who saw the stars for the first time was greatly impressed and intrigued by them. Childlike, she had many questions. Were they there all the time? Why couldn't you see them during the day? Couldn't you see them until it got dark? Her mother replied: "Yes, their beauty is hidden all through the day. You can see them only at night. Aren't they lovely?" And then she added: "Darkness is always beautiful, if we will only look up at the stars instead of into the corners."

How true! If we will just look up at the stars! They tell us that night is the most joyous part of the day. It is the time of homecoming after a hard day's work. We step out of the limited interest of business associates and friends into the boundless love of home and family. In this happy fellowship we relax after the strain of a busy day. Night is the time for rest and for sleep. So it is with death. It is life's night. It is a glorious homecoming. It is a reunion with those who have gone before. It is rest from labor. It is simply to lie back in the Everlastng Arms.

William Wordsworth

But when the great and good depart,
What is it more than this—
That Man, who is from God sent forth,
Doth yet again to God return?—
Such ebb and flow must ever be,
Then wherefore should we mourn?

I hold it true, whate'er befall;
I feel it when I sorrow most;
'Tis better to have loved and lost
Than never to have loved at all.

—Alfred Tennyson

GRIEF SOFTENED BY GRATITUDE

The dreary clouds of grief which gather in the wake of death cast thick gloom over the lives of the bereaved. An aching void, an overpowering loneliness, a fear of facing the future alone, a gnawing pain over the unlived years—all these combine to throw deep darkness over our days. Yet there are small pin points of light that penetrate the overcast. Amidst our grief, if we pause to reflect, we can find, as others have, genuine cause for gratitude. This gratitude may not dispel the gloom but it can relieve it.

Even while we mourn the death of a loved one, there is room in our hearts for thankfulness for that life. We have lost what we have had. For those years of love and comradeship there is no adequate compensation. Impoverished as we are by the passing of our beloved, we should be poorer by far if we had never tasted the joy and richness of that union. Sadder than losing a loved one is never having had a loved one to lose. Helen Hayes expressed this thought most pointedly after the death of her highly gifted daughter. "Tragic that it should have ended," she said of Mary's life, "but how much better than if it had never been."

We can be grateful, too, that while death robs us of our loved ones, it cannot take from us the years that passed and their abiding impression. These have entered into our lives and become part of ourselves. With the poet Georgia Harkness we can say of the loved one we mourn:

77

> To know this life was good—
> It left its mark on me.
> Its work stands fast.

Sober reflection can also lead us to a more sympathetic appreciation of the vital role death plays in the economy of life. Life's significance and zest issue from our awareness of its transiency, its "fragile contingency." The urge to create, the passion to perfect, the will to heal and cure—all the noblest of human enterprises grow in the soil of human mortality. They would vanish if life on earth were an endless, unrelieved process.

To the person of religious faith there remains the profoundest source of gratitude amidst grief. His is the reassuring conviction that the soul is imperishable and "the grave is not its goal." The souls of our loved ones, like our own, come from the great Source of Life, Himself, and flow back into the eternal stream after the earthly pilgrimage is ended.

Thus the pain of parting is mitigated by faith in a divine providence which permits no life to be utterly destroyed. It was this faith which spoke out of Job in his hour of anguish and has since been repeated by countless bereaved believers: "The Lord hath given, The Lord hath taken back, praised be the name of the Lord."

TO MY FATHER
Georgia Harkness

A giant pine, magnificent and old,
Stood staunch against the sky and all around
Shed beauty, grace, and power. Within its fold
Birds safely reared their young. The velvet ground
Beneath was gentle, and the cooling shade
Gave cheer to passers-by. Its towering arms
A landmark stood, erect and unafraid,
As if to say, "Fear naught from life's alarms."

It fell one day. Where it had dauntless stood
Was loneliness and void. But men who passed

Paid tribute—said, "To know this life was good,
It left its mark on me. Its work stands fast."
And so it lives. Such life no bonds can hold—
This giant pine, magnificent and old.

IS IT REALLY THE END?

Rachel (Translated from the Hebrew by the editor)

Is it really the end? The path is still clear.
The mists of life still beckon from afar
The sky is still blue, the grass green;
Autumn is coming.

I shall accept the judgment. My heart harbors no complaint.
How red were my sunsets, how clear my dawns!
And flowers smiled along my path
As I passed.

SHED NOT TOO MANY TEARS

Author unknown

Shed not too many tears when I shall leave;
    Be brave enough to smile.
It will not shorten, howsoe'er you grieve,
    Your loneliness the while.
I would not have you sorrowful and sad,
    But joyfully recall
The glorious companionship we've had,
    And thank God for it all.
Don't let your face grow tear-streaked,
      pale and wan:
    Have heart for mirth and song—
Rejoice, though for a little while I've gone,
    That I was here so long,
For if I thought your faith would fail you so,
    And leave you so distressed,
That sobbing to my body's grave you'd go,
    My spirit could not rest.

SOMEHOW STRENGTH LASTED
Author unknown

Somehow strength lasted through the day,
Hope joined with courage in the way;
The feet still kept the uphill road,
The shoulders did not drop their load,
And unseen power sustained the heart
When flesh and will failed in their part,
    While God gave light
    By day and night,
And also grace to bear the smart.
    For this give thanks.

I THANK GOD SHE WAS MINE FOR THE WHILE I HAD HER
Grace Perkins Oursler and April Armstrong

So it is with love gone. You've had it. In your heart you know you wouldn't trade it for all the riches on earth.

Many people never know it. There are millions who never taste the cup of love, though it is brewed constantly about them, poured before their eyes, left steaming with enticing promises of dreams unfulfilled, and poured out on the ground before dogs. There are those who have never heard a child's call, or looked into eyes that trusted them with overwhelming confidence; men and women who have never been chosen and cherished, however briefly —people who do not know the meaning of friend.

"I've heard so many folks say they would never again have a dog or a bird," a famous statesman, who lost his small daughter, told his father one day, "because it broke their heart so when the pet died. I do not pretend to know why Susan was given to me and snatched away. But I thank God she was mine for the while I had her. I wouldn't have not had her whatever my heartbreak now. And I know that her going brought out whatever of greatness in me that I have. One has to surmount—or fall by the wayside."

John Vance Cheney

The soul would have no rainbow
Had the eyes no tears.

FROM "AT EIGHTY-THREE"
Thomas Durley Landels

Thank God for life, with all its endless store
Of great experiences, of hill and dale,
Of cloud and sunshine, tempest, snow and hail.
Thank God for straining sinews, panting breast,
No less for weary slumber, peaceful rest;
Thank God for home and parents, children, friends,
For sweet companionship that never ends:
Thank God for all the splendor of the earth,
For nature teeming with prolific birth:
Thank God for sea and sky, for changing hours,
For trees and singing birds and fragrant flowers.
And so in looking back at eighty-three,
My final word to you, my friends, shall be:
Thank God for life; and when the gift's withdrawn,
Thank God for twilight bell, and coming dawn.

THE SPARK OF GRATEFULNESS
Joseph I. Weiss

However short, however long the time given to those who are near to us, strength will be fashioned through the gratitude of our hearts for the blessing of life itself. When the days of life are short, shall we curse the moments of beauty for their brevity, or prize them that they came to us at all? When toll is taken in the middle years, shall we be bitter for lack of more, or wall our tears with thanksgiving for what has been? When the bridge of three-score and ten has been crossed, shall we be torn with argument for a longer term, or be grateful for the fullness of the granted time?

Our sages said that all things might be lost save one: the spirit of gratitude that is ever present in the heart of man. They further said that as long as thanksgiving lasts, the world will endure. The waters of sadness are deep, but they will never extinguish the spark of gratefulness that is fed by man's inherent recognition of God's goodness toward him. Let us fan that spark into a flame that will guide us happily into the future.

THEREFORE, WE THANK THEE GOD

Reuben Avinoam (Translated by L. V. Snowman)

The Hebrew poet Reuben Grossman was born in Chicago. His son Noam studied at the Hebrew University, became an officer of Haganah when the fighting started and fell in March, 1948, along with seventeen of his comrades. After the son's death, the poet changed his name to Avinoam which in Hebrew means "father of Noam."

This poem appeared in "Davar," the Hebrew publication, and the following translation is taken from "The Living Rampart," an anthology of stories and poems written in Israel during the war.

At the end of a week of mourning for our son Noam.

Incline Thine ear, O God,
Consider a brief space
In this night hour of sombre rage
The word of parents bewildered by bereavement.
We approach Thee not with regret, nor complaint.
Nor do we come to litigate with Thee,
Only thanks pouring from the wound of our heart we offer
    Thee.
Accept it, O God.
For these three things thanksgiving be to Thee:

For pleasant years,
For one and twenty years
Wherein Thou didst honour us with him and lent him us,
For his steps walking humbly by our side on the little isle
    of life:
Years sown with the peace of his being,
When like a gliding swan he made his way erect with grace;
Years shining with smiles
Which like sunrays he spread around him,

With good-hearted whispers, pardons by concession and
     understanding,
Years shining with the light of his two eyes,
Where dreams yearned, mingled with the sorrow of fate,
Having a pure look and upright before God and man.
For this little gift.
For twenty-one full years of life Thou gavest him and us,
We thank Thee. . . .

And for a hero's death
Thou didst appoint him,
For all the limbs of his body were taut in strength,
And welded in pride
And on all his sinews was spread the essence of power,
The wine kept for the saints of Thy people who hallow its
     land.
Thou didst lead him among the evening-hills in the heights
     of Judah,
No voice being heard but the bidding of the Maccabees of old.
The echoes of their blood set his exultant heart tramping
     to victory,
No other lodestar but the light of his own soul,
A tongue of fire
Born of the flame of Bar Kochba which he kindled,
Marching serene, stepping with confidence
In the height of dread and solitude,
Girt with the armour of hope, encircled with the girdle of
     power,
To meet the beginning of freedom or the end of glory. . .
For death which was like a kiss
At the lips of Mattathias the Hasmonean
With which Thou didst favour him
When he ascended the holy ladder,
We thank Thee. . . .

And for the flowing tear
When Thou didst make Thy host of clouds and
Thy bands of cherubs weep—
When the news of the bereavement reached us—
And when Thou didst roll the sighs of the thunder of Thy
     heart
Among the terrible heights,

And us here on the gloomy earth,
When our soul was clothed with grief for our son!
For Thy tears shed and Thy sigh breathed
Together with those of a father and a mother
We thank Thee. . . .

FROM "ODE: INTIMATION OF IMMORTALITY"

William Wordsworth

What though the radiance which was so bright
Be now for ever taken from my sight,
Though nothing can bring back the hour
Of splendour in the grass, of glory in the flower;
We will grieve not, rather find
Strength in what remains behind;
In the primal sympathy
Which having been must ever be;
In the soothing thoughts that spring
Out of human suffering;
In the faith that looks through death,
In years that bring the philosophic mind.

LIFE OWES ME NOTHING

Author unknown

Life owes me nothing. Let the years
Bring clouds or azure, joy or tears,
Already a full cup I've quaffed;
Already wept and loved and laughed,
And seen, in ever endless days.

Life owes me naught. No pain that waits
Can steal the wealth from memory's gates;
No aftermath of anguish slow
Can quench the soul-fire's early glow.
I breathe, exulting, each new breath,
Embracing Life, ignoring Death.

Life owes me nothing. One clear morn
Is boon enough for being born;
And be it ninety years or ten,
No need for me to question when.
While Life is mine, I'll find it good,
And greet each hour with gratitude.

LET US COUNT THE PAST AS GAIN
Morris Joseph

It is not God's part to spare us suffering—for that is essential
to his plan—but to help us to bear it. If the visitation we dread
finds us—for it may be for our good that it should find us—then
we do right to ask for the strength that will uphold us under the
load, for the insight that reveals the wisdom of it, for the magic
power that will transform it into blessing. And to that prayer there
is always an answer. . . .

Something precious is taken from us, and we think of it as
something we have lost, instead of something we have had. We
remember only how empty our lives are now, we forget how full
and rich they were before; we forget all the many days and years
of happiness we lived while the beloved object was still with us.
We praise God for our treasures while we have them; we cease to
praise him for them when they are fled. But God never gives; He
only lends. What is life itself but a loan? "Everything," cry the old
sages, "is given in pledge" to be restored when the Master wills. . . .
No. When God claims His own shall we rebel or repine? Instead of
murmuring because He takes our precious things from us, let us be
grateful to Him for having spared them to us so long. Let us count
the past happy days not as loss, but as gain. We have had them;
and, now that they are ended, let us turn the loss to glorious gain—
the gain that comes with new courage, with nobler tasks, with a
wider outlook on life and duty. . . .

PRAYER IN SORROW
Sidney Greenberg

Help me, loving Father, to bear bravely the burden of bereavement which weighs upon my heart. May the grief over the death of

my loved one not suffocate the gratitude I owe for the years of life we shared together.

Thou hast created us with a wisdom which we can only partially understand. If it is Thy law that the brightness of noon is followed by the blackness of night and the joy of love by the pain of parting, teach me to accept my sorrow as the spiritual coin with which I pay in part for the blessings of love. Help me to understand, too, that just as the night which blots out the mid-day light fades in turn before the rising sun, so does the death of the body make way for the everlasting life of the soul.

Abide with me in the valley of the shadow. Keep aglow my candle of hope until I shall reach the open meadows of healing and sunshine that lie beyond. *Amen.*

THE TWO SHIPS
Midrash

Two ships were once seen near land. One of them was leaving the harbor, and the other was coming into it. Everyone was cheering the outgoing ship, giving it a hearty send-off. But the incoming ship was scarcely noticed.

A wise man standing nearby explained the people's reaction. "Rejoice not," he said, "over the ship that is setting out to sea, for you know not what destiny awaits it, what storms it may encounter, what dangers lurk before it. Rejoice rather over the ship that has reached port safely and brought back all its passengers in peace."

It is the way of the world, that when a human being is born, all rejoice; but when he dies, all sorrow. It should be the other way around. No one can tell what troubles await the developing child on its journey through life. But when a man has lived well and dies in peace, all should rejoice, for he has completed his journey successfully and he is departing from this world with the imperishable crown of a good name.

DEATH MAKES LIFE MORE MEANINGFUL
Joshua Loth Liebman

The presence of death makes more meaningful all of the values of life. . . . In our rebellious moments we feel, that if we had designed the universe, we would have given man an ever-renewable fountain of youth, so that death could never come and the end of life could never be felt. Yet when we analyze this feeling, we realize that this is the petulant, unreflective desire of a distraught child. . . .

. . . The joy of our striving and the zest of our aspirations, so precious because of their fragile contingency, would vanish if earthly immortality were our inescapable lot and destiny. . . .

. . . The more mature we grow, the more we recognize unsuspected wisdom in the way that nature arranges things. . . .

. . . Apparently, nature does not have the power to create such marvelously sensitive organisms as we human beings are, and at the same time arrange for the durability in us of stone or mountain. This is a universe where everything has a price, and we cannot expect to purchase the fragile beauty of love and consciousness without the suffering of transciency and decay. . . .

. . . The glory of life consists in our very ability to feel deeply and experience widely; it is the part of wisdom to taste of the cup of joy and sorrow without inner rebelliousness, to accept with equanimity the inevitable fact that we and all we possess are transient just because we are such sensitive creatures; that the marvel of our make-up, the superb intricacy of our chemical, physical, spiritual organization gives us our supreme blessings and makes our little day on earth infinitely more significant than all of the rocks and stones which last unchanged but also untouched by the winds of the centuries. . . .

FROM "RUGBY CHAPEL"
Matthew Arnold

And through thee I believe
In the noble and great who are gone,
Pure souls honored and blest
By former ages who else—
Such, so soulless, so poor,
Is the race of men whom I see—
Seem'd but a dream of the heart,
Seem'd but a cry of desire
Yes, I believe that there lived
Others like thee in the past,
Not like the men of the crowd

Who all round me today
Bluster or cringe, and make life
Hideous and arid, and vile,
But souls tempered with fire,
Fervent, heroic, and good,
Helpers and friends of mankind.

Marcus Aurelius

Spend your brief moment according to nature's law, and serenely greet the journey's end as an olive falls when it is ripe, blessing the branch that bare it, and giving thanks to the tree that give it life.

WE ARE FLOODED WITH JOYOUS MEMORIES
William Allen White

A letter written by William Allen White to the late Judge C. A. Leland of El Dorado, Kansas, at the time of Mary's death, and dated June 13, 1921. The letter was first published in the El Dorado Times *in January, 1952.*

I am sure you will pardon my delay in answering your letter about Mary's death. Mrs. White and I appreciated it very much. It is a great comfort to know in sorrow that one's friends are standing by in spirit. Words count for little. Sympathy is not important. But that spiritual sustenance which comes from the thoughtful love of friends—I suppose the thing which some way makes for the answering of prayers—is the only thing that helps in grief, and your letter helped. We want to thank you for it most sincerely.

I wonder if you saw all of the article about Mary that I wrote the day after her funeral. I am taking a chance and enclosing it herewith. It may interest you to know that it has been more widely copied than any other article that ever appeared in the *Gazette*. From Boston to San Diego, in all the towns north, south, east and west, this little article appeared, and I have had literally hundreds of letters from men and women who have been touched by it.

Surely it has brought her life into the lives of others, and I hope for good; by good I mean I hope that she may be an influence to soften other lives and to inspire them with some impulse which will work out for the common good, for some little addition through each heart to our larger social inheritance. These are large words and large thoughts and maybe futile, but anyway they seem to make me feel Mary has had this sure immortality, no matter what else may come, and that helps, too.

Mrs. White and I are standing on our feet, realizing that the loss is heavy and the blow is hard, but not beating our hands against the bars and asking why. On our books Mary is a net gain. She was worth so much more than she cost, and she left so much more behind than she took away that we are flooded with joyous memories and cannot question either the goodness of God or the general decency of man.

LIFE'S LESSON

Anonymous

I learn, as the years roll onward
And I leave the past behind,
That much I had counted sorrow
But proved that God is kind;
That many a flower I'd longed for
Had hidden a thorn of pain
And many a rugged bypath
Led to the fields of ripened grain.
The clouds that cover the sunshine;
They cannot banish the sun,
And the earth shines out the brighter
When the weary rain is done.
We must stand in the deepest shadow
To see the clearest light;
And often through wrong's own darkness
Comes the welcome strength of Right.

> A man should discipline himself to say:
> "Whatever God does, He does for the best."
>
> —Talmud

FAITH IN THE GOODNESS OF GOD

Prince Albert upon his death bed is reported to have said: "I have had wealth, rank and power. But if this were all I had, how wretched I should be now." When we are confronted with the stark reality of death, life's true values become crystallized and our emphasis shifts from the tangibles we so ardently pursue to the intangibles we so persistently neglect. Faith in God may be an elective in our university of daily living. In the presence of death it assumes crucial significance.

For all its urgency, however, faith in God is not easily attained in the hour of grief. Indeed, even the believer finds it difficult to retain his faith in a good God when he is assaulted by the sharp pangs of bereavement and the resultant gnawing doubts fashioned out of his agony. It is undoubtedly for this very reason that Judaism placed such heavy emphasis upon the Kaddish. This prayer which the mourner recites daily for eleven months does not contain a single reference to the deceased. Rather does it embody a powerful affirmation of belief in God in spite of personal sorrow. "Magnified and sanctified be the great name of God throughout the world which He hath created according to His will." But is this a tenable faith? Can we discern any method in what appears like divine madness?

The unprecedented scientific progress of the last century has revealed whole vistas of information which had hitherto been beyond the human ken. At the same time, however, it has served to underscore by how much the unknown still exceeds the known. Our ignorance far outweighs our knowledge.

A very prosaic illustration of this truth is found where physical sight is concerned. Today the scientist informs us that there are en-

tire ranges of wave-lengths which our eyes literally cannot see. The wave-lengths of the visible spectrum range from red at one end to violet at the other. These do not exhaust all the existing wave-lengths. Indeed, these are actually only a small portion of the many wave-lengths which exist. Invisible to our eyes, there are the infra-red beyond the red, and beyond the violet at the other end of the spectrum, there are the ultra-violet wave-lengths. Nor are these all. Beyond these there are many more wave-lengths no human eye has even seen because of its own physical limitations. It would appear then that even in the physical realm we are equipped to see only a fragment of reality, a small arc of the infinite circle.

If this is true in the physical world, is it not also true to a greater degree of the spiritual world? How infinitesimal is the area of our vision, how circumscribed is our spiritual color spectrum. Are we really in a position to comprehend fully the drama of which our present plight is only a fleeting scene?

A mine disaster in England some time ago claimed the lives of forty men. Their stunned and grief-stricken families gathered at the entrance to the mine. The spiritual leader of the community was asked by someone to address the bewildered mourners, to speak some word of comfort or guidance. These are the words he spoke to them: "We stand today in the face of mystery, but I want to tell you about something I have at home. It is a bookmark, embroidered in silk by my mother and given me many years ago. On one side the threads are crossed and recrossed in wild confusion, and looking at it you would think it had been done by someone with no idea of what he was doing. But when I turned it over I see the words beautifully worked in silken threads 'God is Love.' Now we are looking at this tragedy from one side and it does not make sense. Some day we shall be permitted to read its meaning from the other side. Meanwhile, let us wait and trust."

This is the point at which belief in a benign providence becomes so vital. Where knowledge retires, faith awakens. Faith does not dissolve our sorrow nor does it anesthetize us against pain. What it can do for us is to strengthen us for the fierce ordeal which we now regard as part of the divine purpose. Faith goes beyond our range of vision and affirms with Emerson, who himself experienced the tragedy of the death of his young son, "All I have seen teaches me to trust the Creator for all I have not seen." There is much we cannot see but the world we do see about us contains so much of love and beauty, goodness and truth. It attests to a Divine intelligence and points to a universe which has design and plan. A God who fash-

ioned His marvelous universe in so majestic a form is a God who
can be relied upon to care for our loved ones who have gone, to give
courage to us who remain. It has been finely said: "We cannot go
where God is not and where God is, all is well."

AS ONE WHOM HIS MOTHER COMFORTETH
W. L. Alexander

Benighted on a lone and dreary wild,
Perplexed, exhausted, helpless, in despair,
I cast me down, and thought to perish there,
When through the gloom a face appeared and smiled;
And a sweet voice said: "Courage! rise, my child!
And I will guide thee safely on thy way."
As to night-watchers comes the morning ray,
So came that voice to me; and on that face
I seemed a loving tenderness to trace,
That soothed and cheered me as, forlorn, I lay;
I felt as feels the child whose throbbing grief
A mother's love assuages in its source;
And asking strength of Him who gave relief,
I straightway rose, and onward held my course.

Proverbs

The wicked is thrust down in his misfortune;
But the righteous, even when he is brought to death, hath hope.

FAITH CAN OVERCOME BEREAVEMENT
Dean Inge

Bereavement is the deepest initiation into the mysteries of human
life, an initiation more searching and profound than even happy
love. Love remembered and consecrated by grief belongs, more
clearly than the happy intercourse of friends, to the eternal world;
it has proved itself stronger than death.

Bereavement is the sharpest challenge to our trust in God; if faith can overcome this, there is no mountain which it cannot remove. And faith can overcome it. It brings the eternal world nearer to us, and makes it seem more real.

Isaiah

Fear thou not, for I am with thee,
Be not dismayed, for I am thy God;
I strengthen thee, yea, I help thee;

SORROW BUT PROVES US

Stefan Zweig

Have no fear, have no fear, that the Lord will forsake us!
Mistrust him not, brothers, in days that are dark!
For when he debases us, when he afflicts us,
The suffering he sends is but sign of his love.
Then bow ye, my brothers, bend necks to the yoke,
Accept gladly the lot by Jehovah decreed.
Know that sorrow but proves us, that trial uplifts us,
That affliction, though sore, brings us nearer to God.
Each pang that we feel is a step toward his kingdom,
Since the vanquished on earth are in heaven beloved.
Up, brothers, march onward, march onward to God.

FAITH IS ABIDING STRENGTH

Joseph I. Weiss

Our abiding strength is told in terms of faith. For life to have meaning we must believe that the universe represents the purposeful creation of God. We look into the sky and behold the worlds that are the heaven's jewels. We look upon the earth and stand in awe of nature's ordered realm. At every turn we witness the lawful process that bespeaks the accomplishment of an Intelligence far beyond our mental scope. The mind of man never stops in its search for the ultimate truth. What we have learned and what is yet to be known can only lead us to the truth that above and beyond is God, and that the universe is His domain.

Samuel Longfellow

Discouraged in the work of life,
Disenheartened by its load,
Shamed by its failures or its fears,
I sink beside the road;
But let me only think of Thee,
And then new heart springs up in me.

J. E. Saxby

Oh, ask not thou, How shall I bear
The burden of to-morrow?
Sufficient for today its care,
Its evil and its sorrow;
God Imparteth by the way
Strength sufficient for the day.

Isaiah

He giveth power to the faint;
And to him that hath no might He increaseth strength.

FROM "TO A WATER FOWL"

William Cullen Bryant

There is a Power whose care
Teaches thy way along the pathless coast—
The desert and illimitable air—
Lone wandering, but not lost.
He who from zone to zone
Guides through the boundless sky thy certain flight,
In the long way that I must tread alone,
Will lead my steps aright.

I SELL FAITH

Sholom Asch

The following incident forms the conclusion of Sholom Asch's
Kiddush Ha-Shem. *The novel describes the frightful massacre of the*

Jews in seventeenth-century Poland. Shlomo is one of the very few survivors of the decimated Jewish section of Lublin.

In Lublin he came upon refugees from Tulchin, from Bar and from other towns, and he learned from some of the forced converts of the death of his father and mother, who had died for the sanctification of His Name together with the other Jews of Tulchin. But no one knew what had become of Deborah—of Deborah or of the Christian nurse.

But Shlomo knew. He knew that she had gone up to heaven in holiness and purity. In heaven she was, and waiting for him.

He did not mourn for her. Only a great longing for her took possession of him, and for the day when he would again be with her.

And he roamed about through the fair of Lublin among the refugees, among the husbands separated from their wives and the wives separated from their husbands, among the widows and the orphans. He heard the sighs and moans of his people which rose up over the fair. And he pondered deeply on the matter. He sought to understand the meaning of it all. For a minute the meaning escaped him—he could not understand, and he fell in a state of melancholy. And this caused him deep grief, for it is a matter of common knowledge that melancholy is only one degree removed from doubting.

And one day he walked in a narrow street in Lublin where the merchants' stalls were located. And he saw standing before an empty booth an old man who was calling buyers into his booth. And he marveled greatly, for the booth was empty, there was nothing in it to sell. And he walked into the booth and asked the old man: "What do you sell here? Your booth is void and empty, and there is no merchandise in it."

And the old man answered: "I sell faith."

And he looked intently at the old man, and the old man appeared to him familiar as though he had seen him before. . . .

FROM "RESIGNATION"

Henry Wadsworth Longfellow

> Let us be patient! These severe afflictions
>   Not from the ground arise,
> But oftentimes celestial benedictions
>   Assume this dark disguise.

II Chronicles

The Lord is with you, while ye are with Him;
And if ye seek Him, He will be found of you.

Edward Young

Faith builds a bridge across the gulf of death.

WHEN SORROW COMES

Edgar A. Guest

When sorrow comes, as come it must,
In God a man must put his trust.
There is no power in mortal speech
The anguish of his soul to reach,
No voice, however sweet and low,
Can comfort him or ease the blow.

He cannot from his fellow men
Take strength that will sustain him then.
With all that kindly hands will do,
And all that love may offer, too,
He must believe throughout the test
That God has willed it for the best.

We who would be his friends are dumb;
Words from our lips but feebly come;
We feel, as we extend our hands,
That one Power only understands
And truly knows the reason why
So beautiful a soul must die.

We realize how helpless then
Are all the gifts of mortal men.
No words which we have power to say
Can take the sting of grief away—
That Power which marks the sparrow's fall
Must comfort and sustain us all.

When sorrow comes, as come it must,
In God a man must place his trust.
With all the wealth which he may own,
He cannot meet the test alone,
And only he may stand serene
Who has a faith on which to lean.

Victor Hugo

Have courage for the great sorrows of life and patience for the small ones; and when you have laboriously accomplished your daily task, go to sleep in peace. God is awake.

A PRAYER
Thomas Moore

O Thou who dry'st the mourner's tear!
   How dark this world would be,
If, when deceived and wounded here,
   We could not fly to Thee.
The friends, who in our sunshine live,
   When winter comes are flown;
And he, who has but tears to give,
   Must weep those tears alone.
But Thou wilt heal that broken heart,
   Which, like the plants that throw
Their fragrance from the wounded part,
   Breathes sweetness out of woe.

When joy no longer soothes or cheers,
   And e'en the hope that threw
A moment's sparkle o'er our tears,
   Is dimmed and vanished too!
Oh! who could bear life's stormy doom,
   Did not Thy wing of love
Come brightly wafting through the gloom
   Our peace-branch from above?
Then sorrow, touched by Thee, grows bright
   With more than rapture's ray;
As darkness shows us worlds of light
   We never saw by day.

HE KNOWS WHAT IS GOOD FOR US

(From a British aviator's last letter to his mother)

Dearest Mother: Though I feel no premonition at all, events are moving rapidly and I have instructed that this letter be forwarded to you should I fail to return from one of the raids which we shall shortly be called upon to undertake. You must hope on for a month, but at the end of that time you must accept the fact that I have handed my task over to the extremely capable hands of my comrades of the Royal Air Force, as so many splendid fellows have already done.

First, it will comfort you to know that my role in this war has been of the greatest importance. . . . Though it will be difficult for you, you will disappoint me if you do not at least try to accept the facts dispassionately, for I shall have done my duty to the utmost of my ability. No man can do more, and no one calling himself a man could do less.

I have always admired your amazing courage in the face of continual setbacks; in the way you have given me as good an education and background as anyone in the country; and always kept up appearances without ever losing faith in the future. My death would not mean that your struggle has been in vain. Far from it. It means that your sacrifice is as great as mine. . . .

You must not grieve for me, for if you really believe in religion and all that it entails that would be hypocrisy. I have no fear of death; only a queer elation. . . . I would have it no other way. The universe is so vast and so ageless that the life of one man can only be justified by the measure of his sacrifice. We are sent to this world to acquire a personality and a character to take with us that can never be taken from us. Those who just eat and sleep, prosper and procreate, are no better than animals if all their lives they are at peace.

I firmly and absolutely believe that evil things are sent into the world to try us; they are sent deliberately by our Creator to test our mettle because He knows what is good for us. The Bible is full of cases where the easy way out has been discarded for moral principles.

I count myself fortunate in that I have seen the whole country and known men of every calling. But with the final test of war I consider my character fully developed. Thus at my early age my mission is already fulfilled and I am prepared to die with just one regret, and one only—that I could not devote myself to making your declining years more happy by being with you; but you will live in peace and freedom, and I shall have directly contributed to that, so here again my life will not have been in vain.

WHENCE SHALL MY HELP COME?

Psalms

I will lift up mine eyes unto the mountains;
From whence shall my help come?
My help cometh from the Lord,
Who made heaven and earth.

He will not suffer thy foot to be moved;
He that keepeth thee will not slumber.
Behold, He that keepeth Israel
Doth neither slumber nor sleep.

The Lord is thy keeper;
The Lord is thy shade upon thy right hand.
The sun shall not smite thee by day,
Nor the moon by night.

The Lord shall keep thee from all evil;
He shall keep thy soul.
The Lord shall guard thy going out and thy coming in,
From this time forth and for ever.

Isaiah

Though he walketh in darkness,
And hath no light,
Let him trust in the name of the Lord,
And stay upon his God.

HE GIVETH POWER TO THE FAINT
Isaiah

Why sayest thou, O Jacob,
And speaketh, O Israel:
"My way is hid from the lord,
And my right is passed over from my God?"
Hast thou not known? hast thou not heard
That the everlasting God, the lord,
The Creator of the ends of the earth,
Fainteth not, neither is weary?
His discernment is past searching out.
He giveth power to the faint;
And to him that hath no might He increaseth strength.
Even the youths shall faint and be weary,
And the young men shall utterly fall;
But they that wait for the Lord shall renew their strength;
They shall mount up with wings as eagles;
They shall run, and not be weary;
They shall walk, and not faint.

FROM ''RESIGNATION''
Henry Wadsworth Longfellow

We see but dimly through the mists and vapors;
    Amid these earthly damps
What seem to us but sad, funereal tapers
    May be heaven's distant lamps.

OUT OF THE DARK PASSAGES WE EMERGE INTO LIGHT
From "Blessings and Praise"

When suffering comes upon us, as it comes to all, we often fret desparingly and repine. We cannot understand why we should be made the apparent sport of misfortune and calamity. We wonder why tender affection should be created, only to be rudely broken; why agonizing pain should wreck our nerves and consume our flesh;

In moments of great sorrow, the stricken heart is apt to exclaim: "Surely God does not care, or else why does He inflict upon me such cruel pain!" The presence of evil—how baffling it is to our finite understanding!

Yet it is through struggle and sorrow that we learn to know more of the love and faithfulness of God than in any other way! We know only too well that sorrow often breaks the crust of a superficial life, uncovers its deepest realities. Through the dark cloud that envelops us, there breaks forth a new vision of the aim and purpose of our earthly existence. Not always on the heights, sometimes from the depths do we best see God. And seeing Him, we come to realize that our life is not a haphazard occurrence of chance events and circumstances, that a Divine hand and purpose are discernible in all that befalls us. Out of the dark passages of life, we emerge into the light of faith, purified in spirit, more keenly alert and responsive to the soft whisperings of the still small voice ever striving to speak to our hearts.

Mary Frances Butts

Build a little fence of trust around to-day;
Fill the space with loving works, and therein stay;
Look not through the sheltering bars upon tomorrow,
God will help thee bear what comes, of joy and sorrow.

Job

Though He slay me, yet will I trust in Him.

WHAT GOD HATH PROMISED
Annie Johnson Flint

God hath not promised
Skies always blue,
Flower-strewn pathways
All our lives through;
God hath not promised
Sun without rain,
Joy without sorrow,
Peace without pain.

But God hath promised
Strength for the day,
Rest for the labor,
Light for the way,
Grace for the trials,
Help from above,
Unfailing sympathy,
Undying love.

J. G. Holland

Faith draws the poison from every grief, takes the sting from every loss, and quenches the fire of every pain; and only faith can do it.

Nahum

The Lord is good,
A stronghold in the day of trouble;
And He knoweth them that take refuge in Him.

Abraham J. Heschel

Faith is like a flashlight beam thrown ahead of us into the darkness. Its beam is always more visible when grief clouds about us. In some such events, an experience of faith kindles an unquenchable light.

A TREE

Esther M. Campbell

A tree spoke to me today.
Can you see it? A strange sight,
Gnarled and twisted by the fury of the winds and sea.
You say, "How can you find beauty in its jagged form?"
Ah! But to me its message is more appealing
Than the quiet symmetry of a perfect tree.
My tree stands on a rocky crag jutting out over the mighty ocean.

Its footing seems precarious
Yet its roots are twined in and about the rock
Enabling it to withstand the storms that come.
And come they do—fierce gales that bend the tree back toward the
    land.
Whipping off its branches on the seaward side.
Again and again the winds have done their worst.
Trying to uproot my tree,
Trying to tear it from its moorings.
Yes, it has had to bend its back but it has never broken;
Its green arms can always stretch out to land.
The ocean spray has spit upon it,
Laughing at the seeming bravery of a single tree.
The tree is like a life—yours or mine perhaps.
The gales sweep about us
Threatening to tear us from our footing.
Sometimes they are about us; sometimes within us.
And we become twisted and warped,
Not able to maintain the beauty God intended for us.
Yet as we send down our roots of faith
His love and mercy flows through us and heals our scars
And helps us to reach out to others arms of help and kindness,
Enabling His beauty to still be seen in us,
Imperfect though we are.
Help us, O God,
To be as brave and unswerving as my tree.

FROM "TRUST"

John Greenleaf Whittier

    The same old baffling questions! O my friend,
    I cannot answer them. In vain I send
    My soul into the dark, where never burn
    The lamps of science, nor the natural light
    Of Reason's sun and stars! I cannot learn
    Their great and solemn meanings, nor discern
    The awful secrets of the eyes which turn
    Evermore on us through the day and night
    With silent challenge and a dumb demand,
    Proffering the riddles of the dread unknown,
    Like the calm Sphinxes, with their eyes of stone

Questioning the centuries from their veils of sand!
I have no answer for myself or thee,
Save that I learned beside my mother's knee:
"All is of God that is, and is to be;
And God is good." Let this suffice us still.
Resting in childlike trust upon his will
Who moves to his great ends unthwarted by the ill.

EVERYTHING BEAUTIFUL IN ITS TIME

Julius Mark

"God hath made everything beautiful in its time. . . ."

A time for death? Yes, even death can be beautiful in its time and even when death may appear senseless and tragic, men of faith will declare with Job: "The Lord hath given; the Lord hath taken away. Blessed be the Name of the Lord," and derive strength from this confidence in the ways of God.

The late Jacob H. Schiff, perhaps the most distinguished American Jew of his generation, was such a man of complete faith in God. When a brother-in-law of Mr. Schiff's passed away at a comparatively young age, he felt the loss most keenly, since he had been strongly attached to him. From a friend, he received a letter of sympathy in which the former wrote: "Such events create atheists and agnostics, and embitter thinking people against the 'inscrutable ways of Providence.' "

Mr. Schiff replied: "It is true, sometimes goodness and righteousness appear for a time to go for naught, but the ways of God are always right. The laws of nature cannot be changed for anybody, or chaos would result; and even if we pray to God that He may hear us and do this or that for us, we pray for our own benefit and to strengthen ourselves, and not for the benefit of the Almighty. Pardon me, if I should appear to write you a sermon, but such is far from my intention; I only give expression to my own feelings, which have given me strength and courage in many a difficult situation during life."

This is the conviction of a man who believed that "God hath made everything beautiful in its time."

Isaiah

The mind stayed on Thee Thou keepest in perfect peace;
Because it trusteth in Thee.

F. L. Holmes

Faith will turn any course, light any path, relieve any distress, bring joy out of sorrow, peace out of strife, friendship out of enmity, heaven out of hell. Faith is God at work.

ACCEPTANCE OF THE UNANSWERABLE
Zelda Popkin

"Why did it have to happen?" everyone asks. The answer to this is the test of the individual's religious conviction. If his faith is deep and sincere, he replies simply: "This is God's will. This is divine wisdom. There is a higher judgment." Such a man possesses the faith which comforts and heals.

In others, an important recognition must be made—that there are things to which we have no answers at all, and that it is possible to accept what has happened without knowing why. For them, in that acceptance of the unanswerable, is the beginning of wisdom.

WITHOUT GOD WHAT SENSE DOES
LIFE MAKE?
Walter Russel Bowie

What sense can be made out of the existence if rocks and earth and water and the dust beneath our feet go on enduring and human souls, which seem to be the fruition toward which all the slow forces of evolution have been working, should blindly and stupidly be brought to naught? In the face of such a universe, a man might laugh with contempt before he went to his annihilation. But we cannot believe that contemptuous laughter is the ultimate verdict to be passed upon our world. There must be within it something that has caused our own ideals, something akin to our passion for continuing life, and something upon which eternally we can rely.

God must be in it, and God is life, and God is love. Even in the moments when our intellect is baffled, and even in those times when contradictions beset our faith, still we refuse to be put to permanent intellectual and spiritual confusion and still our deepest souls declare that beyond the shadows there is light, and in the depths of the utmost darkness life goes upon its undefeated way.

FROM "THE ONE PRAYER"

James Montgomery

One prayer I have—all prayers in one—
  When I am wholly Thine;
Thy will, my God, thy will be done,
  And let that will be mine.

All-wise, almighty, and all-good,
  In thee I firmly trust;
Thy ways, unknown or understood,
  Are merciful and just.

May I remember that to thee
  Whate'er I have I owe;
And back, in gratitude, from me
  May all thy bounties flow.

And though thy wisdom takes away,
  Shall I arraign thy will?
No, let me bless thy name, and say,
  "The Lord is gracious still."

Talmud

Let us thank God for the evil as well as for the good—indeed even though He take from us all our strength and possessions, for it is written: "Thou shalt love the Lord thy God with all thy might."

I LEAVE IT TO GOD

Joseph Rolnick (Translated from the Yiddish by Joseph Leftwich)

I leave all to God! Let Him lead me
Whither He will and how He will.

In not a thing shall I resist Him,
But like a child will follow still.

On mountain tops, in gaping chasms,
With eyes wide open, and yet blind,
Into the dens of wild beast, even.
Father leads—child follows behind.

Samuel T. Coleridge

He prayeth well who loveth well
Both man and bird and beast;
He prayeth best who loveth best
All things both great and small;
For the dear God who loveth us,
He made and loveth all.

THE BULWARK AGAINST FINAL DESPAIR

Chad Walsh

If a loved one dies, do you feel equal to meeting the loss single-handed? . . . The truth is that we are not built to bear the burden of sorrow and fear and loss alone. In any time of trouble we instinctively turn to our friends, and by their love and sympathy they share their strength with us. But friends are human beings like ourselves, and their strength is limited. They have their own heavy burdens. And sometimes our friends prefer to fade quietly out of the picture and leave us to ourselves and our private griefs and fears.

Only God is strong enough to give us the strength to face—everything that must be faced. . . . He is beside us when death robs us of those dearest to us. No barbed wire and steel doors can keep Him out. This is not mere theorizing. There is testimony from unnumbered voices that the man who carries a real sense of God's presence with him onto the battlefield or into the internment camp finds his Companion more unmistakably with him than before. "Where is your God now?" asked a Nazi guard of a Rabbi in an internment camp. "He is here," answered the Rabbi, "even here."

There is nothing sloppy or sentimental about this discovery. We remain ordinary men and women; our nerves and our emotions are still raw to suffering. But thanks to God, we are not overcome. We are able to endure what must be endured, and to find God in the midst of the worst that can assail us. God is the bulwark against final despair, the one completely solid and trustworthy source of lasting hope.

AT THE PLACE OF THE SEA

Annie Johnson Flint

Have you come to the Red Sea place in your life
    Where, in spite of all you can do,
There is no way out, there is no way back,
    There is no other way but through?
Then wait on the Lord, with a trust serene,
    Till the night of your fear is gone;
He will send the winds, He will heap the floods,
    When He says to your soul, "Go On!"

And His hand shall lead you through, clear through,
    Ere the watery walls roll down;
No wave can touch you, no foe can smite,
    No mightiest sea can drown.
The tossing billows may rear their crests,
    Their foam at your feet may break,
But over their bed you shall walk dry-shod
    In the path that your Lord shall make.

In the morning watch, 'neath the lifted cloud,
    You shall see but the Lord alone,
When He leads you forth from the place of the sea,
    To a land that you have not known;
And your fears shall pass as your foes have passed
    You shall no more be afraid;
You shall sing His praise in a better place,
    In a place that His hand hath made.

Samuel Longfellow

Now our wants and burdens leaving
To his care who cares for all,
Cease we fearing, cease we grieving,
At his touch our burdens fall.

Psalms

The Lord is my light and my salvation; whom shall I fear?
The Lord is the stronghold of my life; of whom shall I be afraid?

Psalms

He shall call upon Me, and I will answer him;
I will be with him in trouble;
I will rescue him, and bring him to honour.

Margaret E. Sangster

Oh, face to face with trouble,
Friend, I have often stood,
To learn that pain hath sweetness,
To know that God is good.
Arise and meet the daylight,
Be strong and do your best,
With an honest heart and a childlike trust
That God will do the rest.

Psalms

God is our refuge and strength, An ever present help in trouble.

Psalms

The sacrifices of God are a broken spirit; a broken and a contrite
heart, O God, Thou wilt not despise.

Marcus Aurelius

Nothing happens to any man which he is not formed by nature
to bear.

Author unknown

My life is but the weaving
Between my God and me.

I only choose the colors
    He weaveth steadily.
Sometimes he weaveth sorrow
    And I in foolish pride
Forget he sees the upper
    And I the under side.

THE BLIND MAN

Margaret E. Sangster

I see a blind man every day
Go bravely down the street;
He walks as if the path were clear
Before his steady feet.
Save when he fumbles with his cane,
I almost feel he sees
The passers-by who smile at him,
The flowers and the trees.

He comes to corners where the crowd
Of traffic swirls about,
But when he hesitates, some hand
Will always help him out.
He crosses pavements fearlessly,
It is as if he knows
That there are unknown, watchful friends
Along the way he goes!

Sometimes we walk through unseen paths,
Sometimes the road ahead
Is shrouded in the mists of fear;
But we are being led
As surely as the blind man is. . . .
And, if we seem to sway,
A hand will find us in the dark
And guide us on our way.

Isaiah

As one whom his mother comforteth,
So will I comfort you;

THE SHEPHERD KNOWS BEST
H. W. Smith

The Shepherd knows what pastures are best for his sheep, and they must not question nor doubt, but trustingly follow him. Perhaps He sees that the best pastures for some of us are to be found in the midst of opposition or of earthly trials. If He leads you there, you may be sure they are green for you, and you will grow and be made strong by feeding there. Perhaps He sees that the best waters for you to walk beside will be raging waters of trouble and sorrow. If this should be the case, He will make them still waters for you, and you must go and lie down beside them, and let them have all their blessed influences upon you.

NOT WITHOUT DESIGN DOES GOD WRITE
John Ruskin

Not without design does God write the music of our lives. Be it ours to learn the time, and not be discouraged at the rests. If we say sadly to ourselves, "There is no music in a rest," let us not forget "there is the making of music in it." The making of music is often a slow and painful process in this life. How patiently God works to teach us! How long He waits for us to learn the lesson!

Midrash

God has compassion like a father and comforts like a mother.

THE ETERNAL GOODNESS
John Greenleaf Whittier

I dimly guess from blessings known
    Of greater out of sight,
And, with the chastened Psalmist, own
    His judgments, too, are right.

I long for household voices gone,
    For vanished smiles I long,
But God hath led my dear ones on,
    And he can do no wrong.

I know not what the future hath
    Of marvel or surprise,
Assured alone that life and death
    His mercy underlies.

And if my heart and flesh are weak
    To bear an untried pain,
The bruised reed he will not break,
    But strengthen and sustain.

No offering of my own I have,
    Nor works my faith to prove;
I can but give the gifts he gave,
    And plead his love for love.

And so beside the Silent Sea
    I wait the muffled oar;
On ocean or on shore
    No harm from him can come to me.

I know not where his islands lift
    Their fronded palms in air,
I only know I cannot drift
    Beyond his love and care.

FROM "SOMETIME"

May Riley Smith

Sometime, when all life's lessons have been learned,
And suns and stars forevermore have set,
The things which our weak judgments here have spurned,
The things o'er which we grieved with lashes wet,
Will flash before us out of life's dark night,
As stars shine most in deeper tints of blue;
And we shall see how all God's plans were right,
And what most seemed reproof was love most true.

FROM "THE END OF SORROW"

Edmond Fleg (Translated by Humbert Wolfe)

We of our sorrows build in the days to come
For the soul of man that tall and ultimate home.
But you that pass tomorrow, as you pass today,
Build you as true as we, and go your way.

And then the sleeper, rising, cried on God:
"Again the torture, and again the road."
And stepping out into the dawn of all
He heard the Jews still weeping by the Wall.

"Dark are thy ways! O who can find them?
O Lord of distance, and yet we see
The day spring a wisp of Thy glory behind them,
The nightfall a step on the path to Thee."

RAISING DOWNCAST EYES

Jay Kaufman

Slowly, with the recitation of the Kaddish and its words of Divine praise, there pierces the shroud of grief the realization that it was God in his endless mercy who had vouchsafed unto us the lifetime of the departed one and thus bequeathed us countless precious hours of exquisite love and sublime companionship. Such treasured memories gleaned in the rich harvest of daily living are not destroyed by death but live on imperishably. Tenderly they minister to aching hearts, these reflections on a life well lived, healing with all the magic of Gilead's balm. Inspiringly, they animate the noblest impulses, these memories of a life which cherished lofty ideals.

In moments when one is cast down, the Kaddish may raise downcast eyes heavenward offering the surest consolation, reassuring the mourner that He who taketh away, giveth in even greater measure.

DEATH SERVES LIFE
Robert W. MacKenna

Practically all the progress that man has made is due to the fact that he is mortal. If man knew that his days on earth were to be endless, all incentive to bestir himself—except to seek food and clothing—would be lost. There would be no desire to make his mark in the world, no stimulating ambition to leave the world a little better than he found it, no hungry aspiration to be remembered after he is dead. If there were no death, life would become a thing stagnant, monotonous and unspeakably burdensome.

Deuteronomy

And thou shalt consider in thy heart, that, as a man chasteneth his son, so the Lord thy God chasteneth thee. . . .

Talmud

God prepares the cure before the hurt.

Henry H. Barry

In "pastures green?" Not always; sometimes He
Who knoweth best, in kindness leadeth me
In weary ways, where heavy shadows be.

So, whether on the hill-tops high and fair
I dwell, or in the sunless valleys, where
The shadows lie, what matter? He is there.

Wisdom of Solomon

For Thou lovest all the things that are, and abhorrest nothing which Thou hast made: for never wouldst Thou have made any thing, if Thou hadst hated it. But Thou sparest all: for they are Thine O Lord, Thou lover of Souls.

MY THOUGHTS ARE NOT YOUR THOUGHTS

Isaiah

For My thoughts are not your thoughts,
Neither are your ways My ways, saith the Lord.
For as the heavens are higher than the earth,
So are My ways higher than your ways,
And My thoughts than your thoughts.
For as the rain cometh down and the snow from heaven,
And returneth not thither,
Except it water the earth,
And make it bring forth and bud,
And give seed to the sower and bread to the eater;
So shall My word be that goeth forth out of My mouth:
It shall not return unto Me void,
Except it accomplish that which I please,
And make the thing whereto I sent it prosper.

WHATEVER HEAVEN DOES IS FOR THE BEST

Moses Chayyim Luzzato (Translated from the Hebrew by Mordecai M. Kaplan)

One mode of reasoning is, "Whatever Heaven does is for the best." This means that even suffering and hardship are only apparently evil; in reality they are good. The surgeon amputates a muscle or a limb which has been injured in order to preserve the health of the rest of the body, and to save the person from death. Though this seems cruel, it is in reality an act of mercy, and meant for the good of the person upon whom it is performed. That patient does not love the surgeon any the less because of what he has done to him; on the contrary, he loves him all the more. In like manner, if a man were to realize that whatever the Holy One, blessed be He, does to him, whether it affects his body or his possessions, is intended for his benefit, neither suffering nor hardship would lessen his love for God in any way, though he may little understand how he is benefited. On the contrary, his love would even become more intense and fervent.

Deuteronomy

The eternal God is a dwelling place, and underneath are the everlasting arms.

IF I WERE GOD
Frank S. Mead

Nasr-ed-Din Hodja, in the heat of the day, sat under a walnut tree looking at his pumpkin vines. He said to himself, "How foolish God is! Here he puts a great heavy pumpkin on a tiny vine without strength to do anything but lie on the ground. And he puts tiny walnuts on a big tree whose branches could hold the weight of a man. If I were God, I could do better than that!"

Just then a breeze dislocated a walnut in the tree, and it fell on the head of the skeptical Nasr-ed-Din Hodja, who rubbed his head, a sadder and a wiser man. "Suppose," he mused, "there had been a pumpkin up there, instead of a walnut. Never again will I try to plan the world for God, but I shall thank God that He has done so well!"

Isaiah

I, even I, am He that comforteth you;

Lamentations

For He doth not afflict willingly,
Nor grieve the children of men.

WHATEVER IS—IS BEST
Ella Wheeler Wilcox

I know as my life grows older
And mine eyes have clearer sight—
That under each rank wrong, somewhere
There lies the root of Right!

That each sorrow has its purpose,
By the sorrowing oft unguessed;
But, as sure as the sun brings morning,
Whatever is—is best.

FROM "IN MEMORIAM"
Alfred Tennyson

Oh, yet we trust that somehow good
    Will be the final goal of ill,
      To pangs of nature, sins of will,
Defects of doubt and taints of blood;

That nothing walks with aimless feet;
    That not one life shall be destroyed,
      Or cast as rubbish to the void,
When God hath made the pile complete;

Behold, we know not anything;
    I can but trust that good shall fall
      At last—far off—at last, to all,
And every winter change to spring.

Ralph Waldo Emerson

The powers of the soul are commensurate with its needs.

THE LOOM OF TIME
Anonymous

Man's life is laid in the loom of time
To a pattern he does not see,
While the weavers work and the shuttles fly
Till the dawn of eternity.

Some shuttles are filled with silver threads
And some with threads of gold,
While often but the darker hues
Are all that they may hold.

But the weaver watches with skillful eye
Each shuttle fly to and fro,
And sees the pattern so deftly wrought
As the loom moves sure and slow.

God surely planned the pattern,
Each thread, the dark and fair,
Is chosen by His master skill
And placed in the web with care.

He only knows its beauty,
And guides the shuttles which hold
The threads so unattractive,
As well as the threads of gold.

Not till each loom is silent
And the shuttles cease to fly,
Shall God reveal the pattern
And explain the reason why

The dark threads were as needful
In the weaver's skillful hand
As the threads of gold and silver
For the pattern which He planned.

DAILY BLESSINGS

Louis Zangwill

In the "Blessings on Various Occasions" we find a very warm jubilation of life—a spontaneous lyric appreciation of earth; joy in the fruits of the tree, the vine and the field; enchantment in the fragrant odours of barks, plants, fruits and spices; exaltation at the sight of stars, mountain, desert, sea and rainbow. Beautiful trees and animals, spring-blossoms equally with scholars and sages—all evoke their grace of appreciation. For storm and evil tidings, too, have their graces—in fortitude! The Hebrew genius could find growth through sorrow; and for the Hebrew, good tidings have their grace, no less than fair sights and experience. Everywhere the infiltration of Earth by Heaven.

FROM "THE MYSTERY OF PROVIDENCE"

William Cowper

God moves in a mysterious way
    His wonders to perform;
He plants his footsteps in the sea,
    And rides upon the storm.

Judge not the Lord by feeble sense,
    But trust him for his grace;
Behind a frowning providence
    He hides a smiling face.

His purposes will ripen fast,
    Unfolding every hour;
The bud may have a bitter taste,
    But sweet will be the flower.

Blind unbelief is sure to err,
    And scan his work in vain;
God is his own interpreter,
    And he will make it plain.

> You cannot prevent the birds of
> sorrow from flying over your
> head, but you can prevent them
> from building nests in your hair.
>
> —Chinese Proverb

HOW TO FACE SORROW

Sorrow tests us as no other experience. It kicks out from under us the social stilts on which we frequently stand and rubs off the veneer we habitually wear. It most accurately mirrors us as we truly are, because in the fearful encounter with it we are compelled to draw most heavily upon our own human resources. Kind friends and loved ones can be of real service, but the ultimate verdict, whether sorrow defeats us or we surmount it, is rendered by our own wisdom and courage. When Macbeth asks the doctor whether he can prescribe "some sweet oblivious antidote" to a sorrowing heart, he answers: "Therein the patient must minister to himself."

This is not to say, however, that there are no outside sources of strength and counsel available to us. Quite the reverse is true. Others before us have endured the agony of grief and from the experience they distilled a measure of wisdom which they have recorded. In more recent times the psychology of grief has been explored more scientifically and the findings, taken together, constitute a genuine strategy for meeting sorrow and subduing it.

The passages which follow in this section can be reduced to three basic principles. In the first place, we ought not to feel ashamed to express the genuine grief we feel. It is for such a time as this that our tear ducts were made. The poet in a romantic mood may speak of "the silent manliness of grief" but it is hardly evidence of manliness to remain silent in grief. Such silence, such repressed emotions may be most dangerous to the mourner when they erupt at some later day in a more violent and damaging form. Ovid stood on firm psychological grounds when he cautioned "Suppressed grief suffocates." Judaism encourages us to "weep for the dead."

The second principle to guide us in our sorrow is that we must avoid the temptation to overindulge our grief. Grief in moderation is beneficial and healing. Taken in excess, it can destroy our will to live and rob us of our initiative. If we do not retain a vigilant emotional watch, grief can easily degenerate into self-pity which Fulton Oursler correctly called "a passport to insanity."

To guard against this psychic pitfall, we resort to a third principle which urges us to accept bravely what we cannot change, to go out of ourselves to transmute sorrow into service, to pass from feeling sorry for ourselves, which paralyzes, to feeling concern for others, which heals. The therapeutic power of this strategy is attested to by a number of genuine experiences which are described in this section. It is also reflected in an old Oriental tale.

There is a legend of a sorrowing woman who came to a wise man with the heart-rending plea that he return to her her only son whom she had just lost. He told her that he could comply with her request on one condition. She would have to bring to him a mustard seed taken from a home entirely free from sorrow. The woman set out on her quest. Years elapsed and she did not return. One day the wise man chanced upon her, but he hardly recognized her, for now she looked so radiant. He greeted her and then asked her why she had never kept their appointment. "Oh," she said in a tone of voice indicating that she had completely forgotten about it, "well, this is what happened. In search of the mustard seed, I came into homes so burdened with sorrow and trouble that I just could not walk out. Who better than I could understand how heavy was the burden they bore? Who better than I could offer them the sympathy they needed? So I stayed on in each home as long as I could be of service. And," she added apologetically, "please do not be angry, but I never again thought about our appointment."

Here is a most profound truth to remember when grief darkens our lives. Trouble and sorrow naturally make us think only of ourselves. But after the first impact of the blow has worn off, our emotional recovery depends upon our ability to forget ourselves. And there is no better way of forgetting about ourselves than by thinking of and serving others. Human experience every day confirms the truth of the legend. He who can do no better after sorrow than engage in the futile search for the mustard seed, to restore the loss which is in fact irretrievable, is destined to spend years of avoidable heartache. But happy is he who can rise from his mourner's bench and so lose himself in the service of others that he finds him-

*self unknowingly climbing the mountain of healing to which the
road of service inevitably leads.*

FROM "AUTUMN SONNETS #23"
Robert Nathan

Hast thou a grief? Go clasp it to thy breast;
Hast thou a poison? Drain it to the end.
Cry then, cry all thy heart out with its pain;
Hearts grow again, and eyes have better sight
After too many tears, as summer rain
Washes the air, and leaves it sweet and bright,
And birds step out on trees, whose happy song
Is often stilled, but never stilled for long.

Henry Seidel Canby

Success, as Shakespeare and Sophocles understood it, is the persistence of man's potential nobility in the teeth of circumstance and up to tragedy and beyond it.

CONVERTING SORROW INTO SERVICE
Sidney Greenberg

A story both sad and inspiring is woven about Leland Stanford University near San Francisco. It is named after the only son of the former governor of California. While on a visit to Italy with his parents, Leland Stanford, Jr., age nine, became ill and died. The grief-stricken parents returned to California and resolved to become the benefactors of other children, to give them the opportunities they could no longer lavish upon their own son. Thus they erected and heavily endowed the university which bears the name of their son. Here boys and girls of every group in America enjoy the opportunity of a university education. This blessing to untold young people was born in the anguish of a personal sorrow which heroic parents converted into a public service.

THE LAWS OF GRIEF

Joshua Loth Leibman

One of the greatest illusions about human nature is that the expression of grief will lead to a breakdown. *Quite the reverse.* No one has ever broken down nervously through the legitimate expression of an emotional reaction. . . . How absurd is that notion current in modern society that men and women must be safeguarded, coddled, and shielded against emotional outbursts. It is not those outbursts which harm the human organism, but the complete avoidance of them, which scars and tears the fabric of the inner soul.

The first law, then, which should be followed in the time of the loss of a loved one is: express as much grief as you actually feel. Do not be ashamed of your emotions. . . . Instead of trying to distract attention from the loss—a procedure that should come much later in the healing process—friends should offer the opportunity and encouragement to the man who has lost a loved one, to talk about his loss, to dwell upon his sorrow, and to rehearse the beauty and the virtues of the departed one.

A second new truth about the grief situation is this: *we must learn how to extricate ourselves from the bondage of the physical existence and coexistence of the loved one.* . . . Too many people make the mistake, in hours of bereavement, of closing the door to the mines of their spirits and permitting no entrance to new friends and comrades who could bring up much precious ore. These grief-stricken lives become abandoned mines with all of the unused shafts covered wth the cobwebs of self-pity.

The melody that the loved one played upon the piano of our life will never be played quite that way again, but we must not close the keyboard and allow the instrument to gather dust. We must seek out other artists of the spirit, new friends who gradually will help us to find the road to life again, who will walk on that road with us. The establishment of new patterns of interaction with other people, beginning with the interaction of language and moving on to new avenues of creative expression, is the second law for the conquest of grief and the conquest of death.

A third law may be expressed as follows: when death destroys an important relationship, it is essential that someone be found partially capable of replacing that relationship. Equilibrium will be restored when the bereaved person discovers some situation demanding the same or similar patterns of conduct. For example, a mother who loses a young child has suffered one of the most tragic bereavements of all. . . . What can be done to bring into play this law of pattern replacement? A mother after the death of her own child should be encouraged, for example, to interest herself in daily work at a nursery school. She should be stimulated to transfer the conduct pattern which she had fashioned in her relationship with her own child into work with a group of children.

It would be unwise for this mother to adopt a baby immediately, because unconsciously she would feel disloyal to her own dead child in this speedy transference of love to a stranger. A very wise solution occurs if the bereaved mother dilutes her affection at first over a wide area in working with the nursery-school children. Then, when the first deep wound has partially healed, she either adopts a child or has one of her own and bestows upon it her mature and devoted affection.

TEARS REFRESH
Leigh Hunt

A Grecian philosopher being asked why he wept for the death of his son, since the sorrow was in vain, replied, "I weep on that account." And his answer became his wisdom. It is only for sophists to contend that we, whose eyes contain the fountains of tears, need never give way to them. It would be unwise not to do so on some occasions. Sorrow unlocks them in her balmy moods. The first bursts may be bitter and overwhelming; but the soil on which they pour would be worse without them. They refresh the fever of the soul. . . .

Where we feel that tears would relieve us, it is false philosophy to deny ourselves at least that first refreshment; and it is always false consolation to tell people that because they cannot help a thing, they are not to mind it. The true way is, to let them grapple with the unavoidable sorrow, and try to win it into gentleness by a reasonable yielding. There are griefs so gentle in their very nature that it would be worse than false heroism to refuse them a tear. . . . The end is an acquittal from the harsher bonds of affliction, from the tying down of the spirit to one melancholy idea.

It is the nature of tears of this kind, however strongly they may gush forth, to run into quiet waters at last. We cannot easily, for the whole course of our lives, think with pain of any good and kind person whom we have lost. It is the divine nature of their qualities to conquer pain and death itself; to turn the memory of them into pleasure; to survive with a placid aspect in our imaginations.

William Cowper

Oh, then indulge thy grief, nor fear to tell
The gentle source from whence thy sorrows flow!
Nor think it weakness when we love to feel,
Nor think it weakness what we feel to show.

TEARS BORDER ON THE SACRED

Grace Perkins Oursler and April Armstrong

What is this taboo on tears? Men hate to see tears. They shy away from crying women, and frown on tears in their own sex. Tears disfigure and ravage, yes. But modern mankind's distress stems from the abuse of weeping. The tears of the morally weak, the infantile personality, the self-indulgent, and the spiritual thief who uses them to burglarize another's principles are so repelling and so degenerating as to give rise to general condemnation of weepers.

But God Almighty gave us tears. It is unlikely that they are meant merely to chap our cheeks when the wind stings our eyes. Or just to keep the eyeballs moist.

No one really denies their importance. We must breathe, eat, sweat, digest, expel—and weep. Tears border on the sacred; they are the only off-casting of our bodies that flows from spiritual and emotional wounds. They are the only channel to release dammed-up sensibilities, letting out the poisonous streams of anxiety that can infect our whole being. Even those we cause ourselves, due to temper, self-will, self-pity, pride, fear of punishment or terror are a safeguard against more disastrous behavior. . . .

We weep at separations that we would not change, but which cut deep at habits and comforts nonetheless. Beyond such weeping are emotions of faith and hope—and great selflessness. . . . The tears for another, the tears of grief, these are holy tears when shed from a pure heart. . . .

So why be ashamed or nonplused at grief, then, or cheat ourselves in denying its expression? Tears are a necessary adjunct to shock. . . .

In Oriental countries one can still find the delicate little tear vases used by the mourners in bereavement. Their philosophy did not discount the cleansing and draining purposes of crying. And they held that the most sacred tears we have are wept for those who have done with this world and are carried on to the mysteries of the next, leaving us to battle out the finish. Those tear bottles were kept and often were buried with the person mourned, where archaeologists now come across them.

Amiel

It is dangerous to abandon one's self to the luxury of grief: it deprives one of courage, and even of the wish for recovery.

Herbert Spencer

He oft finds medicine who his grief imparts.

"DO NOT WEEP TOO MUCH"

Hannah Avrech (Translated from the Hebrew by the editor)

A letter sent to parents of a casualty in Israel's War of Independence by his fiancee. She herself was killed in an airplane accident shortly after she wrote this letter.

Warmest greetings, dear friends:

It is difficult for me to write, for the pain has not yet left my heart and my soul still weeps over the tragedy which befell us.

. . . It happened on the 15th of May, in the battle for Malchiya in Galilee. There were many killed and wounded in this engagement and fate selected us, too. I still do not know all the details. One thing I am certain of, however, is that Yehuda died a hero's death. He knew what he was fighting for and the goal to which he dedicated all his strength and energy. He was always prepared for anything that might happen and I am certain that his last wish was that we should be strong and know how to conquer everything.

. . . I have one request to make: Be brave and do not weep too much. He was one of many and the duty which he fulfilled compels us to carry on in his way. Be courageous and strong! This is the

wish of your daughter whose fiancé fell in battle. It will be easier
for me to carry on if I know that you have gained mastery over
your feelings.

Fulton Oursler

Sometimes it is hard, when life gets tough not to feel sorry for
ourselves. Yet self-pity is deadly as arsenic to peace of the heart.
If we can only keep our souls clean of that poison, we can generally
find a way out of trouble.

THE DANGERS OF SELF-PITY
Louis Binstock

We must see the danger in sorrow when allowed to become a
source of self-pity. Man, even as the lower animals, delights in lick-
ing and nursing his own wounds. It is not only the child that feels
a peculiar pleasure in believing itself to be misunderstood and mis-
treated, but also the adult. One of the basic causes for self-inflicted
injury, and sometimes suicide, is this human tendency to be sorry
for oneself, and to make others also suffer the consequences of the
sorrow. "You'll be sorry," cries the child. The adult does not use
these words, yet his actions clearly express them. Many an adult
becomes a child again when sorrow comes into his life. He cannot
rest content until he has made all those around him share his
sorrow and suffer with him.

Self-pity wastes time and weakens energy. Self-pity dilutes initiative and destroys venturesomeness. That is true of peoples and
nations as well as individuals. Stefan Zweig has written a novel
entitled *Beware of Pity,* in which he warns against the pitfalls of
pity. Self-pity, however, holds hidden for us the deepest and most
dangerous pitfalls of all. Let us understand that it is of no avail for
peoples and nations any more than individuals to spend their days
being sorry for themselves, bewailing their fate. Time and energy
consumed in weeping over a sorrow may be put to much more
intelligent and helpful use if conserved for meeting the grave problems that the sorrow has created. Self-pity never removes the sorrow.
It only delays the solution of the difficulties and the danger out of
which the sorrow grew. And it blinds us to larger and wider sorrows which we share in common with all humanity.

Benjamin Disraeli

Grief is the agony of an instant; the indulgence of grief, the blunder of a life.

Shakespeare

Moderate lamentation is the right of the dead;
Excessive grief the enemy to the living.

THE THREE CHOICES
Harry Lauder

When, during World War I, Sir Harry Lauder, the great Scot comedian, heard that his son had been killed in France, he said: "In a time like this there are three courses open to a man. He may give way to despair, sour upon the world, and become a grouch. He may endeavor to drown his sorrow in drink or by a life of waywardness and wickedness. Or he may turn to God."

COMING THROUGH THE STORM
Charles Lewis Slattery

A story is told of the artist Turner, that one day he invited Charles Kingsley into his studio to see a picture of a storm at sea. Kingsley was rapt in admiration. "How did you do it, Turner?" he exclaimed. Turner answered: "I wished to paint a storm at sea, so I went to the coast of Holland, and engaged a fisherman to take me out in his boat in the next storm. The storm was brewing, and I went down to his boat and bade him bind me to its mast. Then he drove the boat out into the teeth of the storm. The storm was so furious that I longed to lie down in the bottom of the boat and allow it to blow over me. But I could not: I was bound to the mast. Not only did I see that storm and feel it, but it blew itself into me, till I became part of the storm. And then I came back and painted that picture."

Turner's experience is a parable of life. Life is sometimes cloud and sometimes sunshine; sometimes pleasure, sometimes pain; sometimes defeat, sometimes victory. Life is a great mingling of happiness and tragic storm. He who comes out of it rich in living is he who dares to accept it all, to face it all, to let it blow its power and its mystery and its tragedy into the inmost recesses of his soul. The victory, so won in this life, will then be an eternal possession. A loving God allows us to be absorbed in one life at a time, quite ignorant of what is ahead, lest we lose the glory which He provides for our enriching as we pass through it.

FROM "A PRAYER"

Max Ehrmann

Let me do my work each day;
And if the darkened hours of despair overcome me
May I not forget the strength that comforted me
In the desolation of other times.
May I still remember the bright hours that found me
Walking over the silent hills of my childhood,
Or dreaming on the margin of the quiet river,
When a light glowed within me,
And I promised my early God to have courage
Amid the tempests of the changing years.

GREAT GOOD HAS COME FROM BEREAVEMENT

Zelda Popkin

Out of the human understanding which grows from bereavement great good has come. No single force in the modern world has been as constructive as the urge to perpetuate the memory of our beloved dead by service to humanity.

Once, men built pyramids and palaces of stone. Today they add to the goodness of life and to its progress, through the scholarship, the children's ward and the research fund. Each cancer laboratory and hospital is a memorial to some man or woman whose life was cut short.

Damon Runyon is immortalized as much by the Cancer Fund raised in his name as by the stories he wrote. The daughter of a great actress and a famous playwright died of polio at nineteen, but hundreds of children may live because the Mary MacArthur Memorial Fund provides iron lungs and nursing care for polio victims.

The daughter of the Spencer Trasks could not speak clearly when she gave their Saratoga estate its name, but "Yaddo," her childish rhyme for "shadow," has meant to a generation of creative workers a chance to write and paint in gracious, inspiring surroundings.

MEETING SORROW UPRIGHT

Joseph H. Hertz

According to ancient Jewish custom the ceremony of cutting our garments, when our nearest and dearest on earth is lying dead before us, is to be performed standing up. This teaches: meet all sorrow standing upright. The future may be dark, veiled from the eye of mortals—but not the manner in which we are to meet the future. To rail at life, to rebel against a destiny that has cast our lines in unpleasant places, is of little avail. We cannot lay down terms to life. Life must be accepted on its own terms. But hard as life's terms are, life (it has been finely said) never dictates unrighteousness, unholiness, dishonor.

HELPING THE LIVING

Fulton Oursler

This is the story of a miracle.

It was a miracle witnessed by a recording clerk in a cemetery. Every week, for several years, this mild little man had received a letter from a woman he did not know, enclosing a money order and directing him to put fresh flowers on the grave of her son. Then one day he met her face to face. A car drove up to the cemetery gates and a chauffeur hastened into the tiny administration building to speak to the birdlike little clerk whose hands fluttered over the papers on his desk.

"The lady outside is too ill to walk," he explained. "Would you mind coming with me?"

Waiting in the car was a frail elderly woman with a face whose imperious eyes could not hide some deep, long-lasting hurt. In her arms was a great heap of flowers.

"I am Mrs. Adams," she explained. "Every week for years I have been sending you a five-dollar money order—"

"For the flowers!" the clerk exclaimed.

"Yes—to be laid on the grave of my son."

"I have never failed to attend to it," chirped the little man.

"I came here today," Mrs. Adams confided softly, "because the doctors have let me know I have only a few weeks left. I shall not be sorry to go. There is nothing left to live for. But before I die I wanted to drive here for one last look and place the flowers myself."

The little clerk blinked up at her irresolutely. Then, with a wry smile, he made up his mind and spoke.

"You know, ma'am, I was always sorry you kept sending the money for the flowers."

"Sorry?"

"Yes—because the flowers last such a little while! And nobody ever could see them or smell them. It was a shame."

"Do you realize what you are saying?"

"Oh, please don't be angry. I belong to a visiting society. State hospitals. Insane asylums. People in places like that dearly love flowers, and they can see them and can smell them. Lady, there's living people in places like that. But there isn't anybody in that grave. Not really."

The woman did not answer, but sat for a brief while, silently repeating a prayer. When she left, without a word, the little clerk feared that his impulsive frankness might have overcome her, might even have hastened her end.

But some months later he was astonished to have another visit; doubly astonished, in fact, because there was no chauffeur this time; the woman sat at the wheel, driving her car alone.

"I take the flowers to the people myself," she confided with a friendly smile. "You were right; it does make them happy. And it makes me happy. The doctors don't know what is making me well—but I do! I have something to live for now!"

She had discovered what most of us know and forget—in helping others she had miraculously helped herself. It is still true that our chief need in life is somebody who shall make us do what we can. Nothing makes us so strong as a cry for help.

HOW TO BEAR SORROW
Charles Kingsley

I believe that the wisest plan is sometimes not to try to bear sorrow—as long as one is not crippled for one's everyday duties—but to give way to it utterly and freely. Perhaps sorrow is sent that we may give way to it, and in drinking the cup to the dregs, find some medicine in it itself, which we should not find if we began doctoring ourselves or letting others doctor us. If we say simply, "I am wretched—I ought to be wretched," then we shall perhaps hear a voice: "Who made thee wretched but God? Then what can He mean but thy good?" And if the heart answers impatiently: "My good? I don't want it, I want my love," perhaps the voice may answer: "Then thou shalt love both in time."

Miguel de Cervantes

He who loses wealth loses much. He who loses a friend loses more. But he that loses his courage loses all.

Proverbs

If thou faint in the day of adversity, thy strength is small.

Samuel Johnson

Sorrow is the mere rust of the soul. Activity will cleanse and brighten it.

INVICTUS
William Ernest Henley

Out of the night that covers me,
Black as the pit from pole to pole,
I thank whatever gods may be
For my unconquerable soul.

In the fell clutch of circumstance
I have not winced nor cried aloud.
Under the bludgeonings of chance
My head is bloody, but unbowed.

Beyond this place of wrath and tears
Looms but the horror of the shade,
And yet the menace of the years
Finds and shall find me unafraid.

It matters not how strait the gate,
How charged with punishments the scroll,
I am the master of my fate:
I am the captain of my soul.

WE CAN CONQUER SORROW
Louis Binstock

. . . He who has entered within the doors of another's sorrow stands on the threshold of the gates of heaven. He understands the wisdom contained in the old rabbinic teaching: "This also for good." He has caught something of the religious spirit implicit in the two divine truths basic to both Judaism and Christianity: the one fatherhood of God and the one brotherhood of man—"Thou shalt love the Lord thy God with all thy heart, and with all thy soul, and with all thy might, and thou shalt love thy neighbor as thyself." Love of God means, fundamentally, faith in His sorrow and His love for mankind. For sorrow is universal and inevitable —but we can control it, we can conquer it.

WE DO NOT STAND ALONE
Morris Adler

It is an early weekday morn. A quiet residential street of the dynamic city is still enveloped in a drowsy stillness. Soon life will awake in its silent and comfortable houses and noisy children, after a hasty breakfast, will leap through doors, schoolward bound. Men can be seen entering one of the houses. Their bearing is marked by reverence and solemnity. Sorrow has recently visited one of the homes on the street and friends are gathering for the mourning service. Within the residence, candles are lit, tefillin and talesim are quietly donned and the voice of prayer is heard in the hushed atmosphere.

Long ago a people developed this practice so rich in meaning that neither the passing of centuries nor the roaring life of a metropolitan center has been able to render it obsolete. The friends are no longer individuals come to express sympathy, each in his particular way, with the feeling that the degree of his own friendship with the mourners dictates. The individuals have merged into a "minyan," a congregation. They have coalesced into an "eidah," a community. Though this community is small in numbers, it represents in every religious detail the larger K'lal Yisroel of which each identified Jew is part. Thus does a community symbolically and actually share in the sorrow of one of its members. The grief of the individual re-echoes in the life of the group. No Jew stands alone in his bereavement, while his personal anguish serves as a wall between him and all those upon whose way in life the dark shadow has not fallen. A people closes ranks and encircles its stricken member with the warmth of brotherly sympathy.

The religious service of this little group, representing the larger community, takes place in the home. It is a tribute to the central position of the home. Where a family lives and loves and fashions the most intimate bonds to link persons one to the other—you have a sanctuary appropriate for worship. For the home is a sanctuary no less than the Synagogue. Its holiness is of no lesser kind than that with which the formal house of prayer of the entire community is invested. The poignancy and sanctity of grief are best expressed in the intimate sanctuary of the home. The sanctuary of the home can never be replaced by Synagogue or Temple, however large or magnificent.

The prayer is concluded. The imperatives of modern living compel the minyan to dissolve once again into its component individuals who hurry through streets, now filled with romping and laughing children and speeding automobiles, to offices, shops and plants. The mourners remain. They are, however, no longer completely alone. In the atmosphere of their home the prayers linger and bespeak the solace of a tradition and the brotherhood of a community.

William James

Be willing to have it so. Acceptance of what has happened is the first step to overcoming the consequences of any misfortune.

Leigh Hunt

Whenever evil befalls us, we ought to ask ourselves, after the first suffering, how we can turn it into good. So shall we take occasion, from one bitter root, to raise perhaps many flowers.

Chaim Nachman Bialik

Afflictions are really not a good gift—neither they nor their consequences. However, if afflictions do come, it is well that we convert them into afflictions of love. Herein lies the power of man.

TURNING GRIEF INTO THE GIVING OF SUCCOR

John Bright

I was in the depths of grief, I might almost say of despair, for the light and sunshine of my house had been extinguished. All that was left on earth of my young wife, except the memory of a sainted life and a too brief happiness, was lying still and cold in the chamber above us. Mr. Cobden called upon me, and addressed me, as you might suppose, with words of condolence. After a time he looked up and said, "There are thousands of houses in England at this moment where wives, mothers and children are dying of hunger. Now," he said, "when the first paroxysm of your grief is past, I would advise you to come with me, and we will never rest till the Corn Law is repealed."

I accepted his invitation. I knew that the description he had given of the homes of thousands was not an exaggerated description. I felt in my conscience that there was a work which somebody must do, and therefore I accepted his invitation, and from that time we never ceased to labor hard on behalf of the resolution which we had made.

Ben Jonson

To struggle when hope is banished!
To live when life's salt is gone!
To dwell in a dream that's vanished—
To endure, and go calmly on!

THE WISDOM OF ACCEPTING THE INEVITABLE

Fulton Oursler

Much of our happiness and our misery spring entirely from our attitude toward events. It depends on how you look at a thing—how you change it, or else how you accept it. There's no use fighting the inevitable. The only way to argue with a cold wind is to put on your overcoat. And then there's that famous prayer: "God give me the courage to change the things I can change, and the serenity to accept the things I can't change, and the wisdom to know the difference."

Like the soldier who lost his arm. Or did he?

This soldier was wounded in one of the early battles of the Second World War. On the operating table in a field hospital he opened his eyes and saw a doctor bending over him.

"It's all right, kid," the surgeon was saying, "you're going to get well. But I'm afraid you've lost your arm."

The soldier grinned, and in a faint voice replied: "I didn't lose my arm—I gave it."

In great matters and small, what happens to us is not nearly so important as our attitude toward it. The future of that maimed soldier was full of hope because of his positive point of view. He did not yield to despair. Every misfortune in life is an opportunity for advancement in spiritual strength for which we should be truly grateful. It all depends on how we meet God's challenge to us.

Madame Guyon

Ah, if you knew what peace there is in an accepted sorrow!

William Cowper

Beware of desperate steps; the darkest day,
Lived till tomorrow, will have passed away.

TO FACE LIFE WITH DARING
Charles Lewis Slattery

. . . Think of the people great and small who do not accept sorrow with poise and with strength. Think of the people who shelter their children from every peril, till their children, grown fat and useless, cumber the roadway of life. . . .

. . . Think of the people who, when sorrow smites them, go madly afield in gay revels, so hoping to drown their agony in forgetfulness. Think of the people who, having compassed every known device to avoid the inevitable sorrow to which all flesh is heir, and who, having it thrust upon them at the last, still protest against it, cursing God because He allows it and filling the air with their groans. Like children they are, who when sent to bed go because they must, but as they climb the stairs nastily kick each stair, by way of angry protest. One glance at these groups of people who refuse with any sort of grace to accept the sorrow of life, shows one the high relief in which those others stand who, though they know not why, take the sorrow in, and take it consciously in all its bitterness.

. . . Sorrow endures but for a season, and joy comes with the morning. But the joy comes because the sorrow has been felt and gracefully, nobly accepted. Then let us pray for a recklessness which is beyond the recklessness of war; a recklessness which faces life with equal daring whether it presents pleasure or pain, joy or sorrow, life or death.

BEND WITH THE WIND

Grandma Fontaine, one of the tart characters in Margaret Mitchell's Gone With the Wind, *gave forth a bit of wisdom which is worth singling out for reflection right now when some people are finding it hard to sustain their courage.*

"We bow to the inevitable. We're not wheat, we're buckwheat! When a storm comes along, it flattens ripe wheat because it's dry and can't bend with the wind. But ripe buckwheat's got sap in it and it bends. And when the wind has passed, it springs up almost as straight and strong as before."

Bend with the wind—don't let life break your spirit. After your trials and disappointments and discouragements, spring back again like buckwheat! Don't let the things that can't be helped flatten you. Bide your time. Have patience. And after the storm straighten up and go forward.

LORD, HELP ME TO FORGET
Ross L. Holman

I realize, of course, how much easier it is to want to forget than it is to do it, but noted psychiatrists say it can be done not only by the substitution of pleasant memories for unpleasant ones, but by engaging in mind-diverting activities. A married couple lost an only child. The doctor had already told them they could never have another. It looked as though their rose-tinted world had collapsed beneath them. Ever since he was born they had been practically living for that kid.

For months after the child had been laid away, the couple spent much of their time at the grave, mourning their hearts out. The man's business affairs suffered.

Finally their pastor suggested that they could find release by interesting themselves in other people's children. They did. The man organized a basketball team among the boys in his community. In his spare time he led them on hikes and took them on camping trips. The wife found it great fun to invite smaller children in for a party, kiddy games, and refreshments. She directed recreational activities for older girls.

The youngsters of the community idolized this couple and the feeling was shared by their parents. Life took on a new meaning. Their many interests crowded out the aching memory of a tragic event.

W. E. Sangster says: "Conscious memory has a preference for the pleasant. She is always trying to stuff painful experiences down the hole of oblivion and to preserve only the things we are glad to recall. . . . One may not always be able to forget a tragic occurrence . . . the real danger in remembering the wrong things is that we remember them not as facts, but as convulsive experiences."

Robert Louis Stevenson

Quiet minds cannot be perplexed or frightened, but go on in fortune or misfortune at their own private pace, like a clock during a thunderstorm.

Author unknown

When you dig another out of his trouble, you find a place to bury your own.

Midrash

Said Rabbi Elazar ben Jacob: "When sufferings come upon him, man must utter thanks to God, for suffering draws man near unto the Holy One, blessed be He. As it saith: Whom the Lord loveth, He correcteth, even as a father correcteth the son in whom he delighteth. When griefs come upon a man, let him stand up and receive them, thus his reward will be beyond measure."

AS YOU GO THROUGH LIFE
Ella Wheeler Wilcox

This world will never adjust itself
To suit your whims to the letter;
Some things must go wrong your whole life long
And the sooner you know it the better.
It is folly to fight with the Infinite,
And go under at last in the wrestle,
The wiser man shapes into God's plan
As the water shapes into a vessel.

USING THE DARK THREADS
Sidney Greenberg

Oriental rugs which are found in many homes are all woven by hand. Usually, there will be a group of people weaving a single rug together under the directions of an artist who issues instructions to the rest. He determines the choice of colors and the nature of the pattern.

It often happens that one of the weavers inserts the wrong color thread. The artist may have called for blue and instead black was used. If you examine an oriental rug carefully, you may be able to detect such irregularities. What is significant about them is that they were not removed. The skillful artist just proceeded to weave them into the pattern.

Here is a wise procedure that we can follow in life. We should like the pattern of our lives to be woven exclusively of bright-colored threads. But every now and then a dark thread steals into the fabric. If we are true artists of life we can weave even this thread into the pattern and make it contribute its share to the beauty of the whole.

Thomas Carlyle

From the lowest depth there is a path to the loftiest height.

COMFORT IN SERVICE

Helen Hayes

I have found comfort in doing, in visiting those who have been struck down, the children and the parents, in thinking that through Mary's death perhaps she and I were destined to have a little part in the final victory. I have learned ineffable gratitude for the Scriptural commandment to love thy neighbor as thyself. Now at last I know the solace that comes from its meaning. Once I thought it old-fashioned, empty, but it now shines with a new radiance out of the depths of its truth and simplicity.

Before I had only loved myself. My aim was to make others love me. It wasn't selfish or mean, but I had never known what it was to love others as myself. I will not say that my world has been made whole again—it never can be—but there has been acceptance, even happiness, in giving and doing. "For," as Pearl S. Buck has so knowingly written, "there is an alchemy in sorrow. It can be transmuted into wisdom which, if it does not bring joy, can yet bring happiness."

WE MUST NOT EXPECT MIRACULOUS HEALING

Joshua Loth Liebman

We must face grief without any expectation of miraculous healing, but with the knowledge that if we are courageous and resolute we can live as our loved ones would wish us to live, not empty, morose, self-centered, and self-pitying, but as brave and undismayed servants of the greater life. Rabbinic wisdom teaches this approach to grief in the following passages: "When the second Temple in Jerusalem was destroyed, many Jews began to withdraw from life and sank into a state of depressed mourning for the sons and daughters of Israel that had perished and also for the Temple that had gone up in smoke. They refused to eat and to drink." Rabbi Joshua said to them: "My sons, I know that it is impossible not to mourn, but to mourn excessively is forbidden." Why? Because that great Jewish sage felt that we human beings must think not only of the past but of the future. We are commanded by our religion to be the servants of life as long as we live.

Martin F. Tupper

Never give up! If adversity presses,
Providence wisely has mingled the cup,
And the best counsel, in all your distresses,
Is the stout watchword of "Never give up."

George Moore

So long as one does not despair, so long as one doesn't look upon life bitterly, things work out fairly well in the end.

C. F. Deems

To dare is great. To bear is greater. Bravery we share with brutes. Fortitude with saints.

Helen Keller

I thank God for my handicaps, for, through them, I have found myself, my work, and my God.

THE JACKPOT OF COURAGE

Fulton Oursler

The law of recompense for unselfish heroism is seldom talked about. Yet here is a remarkable illustration of the potency of the law.

Take the strange case of Dr. McAlister, the weeping physician of the Eastern Shore, as he was known in Maryland. Dr. McAlister's beautiful wife, whom he loved devotedly, died while still young. The shock of her passing plunged him into a melancholy that was like a paralysis; he would not talk or eat, and he was obsessed with a desire for self-destruction. For years he was guarded by three nurses, on eight-hour duty. Grieving more and more, he became an emaciated shell of his former self; he had to be lifted from his chair to his bed and coaxed to eat. How he detested his three nurses!

In summer he was taken to the seashore, where he liked to sit in his wheel chair on a bluff overlooking the ocean. One afternoon he surprised his nurse by suggesting that she take a swim.

"You can watch me just as well from the water," he said cunningly.

When the nurse, who should have suspected what he was up to, did go in swimming, Dr. McAlister sat quietly watching her, waiting for the opportune moment to throw himself from the cliffs to the rocks below. Then came a scream; the nurse, seized with a cramp, was drowning.

It is a matter of historical record that Dr. McAlister stood up, walked without hesitation to a point on the headland jutting out over the water, and plunged down. Swimming to the help of the screaming nurse, he brought her in to the beach. And, with strength from fathomless sources, he worked over her until she was safely alive. That was the end of Dr. McAlister's melancholy. In restoring life to the nurse, whom he thoroughly disliked, he had lost all desire to die, and thereafter found a new pleasure in living.

Can it be true, what so many believe, that there is some deep therapeutic power in the sacrifice love offers up? A power affecting not only spirit, but body—removing and remedying physical ills?

A NEW HORIZON
Myrtle Dean Clark

Dead wood carried—heavy rot became;
Dead wood burned—a brilliant flame.
Misfortune carried—the very heart grew lame;
Misfortune used—a new horizon came.

Harriet Beecher Stowe

When you get into a tight place and everything goes against you, till it seems as though you could not hold on a minute longer, never give up then, for that is just the place and time that the tide will turn.

THE WEEPING FATHER
Louis I. Newman

An ancient parable of the East tells of the father who daily went to weep at the tomb of his son. The son from his abode of happiness looked with compassion upon his father, and at length, assuming human form again, descended on earth, and throwing himself down near the tomb where his father lay, began to weep with violence. The father, approaching, said: "Young man, why are you weeping?" "I am weeping," replied the youth, "because I yearn for the sun and the moon to make a pair of wheels for my chariot." "Young man," said the father, "you must have lost your reason. We cannot make chariot-wheels out of the sun and the moon?" The youth answered: "You are weeping for a mortal whose transient life has passed away; but I weep for the sun and the moon which I continually have before me."

LET US REJOICE AT OUR TRIALS
Stefan Zweig

Our God, the God of our fathers, is a hidden God; and not until we are bathed in sorrow are we enabled to discern him. He chooses those only whom he has tried, and to none but the suffering does he give his love. Let us therefore rejoice at our trials, brothers, and let us love the suffering God sends. He has broken us with affliction, that he may sink the deeper into the freshly ploughed ground of our hearts, and that we may be ready for the scattering of his seed. He has weakened our bodies that we may strengthen our souls. Let us joyfully enter the smelting furnace of his will, that thereby we may be purified. Follow the example of your forefathers, and thankfully accept the scourgings of the Almighty!

MAKING STEMS OUT OF SCRATCHES
A Parable of the Dubner Maggid

A king once owned a large, beautiful, pure diamond of which he was justly proud, for it had no equal anywhere. One day, the diamond accidentally sustained a deep scratch. The king called in the most skilled diamond cutters and offered them a great reward if they could remove the imperfection from his treasured jewel. But none could repair the blemish. The king was sorely distressed.

After some time a gifted lapidary came to the king and promised to make the rare diamond even more beautiful than it had been before the mishap. The king was impressed by his confidence and entrusted his precious stone to his care. And the man kept his word.

With superb artistry he engraved a lovely rosebud around the imperfection and he used the scratch to make the stem.

We can emulate that craftsman. When life bruises us and wounds us, we can use even the scratches to etch a portrait of beauty and charm.

IT IS WHAT YOU HAVE LEFT
THAT COUNTS
Harold Russell

There is no easy formula for a happy living. Anyone who says he has one is either joking or lying. Even if I could, I have no intention or desire of putting forth any patented, neatly packaged recipe of my own. But there is one simple thought I should like to pass on, if I may. It is no sure-fire prescription for happiness; it is not guaranteed to bring any bluebirds singing in your back yard. I offer it merely because I found it can help prevent much vain regret and self-defeat. It is not what you have lost, but what you have left that counts. Too many of us squander precious energy, time, and courage dreaming of things that were and never can be again, instead of dedicating ourselves to realities and the heavy tasks of today.

HOW TO HELP SOMEONE IN SORROW
Howard Whitman

Most of us want to be helpful when grief strikes a friend, but often we don't know how. We may end up doing nothing because we don't know the right—and helpful—things to say and do. Because that was my own experience recently, I resolved to gather pointers which might be useful to others as well as to myself.

Ministers, priests and rabbis deal with such situations every day. I went to scores of them, of all faiths, in all parts of the country.

Here are some specific suggestions they made:

1. *Don't try to "buck them up."* This surprised me when the Rev. Arthur E. Wilson of Providence, R. I., mentioned it. But the others concurred. It only makes your friend feel worse when you say, "Come now, buck up. Don't take it so hard."

A man who has lost his wife must take it hard (if he loved her). "Bucking him up" sounds as though you are minimizing his loss. But the honest attitude, "Yes, it's tough, and I sure know it is," makes your friend feel free to express grief and recover from it. The "don't take it so hard" approach deprives him of the natural emotion of grief, stops up the safety valve God has given him.

2. *Don't try to divert them.* Rabbi Martin B. Ryback of Norwalk, Conn., pointed out that many people making condolence calls purposely veer away from the subject. They make small talk about football, fishing, the weather—anything but the reason for their visit.

The rabbi calls this "trying to camouflage death." The task of the mourner, difficult as it is, is to face the fact of death, and go on from there. "It would be far better," Rabbi Ryback suggested, "to sit silently and say nothing than to make obvious attempts to distract. The sorrowing friend sees through the effort to divert him. When the visitor leaves, reality hits him all the harder."

3. *Don't be afraid to talk about the person who has passed away.* Well-intentioned friends often shy away from mentioning the deceased. The implication is that the whole thing is too terrible to mention.

"The helpful thing," advised Rabbi Henry E. Kagan of Mount Vernon, N. Y., "is to talk about the person as you knew him in the fullness of his life, to re-create a living picture to replace the picture of death."

Once Rabbi Kagan called on a woman who had lost her brother. "I didn't know your brother too well," he said. "Tell me about him." The woman started talking and they discussed her brother for an hour. Afterward she said, "I feel relieved now for the first time since he died."

4. *Don't be afraid of causing tears.* When a good friend of mine lost a child I said something which made his eyes fill up. "I put my foot in it," I said, in relating the incident to the Rev. D. Russell Hetsler of Brazil, Ind. "No, you didn't," he replied. "You helped your friend to express grief in a normal, healthy way. That is far better than to stifle grief when friends are present, only to have it descend more crushingly when one is all alone."

Fear of causing tears, probably more than anything else, makes people stiff and ineffective. Visiting a friend who has lost his wife, they may be about to mention a ride in the country when they remember the man's wife used to love rides in the country. They don't dare speak of peonies because they were her favorite flower. So they freeze up.

"They really are depriving their friend of probably the greatest help they could give him," Pastor Hetsler commented. "That is, to help him experience grief in a normal way and get over it." Medical and psychological studies back up the pastor's contention that *expressing* grief is good and *repressing* it is bad. "If a comment of yours brings tears," he concluded, "remember—they are healthy tears."

5. *Let them talk.* "Sorrowing people need to talk," explained the Rev. Vern Swartsfager of San Francisco. "'Friends worry about their ability to *say* the right things. They ought to be worrying about their ability to *listen*."

If the warmth of your presence can get your friend to start talking, keep quiet and listen—even though he repeats the same things a dozen times. He is not telling you news but expressing feelings that need repetition. Pastor Swartsfager suggested a measuring stick for the success of your visit: "If your friend has said a hundred words to your one, you've helped a lot."

6. *Reassure—don't argue.* "Everybody who loses a loved one has guilt feelings—they may not be justified but they're natural," Rabbi Joseph R. Narot of Miami pointed out. A husband feels he should have been more considerate of his wife; a parent feels he should have spent more time with his child; a wife feels she should have made fewer demands on her husband. The yearning, "If only I had not done this, or done that—if I only had a chance to do it now," a hallmark of grieving.

These feelings must work their way out. You can give reassurance. Your friend must slowly come to the realization that he or she was, in all probability, a pretty good husband, wife or parent.

7. *Communicate—don't isolate.* Too often a person who has lost a loved one is overwhelmed with visitors for a week or so; then the house is empty. Even good friends sometimes stay away, believing that people in sorrow "like to be alone."

"That's the 'silent treatment,'" remarked Father Thomas Bresnaham of Detroit. "There's nothing worse." Our friend has not only lost his loved one—he has lost us too.

It is in that after-period, when all the letters of sympathy have been read and acknowledged and people have swung back into daily routine, that friends are needed most.

Keep in touch, Father Bresnaham urges. See your friend more often than you did before. See him for any purpose—for lunch, for a drive in the country, for shopping, for an evening visit. He has suffered a deep loss. Your job is to show him, by implication, how much he still has left. Your being with him is a proof to him that he still has resources.

8. *Perform some concrete act.* The Rev. William B. Ayers, of Wollaston, Mass., told me of a sorrowing husband who lost all interest in food until a friend brought over his favorite dish and

simply left it there at suppertime. "That's a wonderful way to help, by a concrete deed which in itself may be small yet carries the immense implication that you care," Pastor Ayers declared.

We should make it our business, when a friend is in sorrow, to do at least one practical, tangible act of kindness. Here are some to choose from: run errands with your car, take the children to school, bring in a meal, do the dishes, make necessary phone calls, pick up mail at the office, help acknowledge condolence notes, shop for the groceries.

9. *Swing into action.* Action is the symbol of going on living.

By swinging into action with your friend, whether at his hobby or his work, you help build a bridge to the future. Perhaps it means painting the garage with him, or hoeing the garden. Or spending an afternoon with a woman friend mending the children's clothes, or browsing through antique shops.

In St. Paul, Minn., the Rev. J. T. Morrow told me of a man who had lost a son. The man's hobby had been refinishing furniture. When he called on him Pastor Morrow said, "Come on, let's go down to the basement." They sanded a table together. When Pastor Morrow left, the man said, "This is the first time I've felt I could go on living."

Sorrowing people, Pastor Morrow pointed out, tend to drop out of things. They're a little like the rider who has been thrown from a horse. If they are to ride again, better get them back on the horse quickly.

10. *"Get them out of themselves,"* advised Father James Keller, leader of the Christophers. Once you have your friend doing things for himself, his grief is nearly cured. Once you have him doing things for others, it *is* cured.

Grief runs a natural course. It will pass. But if there is only a vacuum behind it, self-pity will rush in to fill it. To help your friend along the normal course of recovery, guide him to a new interest.

Volunteer work for a charity, enrollment in a community group to help youngsters, committee work at church or temple are ways of getting people "out of themselves."

If you and I, when sorrow strikes our friends, follow even a few of these pointers, we will be helpful.

Rachel weeps for her children,
She refuses to be comforted.

—Jeremiah

THE DEATH OF THE YOUNG

The grief of a parent for a child is the most difficult of all to bear. Bereaved parents feel keenly the burning anguish of King David's lament: "O my son Absalom, my son, my son Absalom! Would I had died for thee, O Absalom, my son, my son." Almost these very words were found recently by explorers in an Egyptian tomb. Upon the exquisitely carved sarcophagus of a little child there were inscribed the parent's words: "O my life, my love, my little one, would God I had died for thee!"

Jeremiah pictured mother Rachel weeping so bitterly for her children who "are not" that "she refused to be comforted." Indeed is there any comfort equal to the hurt, any solace adequate to the loss?

Nevertheless, the voice of the Divine Comforter speaks softly to the bereft mother: "Refrain thy voice from weeping and thine eyes from tears . . . there is hope for thy future."

There are some genuine sources of hope and courage to tap at such a time. The awareness that other parents have found the strength to endure a similar affliction can be reassuring. Somehow, from somewhere, there comes the endurance and the fortitude equal to our desperate need. The Psalmist undoubtedly experienced this in his own life for he praised God "who healeth the broken in heart and bindeth up their wounds." A measure of comfort may also be derived from the realization that there is a precious store of memories which death cannot take away and which no mother would surrender even if she could thereby be relieved immediately of all her sorrow. In those memories, the ravages of time and decay no longer hold sway. There the child "grows not older," it remains

149

eternally "fair and kind and young." And perhaps the greatest comfort lies in the thought that all of life is but a loan to us and when the Lender asks for the return of the jewel, He promises to care for it better than we can.

HE IS STILL ALIVE
John Gunther

An acquaintance said of Johnny Gunther: "He had the most brilliant promise of any child I have ever known." When he succumbed at the age of seventeen to a vicious brain tumor, his father wrote a moving memoir entitled Death Be Not Proud—*from which the following is taken. Significantly, the very last words the dying lad wrote on the inside back cover of his diary were: "Hebrew Toast:* Le-Hy-eem—*To Life."*

We said goodbye. But to anybody who ever knew him, he is still alive. I do not mean merely that he lives in both of us or in the trees at Deerfield or in anything he touched truly, but that the influence, the impact, of a heroic personality continues to exert itself long after mortal bonds are snapped. Johnny transmits permanently something of what he was, since the fabric of the universe is continuous and eternal. . . .

The whys of this story, why Johnny should have been struck just in that part of him that would have been most fruitful . . . the why above all whys which is why any child should die, the whys and wherefores of the celestial bookkeeping involved, if any, I will not go into here. There are other criteria for measuring a life as well as its duration—quality, intensity. But for us there is no compensation, except that we can go to him though he cannot come to us. For others, I would say that it was his spirit, and only his spirit, that kept him invincibly alive against such dreadful obstacles for so long—this is the central pith and substance of what I am trying to write, as a mournful tribute not only to Johnny but to the power, the wealth, the unconquerable beauty of the human spirit, will and soul.

LOVING LIFE MORE, BEING MORE AWARE

Frances Gunther

Johnny's mother wrote the last chapter in Death Be Not Proud. *The passages which follow are taken from that chapter entitled "A Word From Frances."*

Death always brings one suddenly face to face with life. Nothing, not even the birth of one's child, brings one so close to life as his death.

Johnny lay dying of a brain tumor for fifteen months. He was in his seventeenth year. I never kissed him good night without wondering whether I should see him alive in the morning. I greeted him each morning as though he were newly born to me, a re-gift of God. Each day he lived was a blessed day of grace. . . .

He wasn't just dying, of course. He was living and dying and being reborn all at the same time each day. How we loved each day. "It's been another wonderful day, Mother!" he'd say, as I knelt to kiss him good night. . . .

Since Johnny's death, we have received many letters from many kind friends from all parts of the world, each expressing his condolence in his own way. But through most of them has run a single theme: sympathy with us in facing a mysterious stroke of God's will that seemed inexplicable, unjustifiable, and yet, being God's will, must also be part of some great plan beyond our mortal ken, perhaps sparing him or us greater pain or loss.

Actually, in the experience of losing one's child in death, I have found that other factors were involved.

I did not for one thing feel that God personally had singled out either him or us for any special act, either of animosity or generosity. In a way I did not feel that God was personally involved at all. . . .

During Johnny's illness, I prayed continually to God, naturally. God was always there. He sat beside us during the doctors' consultation, as we waited the long vigils outside the operating room, as we rejoiced in the miracle of a brief recovery, as we agonized when hope ebbed away and the doctors confessed there was no longer anything they could do. They were helpless, and we were helpless, and in His way, God, standing by us in our hour of need, God in

His infinite wisdom and mercy and loving kindness, God in all His omnipotence, was helpless, too. . . .

I wish we had loved Johnny more when he was alive. Of course we loved Johnny very much. Johnny knew that. Everybody knew it. Loving Johnny more. What does it mean? What can it mean now?

Parents all over the earth who lost sons in the war have felt this kind of question, and sought an answer.

To me, it means loving life more, being more aware of life, of one's fellow human beings, of the earth.

It means obliterating, in a curious but real way, the ideas of evil and hate and the enemy, and transmuting them, with the alchemy of suffering, into ideas of clarity and charity.

It means caring more and more about other people, at home and abroad, all over the earth. It means caring more about God.

I hope we can love Johnny more and more till we, too, die, and leave behind us, as he did the love of love, the love of life.

Flora Elizabeth Hastings

Grieve not that I die young. Is it not well to pass away ere life hath lost its brightness?

GOD CALLED HIM

James J. Metcalfe

Your little boy was only five
When he was called away;
And in your dear parental hearts
It was a tragic day.

You heard him laugh and speak to you,
You saw him climb the stair,
And in your fondest memories
You find him everywhere.

You called to him, he called to you,
And you were not alone
Until that sudden moment when
God called him to His own.

But it was God, and only He
Who gave your baby life,
And who withdrew him gently from
The struggle and the strife.

He must have loved your boy so much
He did not want to wait
Until he grew to be a man,
However good and great.

John Milton

Think what a present thou to God has sent,
And render him with patience what he lent.

THE JEWELS
Midrash

While Rabbi Meir was holding his weekly discourse in the House of Study one Sabbath afternoon, his two beloved sons died suddenly at home. The grief-stricken mother carried them to her room and covered them with a sheet. When Rabbi Meir returned after the evening services, he asked his wife, Beruriah, about the boys whom he had missed in the Synagogue. Instead of replying, she asked him to recite the Havdalah service marking the departure of the Sabbath, and gave him his evening meal. When it was over, Beruriah turned to Rabbi Meir and said: "I have a question to ask you. Not long ago, some precious jewels were entrusted to my care. Now the Owner has come to reclaim them. Shall I return them?"

"But of course," said Rabbi Meir. "You know the Law. Naturally they must be returned." Beruriah then took him by the hand, led him to the bed and drew back the sheet. Rabbi Meir burst into bitter weeping. "My sons! My sons!" he lamented. Then Beruriah reminded him tearfully: "Did you not say that we must restore to the Owner what He entrusted to our care? Our sons were the jewels which God left with us and now their Master has taken back His very own."

WEEP NOT FOR THOSE
Thomas Moore

Weep not for those whom the veil of the tomb
In life's happy morning, hath hid from our eyes,
Ere sin threw a blight o'er the spirit's young bloom,
Or earth had profan'd what was born for the skies.

Elbert Hubbard

Whom the gods love die young, no matter how long they live.

WHEN THE FIG IS RIPE
Midrash

In hot weather, a rabbi delivered his discourse to his disciples under the shade of a fig tree. They noticed that each morning the owner would pick his ripened figs. "Perhaps he fears that we will pick his fruit," they thought, and they moved to another place. The owner begged them to return. Believing that they had moved because his presence annoyed them, he resolved not to pick the fruit. In the evening, they beheld the figs dropping from the trees, spoiled by the heat of the sun. The disciples then appreciated why it was necessary for the owner to pick them in the morning.

The rabbi said: "The owner of the figs knows when his fruit should be picked, lest it be spoiled. Thus does God know when to summon His righteous children before they are spoiled. This is the reason why many good and gracious persons are sometimes called by God in their early manhood."

NOTHING IS WASTED
Zelda Popkin

He returned home drained and spent, his sunken eyes dazed and unbelieving. He had just watched a small white coffin being lowered into the earth. No parent in all his days performs a harder task than final farewell to a child.

"Why did it happen?" he cried. "If this is all there is to life, what's the use of going on?"

His father was there. His father had met bereavement before. He said, "Nothing is wasted, son. This is the experience through which you will grow." Then they sat down and quietly talked of the meaning of death.

LOST LOVE

Andrew Lang

In dreams she grows not older,
The lands of dream among,
Though all the world wax colder,
Though all the songs be sung,
In dreams doth he behold her
Still fair and kind and young.

FROM "GONE"

John Greenleaf Whittier

There seems a shadow on the day,
  Her smile no longer cheers;
A dimness on the stars at night,
  Like eyes that look through tears.

Alone unto our Father's will
  One thought hath reconciled;
That He whose love exceedeth ours
  Hath taken home His child.

Fold her, O Father! in Thine arms,
  And let her henceforth be
A messenger of love between
  Our human hearts and Thee.

LINCOLN'S LETTER TO MRS. BIXBY

Dear Madam:

I have been shown in the files of the War Department a statement of the Adjutant General of Massachusetts that you are the mother of five sons who have died gloriously on the field of battle. I feel how weak and fruitless must be any words of mine which should attempt to beguile you from the grief of a loss so overwhelming, but I cannot refrain from tendering to you the consolation that may be found in the thanks of the Republic that they died to save. I pray that the Heavenly Father may assuage the anguish of your bereavement, and leave you only the cherished memory of the loved and lost, and the solemn pride that must be yours to have laid so costly a sacrifice upon the altar of freedom.

Yours very sincerely and respectfully,
Abraham Lincoln

A CHILD'S EPITAPH
Arthur Guiterman

Above a low mound at the cedar tree's root
Is carved on a stone that is moldering dark
"The Dove found no rest for the sole of her foot,
And returned unto Him in the Ark."

DO NOT FEAR FOR THE LITTLE LOVELY VOYAGER
Leigh Hunt

The little innocent face looks so sublimely simple and confiding among the terrors of death. Crimeless and fearless, that little mortal passed under the shadow and explored the mystery of dissolution. There is death in its sublimest and purest image; no hatred, no hypocrisy, no suspicion, no care for the morrow ever darkened that little one's face; death has come lovingly upon it; there yearnings of love, indeed, cannot be stifled; for the prattle and smiles, and all the little world of thoughts that were so delightful, are gone forever. Awe, too, will overcast us in its presence; for we are looking on death. But we do not fear for the little lovely voyager; for the child has gone, simple and trusting, into the presence of its all-wise Father. . . .

AT A CHILD'S GRAVE

Robert Ingersoll

My friends: I know how vain it is to gild a grief with words, and yet I wish to take from every grave its fear.

Here in this world, where life and death are equal kings, all should be brave enough to meet what all the dead have met. The future has been filled with fear, stained and polluted by the heartless past. From the wondrous tree of life the buds and blossoms fall with ripened fruit, and in the common bed of earth, patriarchs and babes sleep side by side.

Why should we fear that which will come to all that is? We cannot tell, we do not know, which is the greater blessing—life or death. We cannot say that death is not a good. We do not know whether the grave is the end of this life, or the door of another, or whether the night here is not somewhere else a dawn.

Neither can we tell which is the more fortunate, the child dying in its mother's arms, before its lips have learned to form a word— or he who journeys all the length of life's uneven road, painfully taking the last slow steps with staff and crutch.

Every cradle asks us "whence?" and every coffin "whither?" The poor barbarian, weeping above his dead, can answer these questions just as well as the robed priest of the most authentic creed. The tearful ignorance of the one is as consoling as the learned and unmeaning word of the other. No man, standing where the horizon of a life has touched a grave, has any right to prophesy a future filled with pain and tears.

May be that death gives all there is of worth to life. If those we press and strain within our arms could never die, perhaps that love would wither from the earth. May be this common fate treads from out the paths between our hearts the weeds of selfishness and hate. And I had rather live and love where death is king than have eternal life where love is not. Another life is nought, unless we know and love again the ones who love us here.

They who stand with breaking hearts around this little grave need have no fear. The larger and the nobler faith in all that is, and is to be, tells us that death, even at its worst, is only perfect rest. We know that through the common wants of life—the needs and duties of each hour—their grief will lessen day by day, until at last this grave will be to them a place of rest and peace—almost of joy. There is for them this consolation: the dead do not suffer. If they live again, their lives will surely be as good as ours. We have no fear; we are all children of the same mother, and the same fate awaits us all. We, too, have our religion, and it is this: Help for the living—hope for the dead.

Julianus

Life's pleasure hath he lost—escaped life's pain,
Nor wedded joys nor wedded sorrows knew.

THE SLEEP OF THE DILIGENT
Midrash

When Rabbi Bun died, Rabbi Zeira eulogized as follows: "To what is the case of Rabbi Bun like? To a king who has hired workmen for his garden, and he observes that one of them works expertly and efficiently. He calls him over and walks with him about the garden. In the evening, when the king pays his workmen, he gives to the capable man the same pay as to the others. The latter protest to the king: 'But he has worked only two hours, and we have worked for eight.' 'True,' answers the king, 'but he has accomplished more in two hours than you in eight.' Likewise, 'My beloved is gone down to His garden.' (Song of Songs 6:2) Rabbi Bun has labored in the Torah during his twenty-eight years more than another fine student in a hundred years. Therefore God summoned him to walk with Him. May 'the sleep of the diligent worker be sweet.'" (Eccl. 5:11)

Robert Burns

Here lies a rose, a budding rose,
  Blasted before its bloom;
Whose innocence did sweets disclose
  Beyond that flower's perfume.
To those who for her loss are griev'd
  This consolation's given,—
She's from a world of woe receiv'd
  And blooms a rose in Heaven.

Leigh Hunt

Those who have lost an infant are never, as it were, without an infant child. They are the only persons who, in one sense, retain it always. . . . The other children grow up to manhood and womanhood, and suffer all the changes of mortality. This one alone is rendered an immortal child. Death has arrested it with his kindly harshness, and blessed it into an eternal image of youth and innocence.

THE FLOWER PLUCKED BY THE MASTER
Author unknown

A gentleman's gardener had a darling girl whom he loved dearly. At a tender age she was fatally stricken. The father was terribly distressed and murmured at the dealings of Providence.

The gardener had in one of his flower-beds a favorite rose. It was the fairest flower he had ever seen on the tree, and he daily marked its growing beauty, intending, when it was full blown, to send it to his master's mansion. One morning it was gone: someone had plucked it. Mortified at what he thought was the improper conduct of one of the servants, he tried to find out the culprit. He was, however, much surprised to find that it was his master who, on walking through the garden, had been attracted by the beauty of the rose, and, plucking it, had carried it to one of the beautiful rooms in the hall. The gardener's anger was changed into pleasure. He felt reconciled when he heard that his master had thought the flower worthy of such special notice.

"Ah, Richard," said the gentleman, "you can gladly give up the rose, because I thought it worthy of a place in my house. And will you repine because your heavenly Father has thought wise to remove your child from a world of trial and hardship to be with Himself in Heaven?"

EPITAPH ON AN INFANT
Samuel T. Coleridge

Ere sin could blight or sorrow fade,
Death came with friendly care;

The opening bud to Heaven conveyed,
And bade it blossom there.

HE IS MORE ALIVE THAN WE ARE

Canon W. H. Elliott

We do not think of our Robin as dead—he who was always so much alive. He is not dead. He is much more alive than we are, his eyes on far horizons that we cannot see, his warm young heart aglow with love and hope, his whole eager nature intent already on the thrilling work that God is giving him to do.

He is not asleep, as some may think. What we have laid reverently away was his overcoat, as we describe it to his little brother Michael. He himself in his shining uniform—too full of light for eyes like ours to see it—has gone on.

Yet he has not gone from us. How we miss him in his coming and going, no words can tell. But we know that he does come and go—more than ever; that he is with us round the fire in a home circle still unbroken. But for his great shining we should see him. Nevertheless in his own way, he will make himself known and speak to us of his life and our life—more deeply shared than ever before—and of what the Wise Ones say.

We do not believe that God called him—even for some higher service. What we do believe is that, when a thing like this happens, God can take it and weave it so gloriously into the pattern of our lives that one day we shall shout when we behold it—for wonder and for joy. It is for us to see to it, that, in quiet faith and humility of heart and surrender of our wills to the Great Loving Will, we help and never hinder the hand of God which is at work upon us.

Being then so very confident of all this—that there is no death here, nor separation, nor loss—we do not feel that Robin's young life has been cut off in the fresh spring blossom of its promise. There is no "might have been" for him. If he might have been a great artist, as we think—for he drew and painted wonderfully—he will still be that. He will roam across wide landscapes, unknown as yet to any of us, where colors change and blend as no mortal eye can see them and sing themselves into music as they shine. There shall he "draw the thing as he sees it for the God of things as they are."

If, as both his schools had hoped, he might have been a leader of men, he still shall lead, and find the way for us and them the more easily from the high plane of his life. And in all that he was and is—his deep love for us, his strong sense of justice and fair play, his great compassion for suffering folk (including the animals), his will at every turn to be unselfish and to do his duty—he goes from strength to strength. For his young untiring energies and for his eager burning spirit he shall find wondrous scope both here on earth and in those wider ranges of the soul that we call heaven.

So we think of our very dear Robin. Help us to think that always. Our only picture of him is of a happy-hearted, laughing boy. That is what he was and still is. We shall never say, "How Robin would have laughed!" but, as we have said already, "How Robin must be laughing!" For he is not a proud and happy memory. He is a radiant, living, loving person, round about us. We know it.

That is our faith. So help us, God.

THREE DUTIES

Grace Perkins Oursler and April Armstrong

Those who have lost a child have three great duties to the living: to husband or wife, to the rest of the family, and to children everywhere. These three duties are like sides of a great triangle, each one supporting the other.

No other can take your lost child's place, but by loving and caring for some needy little one, you can raise a lasting tribute to the spirit that did not need to live out the full years.

There are so many ways to do this! Think of the love-starved children in this lonely world who have lost their parents, or whose parents are too poor to care for them. Pour your love out on these friendless ones, in your own home, in their orphanages, by your financial, moral, or actual physical help! Even occasional visits and contacts are mutual blessings.

A parent's love does not die with the child. A mother's love is unquenchable: it is born of God, and in its eternal strength it demands an outlet. What, then, when the child is gone, when no longer there is a little one to tend, to wash and cook and mend for, to comfort? You cannot expect simply to take up life casually once he is gone. That love was given you for a purpose; use it wisely even when at first it seems that you are deprived of its main object.

If circumstances prevent actual adoption of a child, you might board one, work in a day nursery, support one. Even with other remaining children, people have found it wise to fill the place of the lost one. There was enough money, enough time, enough love before—there still is now.

In Miami there is an elderly couple who run a roadstand. They are a bit proud to be able to say: "We have sent five little Ellens through college," since they could never send their own Ellen. They had started her college fund the day she was born, but she was taken from them in a schoolyard accident in the eighth grade. Not all their five Ellens are actively grateful, but that doesn't seem to spoil their quiet pride and achievement. They are doing what they did—for Ellen.

BE CAREFUL LEST YOU LOSE THOSE LEFT TO YOU

Grace Perkins Oursler and April Armstrong

Rebecca N. Porter, in an article in Today's Woman, *January, 1949, speaking from the schoolteacher's view, painted a vivid picture of the effect on one child of the loss of another. Ralph's parents had made a common mistake: to their dead son Earl they had attributed every virtue a boy could have. Earl had been talented, friendly, popular, good at baseball and studies. And Ralph?*

As Mrs. Porter says: "By spoken word, by implication, Ralph was made to feel that he fell short of what his parents would have had in their elder son. So he had come secretly to hate this dead brother. He fiercely resolved, perhaps unconsciously, to be unlike him in every way. Earl had been popular—Ralph would show people he could get along without them. He wouldn't even get as good grades as he knew he could. Struggling with his own sense of inadequacy, he may cry in his secret soul: 'I don't believe Earl was as perfect as that!' But he is forever helpless to disprove it.

"You parents who have lost a child, be doubly careful lest in other ways you lose those left to you. Let the brother or sister who is gone be, not an impossible paragon, an absentee tyrant, but a cherished memory of an imperfect but loved real child."

William Wordsworth

Three years she grew in sun and shower,
Then Nature said: "A lovelier flower

> On earth was never sown;
> This child I to myself will make
> A lady of my own."

IN MY DARKEST HOUR—HOPE
Helen Hayes

On each New Year's Eve the mail brings me a gift that is done up in ordinary brown paper, yet is precious beyond price. It is from Mr. and Mrs. Isaac Frantz, Brooklyn. To understand the value of this gift you must know something about the Frantzes.

They came into my life in 1949, just after my daughter, Mary, had died of polio and I was being tortured by the unanswerable question—Why? Mary had been so lovely and talented, so young and free from sin. Why had this happened to her? I could only feel that her death had been a cruel, senseless thing.

This was a self-destroying mood, for an artist needs the belief that life holds some beauty and meaning. I could not create beauty or meaning on the stage if there was none within me. So to save myself I began to search for God. I read St. Thomas Aquinas, explored the life and works of Gandhi, read the Bible. But the search failed. My daughter was dead! That brutal fact overwhelmed me, blinded my heart.

All during this time I accepted no professional or social engagements and saw only my family and most intimate friends. But, in this self-imposed isolation, I became aware that a Mr. Isaac Frantz was telephoning almost every day, trying to get through to me. My husband finally talked to him and reported: "He has just lost a little boy with polio and he seems to think it would help his wife if she could see you."

"Oh, Charles—no! I have no strength to give her. I have barely enough for myself. I simply can't do it."

"Of course, darling. That's what I told him."

But Isaac Frantz kept telephoning and we finally agreed to let him bring his wife to our home.

I steeled myself for the ordeal.

When they arrived in their Sunday best, they were ill at ease, but they had a quiet dignity that surmounted their painful self-consciousness. Coming face to face with us was obviously something that demanded all their courage. Charles and I tried to put them at ease.

Now I discovered the truth about their visit. It had been the husband's idea entirely and he had arranged it without his wife's knowledge. But he was so sure that a meeting would bring some comfort to his wife that he forced himself to ask it. As for his wife, she was appalled when she heard of the completed arrangements, but knowing how difficult it had been for her husband, and how important to him, she consented to come. Each was doing this for the other—in the moment of great need.

The Frantzes owned a tiny stationery store and obviously had to struggle for the necessities of life. Charles and I had never known anything but success, fame, luxury. And yet the four of us suddenly had one thing to share, the tragic loss of our children.

Mrs. Frantz soon began talking about her son in a most natural manner, and, before I quite knew what was happening, I had plunged into a series of stories about Mary. Then a glance at Charles's surprised face made me realize that I was actually mentioning her name for the first time since her death. I had taken her memory out of hiding, and I felt better for it.

Then Mrs. Frantz told us of her plans to adopt an orphan from Israel, and for a moment I was shocked.

"You are thinking I am letting him take my little boy's place?" she asked gently, guessing my thoughts. "No one could ever do that. But in my heart there is still love and maybe wisdom, too. Should I let these dry up and go to waste?"

"I—I don't know, Mrs. Frantz," I said.

"No, my dear, we cannot die because our children die. I should not love less because the one I loved is gone—but more should I love because my heart knows the suffering of others."

While she talked I thought about my child. Mary had been a big and wonderful part of my life. Even though that part had ended, I was a better human being for having had Mary, for having hoped and dreamed and worked for her. Tragic that it should have ended, but how much better than if it had never existed.

These were the things that Mrs. Frantz was saying, in her own way. These were the things that I now understood. Then I thought how ironic it was that I hadn't wanted Mrs. Frantz to come because I feared she would draw upon my feeble strength. It was I who drew upon hers!

When they finally rose to leave, I realized why my search for God had been fruitless—I had looked in the wrong places. He was not to be found between the covers of a book, but in the human heart.

We never met after that. Charles and I invited them back a couple of times, but they were always busy with their store and their new son. I think they understood that our worlds were meant to touch but briefly.

Every New Year's Eve since then I have received from them a box of candy wrapped in plain brown paper. Perhaps you can understand why it is so precious to me. For it was through these simple people that I learned humility, and God's pattern finally came clear. Now I know that when He afflicts the celebrated of the world, it is His way of saying, "None is privileged. In My eyes, all are equal."

CAN I BRING HIM BACK?

II Samuel

When King David's child became very ill, David prayed to God for the child. He also fasted and lay all night upon the earth. And the elders of his house arose and stood beside him to raise him up from the earth; but he would not, neither did he eat bread with them.

On the seventh day, the child died. And the servants of David were afraid to tell him that the child was dead; for they said: "Behold, while the child was yet alive, we spoke unto him, and he did not listen to us; how then shall we tell him that the child is dead? He may do himself some harm."

When David saw that his servants whispered together, David understood that the child was dead; and David said to his servants: "Is the child dead?" And they said: "He is dead." Then David arose from the earth and washed and anointed himself, and changed his apparel; and he came into the house of the Lord, and worshipped. Then he came to his own house; and when he requested it, they set bread before him, and he ate. Then his servants said to him: "What is this that you have done? You fasted and wept for the child while he was alive; but when the child died, you rose up and ate bread."

And David said; "While the child was yet alive, I fasted and wept; for I said: 'Who knows whether the Lord will not be gracious to me, that the child may live?' But now he is dead, why should I fast? Can I bring him back again? I shall go to him, but he will not return to me."

BEREAVED

James Whitcomb Riley

Let me come in where you sit weeping—aye,
Let me, who have not any child to die,
Weep with you for the little one whose love
I have known nothing of.
The little arms that slowly, slowly loosed
Their pressure round your neck; the hands you used
To kiss. —Such arms—such hands I never knew.
May I not weep with you?
Fain would I be of service—say some thing,
Between the tears, that would be comforting,—
But ah! So sadder than yourselves am I,
Who have no child to die.

ON A DEAD CHILD

Richard Middleton

Man proposes, God in His time disposes,
And so I wander'd up to where you lay,
A little rose among the little roses,
And no more dead than they.

It seem'd your childish feet were tired of straying,
You did not greet me from your flower-strewn bed,
Yet still I knew that you were only playing—
Playing at being dead.

I might have thought that you were really sleeping,
So quiet lay your eyelids to the sky,
So still your hair, but surely you were peeping,
And so I did not cry.

God knows, and in His proper time disposes,
And so I smiled and gently called your name,
Added my rose to your sweet heap of roses,
And left you to your game.

LOVE AND SYMPATHY COUNT FOR SOMETHING
Thomas H. Huxley

It is very sad to lose your child just when he was beginning to bind himself to you, and I don't know that it is much consolation to reflect that the longer he had wound himself up in your heart-strings, the worse the tear would have been, which seems to have been inevitable sooner or later. One does not weigh and measure these things while grief is fresh, and in my experience a deep plunge into the waters of sorrow is the hopefulest way of getting through them in one's daily road of life again. No one can help another very much in these crises of life; but love and sympathy count for something.

ACCEPT THE VERDICT WITH HUMILITY
Jerusalem Talmud

When Rabbi Abbahu's child died, he said: "We are taught that after the execution of a person condemned by an earthly court, where lies, deception, favoritism and bribery may have existed, whose judges are but mortal beings, the kinsfolk come and pleasantly greet the judges and witnesses to demonstrate that they have no grievance in their heart against them, because they have judged truthfully. How much the more then, after a person has surrendered his life according to the decree of the Heavenly Tribunal, where no human defects and shortcomings exist, should we not receive with humility and submission the verdict of Heaven."

Wisdom of Solomon

Being found well pleasing unto God he was beloved of Him,
He was carried away lest wickedness should change his understanding,
Or guile deceive his soul.
Being perfect in a little while, he fulfilled long years;
For his soul was pleasing unto the Lord. . . .

> It is better to go to the house of
> mourning, than to go to the
> house of feasting; for that is the
> end of all men, and the living
> will lay it to his heart.
>
> —Ecclesiastes

DEATH TEACHES LIFE

*The existence of death has ever served as a lesson to life. Man can-
not for long evade the consciousness of his mortality nor fail to
draw therefrom some fundamental attitudes on how his life shall
be conducted.*

*Death, however, has not taught the same lesson to all people. To
some, the presence of death has been a spur to unbridled self-
indulgence and the uninhibited pursuit of pleasure. Thus among
the Romans, a human skeleton was frequently exhibited among
the celebrants at festive parties with the exhortation: "Let us
enjoy life while we may." Herodotus tells us that a similar custom
prevailed among the Egyptians. At joyous occasions, the image of
a dead man carved in wood, or a coffin containing the embalmed
remains of some ancestor, would be presented to each guest by a
person whose function it was to pronounce distinctly as he did so:
"Look upon this and be merry; for such as this, when dead, shalt
thou be." The prophet Isaiah sums up the slogan of those to whom
life's brevity is a stimulant to unrestrained hedonism in the words:
"Let us eat and drink, for tomorrow we die."*

*This approach to life testifies to a failure of nerve and leads to
moral bankruptcy. It is a philosophy of despair which not only
fails to bring satisfaction but overlooks the many sources of real
joy that life generously affords. Where the sole objective of living
is reduced to an endless round of pleasure-seeking, the ultimate
verdict must be a cynical refrain of disillusionment: "Futility of
futilities, all is futility."*

There are others whom death has instructed more wisely. To them life's brevity has been an incentive to live more nobly, more generously, more creatively. They have recognized that while a limit has been set to the length of our days, we alone determine their breadth and their depth. Thus Joshua Loth Liebman counsels: "We must make up for the . . . brevity of life by heightening the intensity of life." Frances Gunther urges us to embrace life and those we love "with a little added rapture and a keener awareness of joy." Bertrand Russell, in a somewhat bleaker mood, realizes that we and our comrades alike are subject to "the silent orders of omnipotent Death." He would therefore have us "shed sunshine on their path . . . lighten their sorrows by the balm of sympathy . . . strengthen failing courage . . . instill faith in hours of despair." The Psalmist of an earlier age contemplated life's transiency and prayed: "So teach us to number our days that we obtain a heart of wisdom."

In the hour of bereavement the death of a loved one can teach us to pitch our lives at the highest level. Yes, life is brief, but we determine its quality. Indeed, precisely because of its brevity, we must be very discriminating as to what we put into it. We are like a man leaving on a journey with a small leather pouch. Shall he fill it with mud when he can take along diamonds? Shall we fill our days with selfishness and pettiness when close at hand is generosity and kindness? George Bernard Shaw's declaration might well serve as our watchword: "Life is no brief candle for me. It is a sort of splendid torch which I have got hold of for a moment and I want to make it burn as brightly as possible before handing it on to future generations."

DO NOT SQUANDER TIME
Benjamin Franklin

Dost thou love life? Then do not squander time; for that's the stuff life is made of.

If time be of all things the most precious, wasting time must be the greatest prodigality; since lost time is never found again and what we call time enough always proves little enough. Let us then be up and doing, and doing to the purpose; so by diligence shall we do more with less perplexity. Sloth makes all things difficult, but industry all easy.

Employ thy time well, if thou meanest to gain leisure. Since thou are not sure of a minute, throw not away an hour.

THE GOAL OF LIFE
Joshua Loth Liebman

The religion of Judaism can teach us . . . how to understand the goal of life in the presence of mortality. That goal is that we should create a pattern that will be a blessing and inspiration to those who come after us. When we die, those who have been touched and illumined by the flame of our being should rejoice to think of us with joyous reminiscence.

We can face death nobly when we resolve so to live and to work in the years allotted to us that no one shall cry in frustration or anger when we have gone, that no one shall silently curse the day of our birth but rather that they shall recall our day upon earth in the concert hall of memory and shall laugh, with the overbrimming joy that a dear one walked the earth bravely and lovingly once upon a time.

The thought of death need not fill us with dark and despairing anxiety but rather with a creative determination to be for the little world of which we are a part the center of the target toward which all the archers shall send the arrows of their aspiration, to be the oak tree, tall and stately, in the shelter of whose branches the young can sit and play and the old can find shade from the heat of the day. Let us live in such a way that our spirit shall be the rain causing the soil of other souls to grow moist and verdant, to be the sunlight making chlorophyll in the filigree leaves of other hearts and other minds, to be the star, the guiding North Star, by which the mariners and the navigators in our family and in our circle of friends can set their compass across the unchartered sea of being. This is the goal of life, so to live that men shall rehearse the story of our being with inspiration and with deep gratitude that we have walked the earth rejoicing to tell of our strong youth, the manliness of our maturity, the wisdom of our old age. Then indeed our memory shall be a blessing.

LIFE IS WORTH LITTLE UNLESS . . .
Eldad Pan (Translated from the Hebrew by the editor)

Eldad Pan was killed in Israel's War of Independence at the age of twenty, a veteran of many battles.

Lately I have been thinking about what the goal of life should be. At best, man's life is short. His life may be kind or harsh, easy or difficult, but the time passes before he realizes it. An old person wants to live no less than a young person. The years of life do not satisfy the hunger for life. What then shall we do during this time?

We can reach either of two conclusions. The first is that since life is so short we should enjoy it as much as possible. The second is that precisely because life is short and no one can completely enjoy it (for we die with half our desires unsatisfied), therefore we should dedicate life to a sacred and worthy goal, to sacrifice it for something which will be valued above life. At times the first feeling is stronger and at others the second one. Of late, however, I think that the second feeling is dominant. It seems that I am slowly coming to the conclusion that life by itself is worth little unless it serves something greater than itself.

LIFE IS TOO BRIEF

W. M. Vories

Life is too brief
Between the budding and the falling leaf.
Between the seed time and the golden sheaf,
   For hate and spite.
We have no time for malice and for greed;
Therefore, with love make beautiful the deed;
   Fast speeds the night.

Life is too swift
Between the blossom and the white snow's drift,
Between the silence and the lark's uplift,
   For bitter words.
In kindness and in gentleness our speech
Must carry messages of hope, and reach
   The sweetest chords.

Life is too great
Between the infant's and the man's estate,
Between the clashing of earth's strife and fate,
   For petty things.
Lo! we shall yet who creep with cumbered feet
Walk glorious over heaven's golden street,
   Or soar on wings!

TODAY IS THE DAY
Grenville Kleiser

There are many fine things which you mean to do some day, under what you think will be more favorable circumstances. But the only time that is surely yours is the present, hence this is the time to speak the word of appreciation and sympathy, to do the generous deed, to forgive the fault of a thoughtless friend, to sacrifice self a little more for others. Today is the day in which to express your noblest qualities of mind and heart, to do at least one worthy thing which you have long postponed, and to use your God-given abilities for the enrichment of some less fortunate fellow traveler. Today you can make your life . . . significant and worth while. The present is yours to do with it as you will.

THE TIME IS SHORT
Phillips Brooks

You who are letting miserable misunderstandings run on from year to year, meaning to clear them up some day;

You who are keeping wretched quarrels alive because you cannot quite make up your mind that now is the day to sacrifice your pride and kill them;

You who are passing men sullenly upon the street, not speaking to them out of some silly spite, and yet knowing that it would fill you with shame and remorse if you heard that one of those men were dead tomorrow morning;

You who are letting your neighbor starve, till you hear that he is dying of starvation; or letting your friend's heart ache for a word of appreciation or sympathy, which you mean to give him some day;

If you only could know and see and feel, all of a sudden, that "the time is short," how it would break the spell! How you would go instantly and do the things which you might never have another chance to do.

Louis D. Brandeis

I have only one life and it's short enough; why waste it on things I don't want most.

HOW SWIFTLY ALL THINGS PASS AWAY
Marcus Aurelius

Think often of how swiftly all things pass away and are no more —the works of man. The substance of the Universe, matter, is like unto a river that flows on forever. All things are not only in a constant state of change, but they are the cause of constant and infinite change in other things. Upon a narrow ledge thou standest! Behind thee, the bottomless abyss of the Past! In front of thee, the Future that will swallow up all things that are now. Over what things, then, in this present life wilt thou, O foolish man, be disquieted or exalted—making thyself wretched; seeing that they can vex thee only for a time—a brief, brief time!

Wisdom of Ben Sira

Remember that death will not tarry;
Do well unto thy friend before thou die;
And according to thy ability stretch out thy hand and give to him.

Horace Mann

Be ashamed to die until you have won some victory for humanity.

WHAT WOULDST THOU BE FOUND DOING. . . ?
Epictetus

What wouldst thou be found doing when overtaken by Death? If I might choose, I would be found doing some deed of true humanity, of wide import, beneficent and noble. But if I may not be found engaged in aught so lofty, let me hope at least for this— what none may hinder, what is surely in my power—that I may be found raising up in myself that which had fallen; learning to deal more wisely with the things of sense; working out my own tranquillity, and thus rendering that which is its due to every relation of life. . . .

If death surprise me thus employed, it is enough if I can stretch forth my hands to God and say, "The faculties which I received at Thy hands for apprehending this thine Administration, I have not neglected. As far as in me lay, I have done Thee no dishonour. Behold how I have used the senses, the primary conceptions which Thou gavest me. Have I ever laid anything to Thy charge? Have I ever murmured at aught that came to pass, or wished it otherwise? Have I in anything transgressed the relations of life? For that Thou didst beget me, I thank Thee for that Thou hast given; for the time during which I have used the things that were Thine, it suffices me. Take them back and place them wherever Thou wilt! They were all Thine, and Thou gavest them me." If a man depart thus minded, is it not enough? What life is fairer or more noble, what end happier than his?

William James

The great use of life is to spend it for something that will outlast it.

INVOCATION OF THE DAWN

Anonymous
From "Kalidasa"

Look to this day!
For it is life, the very life of life.
In its brief course lie all the verities,
All the realities of existence:
The bliss of growth,
The glory of action,
The splendor of beauty;

For yesterday is already a dream,
And tomorrow is only a vision;
But today, well lived,
Makes every yesterday a dream of happiness,
And every tomorrow a vision of hope.
Look well, therefore, to this day!

DEATH IS ALL WE HAVE MISSED
Israel Zangwill

Whoever dies in the full tilt of his ambitions is buried alive, and whoever survives his hopes and fears is dead, unburied. Death for us is all we have missed, all the periods and planets we have not lived in, all the countries we have not visited, all the books we have not read, all the emotions and experiences we have not had, all the prayers we have not prayed, all the battles we have not fought. Every restriction, negation is a piece of death.

Wisdom of Ben Sira

In all thy matters remember thy last end,
And thou shalt never do amiss.

James Russell Lowell

Emerge thou mayst from the last whelming sea,
And prove that death but routs life into victory.

FROM "IF WE KNEW"
May Riley Smith

Strange we never prize the music
    Till the sweet-voiced bird has blown;
Strange that we should slight the violets
    Till the lovely flowers are gone;
Strange that summer skies and sunshine
    Never seem one half so fair
As when winter's snowy pinions
    Shake their white down in the air!

Let us gather up the sunbeams
    Lying all around our path;
Let us keep the wheat and roses,
    Casting out the thorns and chaff;

Let us find our sweetest comfort
In the blessings of today,
With a patient hand removing
All the briars from the way.

Ralph Waldo Emerson

Life wastes itself whilst we are preparing to live.

TO CONTRIBUTE TO THE INHERITANCE
OF MANKIND

John Erskine

Though I have little fear of death, yet I cannot contemplate with equanimity the fact that on this earth I shall some day be altogether forgotten, and my place shall know me no more. This sentiment is not peculiar with me. Every man and woman who thinks at all recoils from the prospect of mortal oblivion, even though confident of continued existence elsewhere.

The wish to live on men's tongues or on perpetual tombstones is ignoble and futile. But to contribute to the inheritance of mankind, and in our works to continue even after our names are lost, this is a kind of survival neither futile nor unworthy. The hope to gain it spurs us on. Let me correct myself—not the hope to gain but to deserve it.

Henri F. Amiel

Life is short and we have not too much time for gladdening the hearts of those who are traveling the dark way with us. Oh, be swift to love! Make haste to be kind!

FROM "A FREE MAN'S WORSHIP"

Bertrand Russell

United with his fellow-men by the strongest ties of all ties, the tie of a common doom, the free man finds that a new vision is with him always, shedding over every daily task the light of love. The life of Man is a long march through the night, surrounded by invisible foes, tortured by weariness and pain, towards a goal that few can hope to reach, and where none may tarry long. One by one, as they march, our comrades vanish from our sight, seized by the silent orders of omnipotent Death. Very brief is the time in which we can help them, in which their happiness or misery is decided. Be it ours to shed sunshine on their path, to lighten their sorrows by the balm of sympathy, to give them the pure joy of a never-tiring affection, to strengthen failing courage, to instill faith in hours of despair. Let us not weigh in grudging scales their merits and demerits, but let us think only of their need—of the sorrows, the difficulties, perhaps the blindnesses, that make the misery of their lives; let us remember that they are fellow-sufferers in the same darkness, actors in the same tragedy with ourselves. And so, when their day is over, when their good and their evil have become eternal by the immortality of the past, be it ours to feel that, where they suffered, where they failed, no deed of ours was the cause; but wherever a spark of the divine fire kindled in their hearts, we were ready with encouragement, with sympathy, with brave words in which high courage glowed.

Ethics of The Fathers

This world is like a vestibule before the World to Come; prepare thyself in the vestibule that thou mayest enter the Hall.

A NEW AWARENESS OF THE VALUE OF LIFE
Zelda Popkin

The understanding which grows out of personal loss is not merely in the ability to share the world's sorrows but in a new awareness of the value of life. "When my mother died," a man said to me, "my own children were at once closer and dearer to me."

"Losing my father," a young man said, "made us all realize how much we had wasted. We'd never gotten to know each other. There never seemed to be time. I hope to live differently with my own family. I've gotten a new sense of values from this."

Ethics of the Fathers

The day is short, the work is immense, the laborers are sluggish, the reward is great and the Master of the house is insistent.

JOURNEY'S END

Evelyn H. Healey

We go from God to God—then, though
    The day be long,
We shall return to Heaven our home
    At evensong.

We go from God to God—so let
    The space between
Be filled with beauty, conquering
    Things base and mean.

We go from God to God—lo! what
    Transcendent bliss,
To know the journey's end will hold
    Such joy as this!

NOW

George H. Candler

The clock of life is wound but once,
And no man has the power
To tell just when the hands will stop—
At late or early hour.
Now is the only time you own:
Live, love, work with a will.
Place no faith in tomorrow, for—
The clock may then be still.

Marcus Aurelius

Short is the little that remains to thee of life. Live as on a mountain!

LIFE IS TOO SHORT TO BE LITTLE
Author unknown

My favorite quotation is the sentence above, written by Disraeli. It has helped through many a painful experience. Often we allow ourselves to be upset by small things we should despise and forget. Perhaps some man we helped has proved ungrateful . . . some woman we believed to be a friend has spoken ill of us . . . some reward we thought we deserved has been denied us. We feel such disappointments so strongly that we can no longer work or sleep. But isn't that absurd? Here we are on this earth, with only a few more decades to live, and we lose many irreplaceable hours brooding over grievances that, in a year's time, will be forgotten by us and by everybody. No, let us devote our life to worthwhile actions and feelings, to great thoughts, real affections and enduring undertakings. For life is too short to be little.

AS A TALE THAT IS TOLD
Psalms

We bring our years to an end as a tale that is told.
The days of our years are three-score years and ten,
Or even by reason of strength four-score years;
Yet is their pride but travail and vanity;
For it is speedily gone, and we fly away.
So teach us to number our days
That we may obtain a heart of wisdom.

Goethe

A useless life is only an early death.

IN DYING . . . ONE GIVES SIGNIFICANCE
John Gardner

If a soldier dies merely through the hazards of war, that is one thing. But if he dies for a cause to which his country has linked its destiny, such as human freedom or the maintenance of justice, he has linked himself to a cause which is great and glorious. If that cause is eternal, an eternal significance is given to his dying. But if not, his attachment to it gives him the distinction of a patriot and a hero, but not necessarily that of a saint. To die for justice or for freedom, links a man to something different from mere devotion to a flag. Justice is not temporal, it is eternal. In dying for it, one gives significance to his final act. If a man will link himself to the will of God and the reign of God over all human affairs; if he lives for it, dies for it, his life and death are merged in the life and purpose of God and therefore he is indestructible.

Epictetus

Remind thyself that he whom thou lovest is mortal—that what thou lovest is not thine own; it is given thee for the present, not irrevocably nor forever, but even as a fig or a bunch of grapes at the appointed season of the year. . . .

Deuteronomy

If they were wise, they would consider their latter end.

THE SCHOOL OF ADVERSITY

Joseph Krauskopf

Affliction is a stern teacher, but the best. From it alone we know how to value justly things below. He who wrestles with us strengthens our nerves and increases our skill. Our antagonist is our helper. He that has never known adversity is but half-acquainted with others or with himself. . . .

Much depends upon how we acquit ourselves under our crushing trials. . . . The sharpest sting of adversity is borrowed from our own impatience. . . . There are chemical solutions that deposit their precipitates in the shade and stillness of night; so in the dark hours of trouble the latent virtues of noble character are developed. . . .

DEATH BRINGS AWARENESS
Frances Gunther

All the wonderful things in life are so simple that one is not aware of their wonder until they are beyond touch. Never have I felt the wonder and beauty and joy of life so keenly as now in my grief that Johnny is not here to enjoy them. Today, when I see parents impatient or tired or bored with their children, I wish I could say to them, But they are alive, think of the wonder of that! They may be a care and a burden, but think, they are alive! You can touch them—what a miracle! All parents who have lost a child will feel what I mean. Others, luckily, cannot. But I hope they will embrace them with a little added rapture and a keener awareness of joy.

BE PREPARED AT ALL TIMES
Earl of Warwick

There is nothing more certain than death, nothing more uncertain than the time of dying. I will, therefore, be prepared for that at all times, which may come at any time, must come at one time or another. I shall not hasten my death by being still ready, but sweeten it. It makes me not die the sooner, but the better.

Midrash

A man cannot say to the Angel of Death: "I wish to arrange my affairs before I die."

PORTRAIT PAINTERS OF THE SOUL
Joshua Loth Liebman

Judaism is the religion of life which makes no cult out of death, which seeks no private salvation from the grave, which accepts with confidence and trust both the miracle of birth and the mystery of death. Our faith does not close its eyes to tragedy and does not deny that we human beings shall never possess the everlastingness of stone, the silent perduring quality of the mountain peak, but we have other gifts, conscious minds, aspiring hearts, far-visioned souls. Our faith tells us that God has given to each human being the ability to paint a portrait large or small, beautiful or ugly, radiant or blooming, and our faith summons us to become a portrait painter of a soul-landscape that shall be worthy to be hung in any art gallery of the spirit. Judaism proclaims that God has arranged our journey so that in years brief or many we can find love, joy and the fruits of fulfilment, partial and relative though they be, and that when our day is finished, we should accept its final note with the same calm trust that we greet the skylark's song at sunrise. True, "each one of us has his toad to swallow every morning." Yet we can become what Goethe once said is the true task of man— "Life-worthy."

Ecclesiasticus

Remember thy last end, and cease from enmity.

'TIS A LITTLE JOURNEY

Anonymous

'Tis a little journey
This we walk;
Hardly time for murmurs—
Time for talk.

Yet we learn to quarrel
And to hate;
Afterwards regret it
When too late.

Now and then 'tis sunshine—
Sometimes dark;
Sometimes care and sorrow
Leave their mark.

Yet we walk the pathway
Side by side;
Where so many others
Lived and died.

We can see the moral,
Understand;
Yet we walk not always
Hand in hand.

Why must there be hatred?
Greed and strife?
Do we need such shadows
Here in life?

'Tis a little journey
Soon gone by;
Let's be friends together
Ere we die

OPPORTUNITY
Anonymous

I shall pass through this world but once.
Any good therefore that I can do or any kindness that I can show
to any human being let me do it now.
Let me not defer or neglect it, for I shall not pass this way again.

ROB DEATH OF ULTIMATE VICTORY
Jacob P. Rudin

Death will come. Its hand will not be stayed even an instant; nor
can we enter into judgment with it. Our question "Why?" will go
unanswered. But this does not mean that we are helpless in the
face of death. We can and we do rob death of ultimate victory,
by living life as long as it is ours to live. To ask of death that it
never come is futile, but it is not futility to pray that when death
does come for us, it may take us from a world one corner of which
is a little better because we were there.

When we are dead, and people weep for us and grieve, let it be
because we touched their lives with beauty and simplicity. Let it
not be said that life was good to us, but, rather, that we were good
to life.

OF EVERY TEAR SOME GOOD IS BORN
Charles Dickens

When Death strikes down the innocent and young, for every fragile form from which he lets the panting spirit free a hundred virtues rise, in shapes of mercy, charity, and love, to walk the world and bless it. Of every tear that sorrowing mortals shed on such green graves some good is born, some gentler nature comes. In the Destroyer's steps there spring up bright creations that defy his power, and his dark path becomes a way of light to heaven.

A GOOD NAME IS BETTER THAN GOOD OIL
Talmud

When Rabbi Johanan concluded the Book of Job, he said thus: The end of man is death, and the end of cattle is slaughter, and everything is designated for death. Blessed is he that has been reared in the Law, and whose toil is in the Law, and acts so as to please his Creator, and has grown up with a good name, and departed life with a good name, Concerning him, Solomon said (Ecclesiastes: VII, 1): "A good name is better than precious oil; and the day of death than the day of one's birth."

TO LIVE FULLY, RICHLY, NOBLY
Joshua Loth Liebman

And while we live, we should try to make each day a year as far as beauty, nobility, and a warm sense of brotherhood are concerned. In a time when there is so much cruelty abroad, we must generate the oxygen of love to keep the soul of the world still breathing. Religion should summon all of us to deepen the quality of life as a compensation for the diminution of its quantity, to treasure each other in the recognition that we do not know how long we shall have each other, to make life strong and brave and beautiful as our answer to the forces of death abroad in the world. We must make up for the threatened brevity of life by heightening the intensity of life. The crimes and sin for which there should be little forgiveness during this epoch are hardheartedness, selfishness, mutual cruelty, lovelessness—all of the little weapons which we use to shorten the lives of others. Our very understanding of each other can serve to deepen life even when we cannot lengthen it.

All men today need the healthy-mindedness of Judaism, the natural piety with which the Jew declares, "One world at a time is enough." For just as we can rely without fear upon the Power greater than ourselves during this earthly journey; just as we can rest and do rest securely upon the bosom of mystery every time we fall asleep at night—so we can trust the universe beyond time also, recognizing that it is the part of wisdom not to seek to remove the veil from before birth or after death, but to live fully, richly, nobly, here and now, and make possible a society where other men can so live.

John Henry Newman

Fear not that thy life shall come to an end, but rather fear that it shall never have a beginning.

A RIGHTEOUS JUDGE

Ben Zion Bokser

Simon mourned excessively for his departed friend. He was inconsolable in his grief. One night in a vision he heard a voice say to him reprovingly: "Why do you grieve so much? Is not death an inevitable incident in the cycle of life? Would you change the plan of the universe and make man immortal?"

Simon gathered courage and he talked back: "Why not, O Lord? Thou canst do all things. My friend—and others like him—why should there be an end to lives as wonderful as theirs?"

And the voice replied: "So you deny the service of death to the economy of life! Very well, then. We shall set you into a world where immortality prevails, and see how you like it."

Simon looked at the countryside and understood the meaning of his dream. All this magnificence will endure forever. Nothing of it will perish. And so it indeed turned out to be.

Not a flower died on its stalk. Not a blossom fell from the lilac bushes. Summer gave way and autumn came, but not a leaf withered, not a tree lost its foliage. The world in all its beauty had been given a kind of fixed permanence, and it shone in the self-same lustre. At last life seemed to be freed from the ravages of time and circumstance.

But gradually Simon felt palled. Nothing died in his world, but nothing was born in it either. He was spared the ravages of age, but he missed seeing the wondrous dance of youth. His eyes tired at the beauty of flowers forever the same in hue. He longed to witness the glory of a new flower's unfolding. He was ready to renounce the gift of immortality when he suddenly awoke from his dream.

He brooded for a while over his strange experience and then he said: "O Lord, I thank Thee that Thou hast made a mortal of flesh and blood. Someone died that I might be born and I am willing to die that there may be growth and the emergence of new life in Thy world. Thou art a righteous Judge."

Madam Guyon

> Our days are numbered: let us spare
> Our anxious hearts a needless care:
> 'Tis Thine to number out our days;
> 'Tis ours to give them thy Praise.

NOAM GROSSMAN

(Translated from the Hebrew by Eliezer Whartman)

Noam Grossman was born in Brooklyn. At an early age he was brought to Palestine, and later entered the Hebrew University, where he excelled in historical criticism. His career never came to full flower, for he was cut down at the age of twenty while on a mission in the Judean hills. . . .

One of the most heart-rending documents to come out of the war is Noam's will, the last message which his parents received. It was found among his things after his death. Upon the envelope was written: "To be opened only after my death."

LAST WILL AND TESTAMENT

This will is written in haste without time to say goodbye.

1. Bury me in the Nahlat Yitzhak cemetery in Tel Aviv.
2. Do not print any tributes to me in the newspapers.

3. My salary and my money due me is to be turned over to my family to establish a fund with which to buy rifles for the Haganah.
4. My personal effects are to be forwarded to my family.
5. Do not mourn for me; I did only that which I was called upon to do.

Ethics of the Fathers

It is not thy duty to complete the work but neither art thou free to desist from it.

THE WATER MILL
Sarah Doudney

Listen to the water mill, through the livelong day,
How the clanking of its wheels wears the hours away.
Languidly the autumn winds stir the greenwood leaves;
From the field the reapers sing, binding up the sheaves;
And a proverb haunts my mind, a spell is cast;
"The mill will never grind with the water that has passed."

Take a lesson to thyself, loving heart and true;
Golden years are fleeting by, youth is passing, too;
Learn to make the most of life, lose no happy day;
Time will never bring thee back chances swept away.
Leave no tender word unsaid, love while life shall last;
"The mill will never grind with water that has passed."

Work while the daylight shines, man of strength and will
Never does the streamlet glide useless by the mill.
Wait not till tomorrow's sun beams up the way;
All thou canst call thy own lies in thy today.
Power, intellect and health may not, cannot last;
"The mill will never grind with water that has passed."

Oh, the wasted hours of life that have drifted by,
Oh, the good we might have done, lost without a sigh;
Love that we might once have saved by a single word,
Thoughts conceived but never penned, perishing unheard,
Take a proverb to thine heart, take it, oh, hold it fast;
"The mill will never grind with water that has passed."

Talmud

Blessed shalt thou be when thou comest in, and bless shalt thou be when thou goest out (Deuteronomy: XXXVII, 6). May thy departure from this world be like thy coming into this world. As thou didst enter into this world without sin, so mayest thou depart from this world without sin.

Carroll Binder

I love life but I am not worried about death. I do not feel that I have lost my son and a host of others dear to me by death. . . . Death, I believe, teaches us the things of deathlessness.

THE PURPOSE OF LIFE
Albert Einstein

How extraordinary is the situation of us mortals Each of us is here for a brief sojourn; for what purpose he knows not though he sometimes thinks he senses it. But without going deeper than our daily life, it is plain that we exist for our fellow-men—in the first place for those upon whose smiles and welfare our happiness depends, and next for all those unknown to us personally but to whose destinies we are bound by the tie of sympathy. A hundred times every day I remind myself that my inner and outer life depend on the labors of other men, living and dead, and that I must exert myself in order to give in the measure as I have received and am still receiving.

A THOUSAND YEARS IN THY SIGHT
Psalms

Lord, Thou hast been our dwelling place in all generations.
Before the mountains were brought forth,
Or ever Thou hadst formed the earth and the world,
Even from everlasting to everlasting, Thou art God.
Thou turnest man to contrition;
And sayest: "Return, ye children of men."

For a thousand years in Thy sight
Are but as yesterday when it is past,
And as a watch in the night.

Helen Keller

Each day comes to me with both hands full of possibilities, and in its brief course I discern all the verities and realities of my existence, the bliss of growth, the glory of action, the spirit of beauty.

A ROSE TO THE LIVING
Nixon Waterman

A rose to the living is more than
Sumptuous wreaths to the dead;
In filling love's infinite store,
A rose to the living is more—
If graciously given before the
Hungering spirit is fled,
A rose to the living is more than
Sumptuous wreaths to the dead

Francis Quartes

If thou expect death as a friend, prepare to entertain it; if thou expect death as an enemy, prepare to overcome it; death has no advantage, but when it comes a stranger.

I SHALL NOT PASS THIS WAY AGAIN
Eva Rose York

I shall not pass this way again—
    Although it bordered be with flowers,
    Although I rest in fragrant bowers,
        And hear the singing
        Of song-birds winging
To highest heaven their gladsome flight;
Though moons are full and stars are bright,

And winds and waves are softly sighing,
While leafy trees make low replying;
Though voices clear in joyous strain
Repeat a jubilant refrain;
Though rising suns their radiance throw
On summer's green and winter's snow,
In such rare splendor that my heart
Would ache from scenes like these to part;
    Though beauties heighten,
      And life-lights brighten,
And joys proceed from every pain—
I shall not pass this way again.

Then let me pluck the flowers that blow,
And let me listen as I go
    To music rare
    That fills the air;
    And let hereafter
    Songs and laughter
Fill every pause along the way;
And to my spirit let me say:
"O soul, be happy; soon 'tis trod,
The path made thus for thee by God.
Be happy, thou, and bless His name
By whom such marvellous beauty came."
And let no chance by me be lost
To kindness show at any cost.
I shall not pass this way again;
Then let me now relieve some pain,
Remove some barrier from the road,
Or brighten someone's heavy load;
A helping hand to this one lend,
Then turn some other to befriend.

    O God, forgive
    That now I live
As if I might, sometime, return
To bless the weary ones that yearn
For help and comfort every day—
For there be such along the way.
O God, forgive that I have seen
The beauty only, have not been

Awake to sorrow such as this;
That I have drunk the cup of bliss
Remembering not that those there be
Who drink the dregs of misery.

I love the beauty of the scene,
Would roam again o'er fields so green;
But since I may not, let me spend
My strength for others to the end—
For those who tread on rock and stone,
And bear their burdens all alone,
Who loiter not in leafy bowers,
Nor hear the birds nor pluck the flowers.
A larger kindness give to me,
A deeper love and sympathy;
   Then, O one day
      May someone say—
Remembering a lessened pain—
"Would she could pass this way again."

Talmud

Rabbi Eliezer declared: "Repent one day before your death."
Whereupon his disciples asked: "How does one know which day
that is?" "Exactly," answered the Sage, "for that reason we ought
to live every day as though it were our last."

Edward Capel Cure

What a man has is too often the standard of worth while a man
is living; what he has done is the ultimate standard of the world;
what he has been is God's standard.

DEATH SERVES LIFE

In the University of Oxford, above the entrance to the Department of Anatomy, there is the following inscription: "This is the
place where death serves life."

FROM "THE CHOIR INVISIBLE"
George Eliot

Oh, may I join the choir invisible
Of those immortal dead who live again
In minds made better by their presence; live
In pulses stirred to generosity,
In deeds of daring rectitude, in scorn
For miserable aims that end with self,
In thoughts sublime that pierce the night like stars,
And with their mild persistence urge man's search
To vaster issues!
    This is life to come,
Which martyred men have made more glorious
For us to strive to follow. May I reach
That purest heaven, be to other souls
The cup of strength in some great agony,
Enkindle generous ardor, feed pure love,
Beget the smiles that have no cruelty,
Be the sweet presence of a good diffused,
And in diffusion ever more intense.
So shall I join the choir invisible
Whose music is the gladness of the world.

George Eliot

If endless morrows had stretched before man's vision
He would never have accomplished anything today.

FORGIVENESS
John Greenleaf Whittier

My heart was heavy, for its trust had been
 Abused, its kindness answered with foul wrong;
So, turning gloomily from my fellowmen,
 One summer Sabbath day I strolled among
The green mounds of the village burial-place;
 Where pondering how all human love and hate

Find one sad level; and how, soon or late,
Wronged and wrongdoer, each with meekened face,
And cold hands folded over a still heart,
Pass the green threshold of our common grave,
Whither all footsteps tend, whence none depart,
Awed for myself, and pitying my race,
Our common sorrow, like a mighty wave
Swept all my pride away, and trembling I forgave!

THE MEASURE OF MAN

Anonymous

Not—"How did he die?" But—"How did he live?"
Not—"What did he gain?" But—"What did he give?"
These are the units to measure the worth
Of a man as a man, regardless of birth.

Not—"What was his station?" But—"Had he a heart?"
And—"How did he play his God-given part?
Was he ever ready with a word of good cheer,
To bring back a smile, to banish a tear?"

Not—"What was his shrine?" Nor—"What was his creed?"
But—"Had he befriended those really in need?"
Not—"What did the sketch in the newspaper say?"
But—"How many were sorry when he passed away?"

MAN CARRIES NOTHING AWAY EXCEPT . . .

Talmud

A hungry fox was eyeing some luscious fruit in a garden, but to his dismay, he could find no way to enter. At last he discovered an opening through which, he thought, he might possibly get in, but he soon found that the hole was too small to admit his body. "Well," he thought, "if I fast three days I will be able to squeeze through." He did so; and he now feasted to his heart's delight on the grapes and all the other good things in the orchard. But lo! when he wanted to escape before the owner of the garden would find him, he discovered to his great distress, that the opening had again become too small for him. Poor animal! Again he had to fast three days, and as he escaped, he cast a farewell glance upon the scene of his late revels saying: "O garden, charming art thou, delicious are thy fruits! But what have I now for all my labor and cunning?"

So it is with man. Naked he comes into the world, naked must he leave it. After all his toil therein he carries nothing away with him except the good deeds he leaves behind.

Benjamin Franklin

A long life may not be good enough but a good life is long enough.

Stephen Vincent Benét

Life is not lost by dying!
Life is lost minute by minute, day by dragging day
In all the thousand, small, uncaring ways.

BEHOLD, O EARTH

Saul Tchernichovsky (Translated from the Hebrew by Sholom J. Kahn)

Behold, O Earth, what spendthrifts we are
    indeed!
Where blessing dwells, in your hidden lap, we
    have buried seed . . .
Not grains of heavy wheat, pearls of spelt with
    glossy coats,
No gold-sheathed barley seed, nor timid ears
    of oats.

Behold, O Earth, what spendthrifts we are
    indeed!
In you we have hid our choicest flowers, most
    splendid of the breed,
Kissed by the sun's first kiss, concealing still

Their grace on lovely stalks, cups of incense
    ready to fill.
Before they could know their noon, at innocent
    sorrow's core,
Or drain the dew for dreams of light that their
    sprouting bore.

Take you the best of our sons, youth's visions
    of purest worth,
Pure of heart, clean of hands, not soiled with
    filth of earth,
The fabric of their lives still weaving, with hopes
    of a day more fair.
We have none that are better than these. Have
    you? Then where?

And you shall cover all these. May the plant
    arise at length!
To its homeland's people sacred, in hundred-
    fold splendor and strength!
Blest be their offering of death, by whose glory
    our lives are freed . . .
Behold, O Earth, what spendthrifts we are
    indeed!

Virgil

Death plucks my ear and says, Live— I am coming.

FROM "THANATOPSIS"

William Cullen Bryant

So live, that when thy summons comes to join
The innumerable caravan, which moves
To that mysterious realm, where each shall take
His chamber in the silent halls of death,
Thou go not, like the quarry-slave at night,
Scourged to his dungeon, but, sustained and soothed
By an unfaltering trust, approach thy grave
Like one who wraps the drapery of his couch
About him, and lies down to pleasant dreams.

I walked a mile with Sorrow
And ne'er a word said she
But oh the things I learned from her
When Sorrow walked with me.

—Robert Browning Hamilton

THE THINGS WE LEARN
FROM SORROW

The moment of bereavement is the most dreaded of all moments. So deeply do we fear separation from those we love that we try desperately to prevent the very thought of it from stealing into our consciousness. When in unguarded moments it succeeds in breaking through, we hasten to expel the unwelcome intruder. It is therefore not altogether strange that sorrow finds us emotionally unprepared and perhaps even rebellious and resentful.

If we are wise, however, we will accept sorrow courageously now that it has forced its way into our lives. Despite its forbidding countenance, sorrow possesses great potential power to expand our lives, to enlarge our vision and to deepen our understanding. It has played a beautiful and transforming role in the lives of countless bereaved who could say in a mood of melancholy gratefulness with Wordsworth: "A deep distress hath humanized my soul."

Through the portals of sorrow we can enter into the suffering of others. Our human compassion is kindled. Our sympathies are awakened. Grief can also help purge us of pettiness and selfishness. It can elicit from us powers of fortitude and patience which, but for it, might have never been quickened into life. Sorrow can thus bring us closer to our fellow man and help introduce us to ourselves. The recorded experience and testimony of poet, psalmist and philosopher all tend to confirm overwhelmingly the observation of Jean Paul: "There is a purity which only suffering can impart; the stream of life becomes snow-white when it dashes against the rocks."

The abundance of elegaic poetry and music in world culture points up another benevolent service which sorrow frequently renders. Where we do not permit it to embitter us or crush us, it often arouses deep latent powers of creativity by which the human spirit transmutes suffering into song, adversity into artistry, and pain into poetry.

Thus it is quite possible to emulate those of whom the Psalmist wrote: "They pass through a valley of tears and convert it into a life-giving fountain." Our sorrows can serve as "needles with which God sews our souls to eternal truths." If we face sorrow affirmatively and creatively we can use it to enhance life's meaning and beauty for others no less than for ourselves.

This truth seems to be symbolized by a strange tree which grows near Bombay. It is called "The Sorrowful Tree" because it has the remarkable characteristic of blooming only in the night. Just as soon as the sun sets, the flowers come bursting out. May not this also reflect our uniquely human endowment? Like that tree we can also bring forth flowers of surpassing beauty in the dark night of sorrow.

VICTORY IN DEFEAT

Edwin Markham

Defeat may serve as well as victory
To shake the soul and let the glory out.
When the great oak is straining in the wind,
The boughs drink in new beauty and the trunk
Sends down a deeper root on the windward side.
Only the soul that knows the mighty grief
Can know the mighty rapture. Sorrows come
To stretch out spaces in the heart for joy.

LOST AND FOUND

George MacDonald

I missed him when the sun began to bend;
I found him not when I had lost his rim;

With many tears I went in search of him,
Climbing high mountains which did still ascend,
And gave me echoes when I called my friend;
Through cities vast and charnel-houses grim,
And high cathedrals where the light was dim,
Through books and arts and works without an end,
But found him not—the friend whom I had lost.
And yet I found him—as I found the lark,
A sound in fields I heard, but could not mark;
I found him nearest when I missed him most;
I found him in my heart, a life in frost,
A light I knew not till my soul was dark.

I THANK THEE, GOD! FOR WEAL AND WOE

Eliza Cook

I thank Thee, God! for all I've known
Of kindly fortune, health, and joy;
And quite as gratefully I own
The bitter drops of life's alloy.

Oh! there was wisdom in the blow
That wrung the sad and scalding tear;
That laid my dearest idol low,
And left my bosom lone and drear.

I thank Thee, God! for all of smart
That thou hast sent; for not in vain
Has been the heavy, aching heart,
The sigh of grief, the throb of pain.

What if my cheek had ever kept
Its healthful color, glad and bright?
What if my eyes had never wept
Throughout a long and sleepless night?

Then, then, perchance, my soul had not
Remembered there were paths less fair;
And, selfish in my own blest lot,
Ne'er strove to soothe another's care.

But when the weight of sorrow found
My spirit prostrate and resign'd,
The anguish of the bleeding wound
Taught me to feel for all mankind.

Even as from the wounded tree
The goodly precious balm will pour;
So in the riven heart there'll be
Mercy that never flow'd before.

'Tis well to learn that sunny hours
May quickly change to mournful shade;
'Tis well to prize life's scatter'd flowers,
Yet be prepared to see them fade.

I thank Thee, God! for weal and woe;
And, whatsoe'er the trial be;
'Twill serve to wean me from below,
And bring my spirit nigher Thee.

SHAPING THE RAW MATERIAL
OF SORROW
Charles Lewis Slattery

We may turn this gift of sorrow as men turn a diamond in the
sun and see new shafts of light from it. We may think of sorrow
as harsh raw material which God gives to us, asking us to cooperate
with Him in His creative power and, by using our ingenuity and
our faith, to make this raw material into something glorious, and
so give it back to Him as our own gift for His happiness.

We may think of an earthly father who presents to his son a
tree, and then, giving him certain tools, such as an axe and saw
and chisel, bids him turn that tree into something beautiful.
Through the years, with increasing strength and increasing skill
and imagination, the youth fells the tree and makes its wood at
last into a great chest, which he carves with the images of animals
and plants. When the carving is all that he can make it, when he
has filled every angle and curve with the love which he bears his
father, he brings his finished gift home. The happiness on the
father's face is beyond all description; this chest, he commands,

shall be bequeathed from generation to generation as a precious heirloom as long as his family shall endure. So God's human children may take the raw material of sorrow and fashion it, by years of faithfulness and labor and love, into a glorious thing, a fitting gift for the loving Father on High.

SORROW—THE SOLEMN INITIATION
George Eliot

For the first sharp pangs there is no comfort. Whatever goodness may surround us, darkness and silence still hang about our pain. But, slowly, the clinging companionship with the dead is linked with our living affections and duties, and we begin to feel our sorrow as a solemn initiation, preparing us for that sense of loving, pitying fellowship with the fullest human lot, which, I must think, no one who has tasted it will deny to be the chief blessedness of our life.

Leigh Hunt

We may conceive it possible for beings to be made entirely happy; but in our composition something of pain seems to be a necessary ingredient, in order that the materials may turn to as fine account as possible, though our clay, in the course of ages and experience, may be refined more and more.

FRIEND SORROW
Adelaide Ann Procter

Do not cheat thy heart and tell her
   "Grief will pass away.
Hope for fairer times in future,
   And forget to-day."
Tell her, if you will, that sorrow
   Need not come in vain;
Tell her that the lesson taught her
   Far outweighs the pain.

Thomas Fuller

That which is bitter to endure may be sweet to remember.

A MESSAGE FOR BETSY ANN
Fulton Oursler

No other letter I have ever received was as hard to answer as the one from Betsy Ann. Here is what Betsy Ann wrote:

"My dog is named Jigger. I love him like a little brother. He got sick and the vet said he could never get well. So I prayed to God, but Jigger died early this morning, before I went to school. Please print the answer to that: Why on earth didn't God answer my prayer?"

Why on earth? Grownups know that we cannot understand the mind of God. But how do you comfort a grieving child?

For one thing, I hope Betsy Ann gives a home to some poor home-less dog. Of course, I know she feels there can never be another Jigger; she's right about that. But she has so much love to give, and there are little dogs that the kind people at the S.P.C.A. would hate to see wind up in the pound. And if Jigger had a soul, he could never be happy in a dog heaven while his little mistress was so lonely. He would bark his joy across the sky, if she would try to help some friendless little dog.

When sorrows come, we are all tempted to feel bitter and cry out: "Why should this happen to me? What did I do to deserve it?"

But there is an answer. Often, I am sure, Betsy asks a favor of her earthly father. She climbs up on his knee and pleads with him, per-haps to stay home tonight and play games. And sometimes Daddy has to refuse. His reasons for saying no may be too hard for a little girl to understand, but just the same she is perfectly sure that Daddy loves her. We must be sure of God's love, too.

And now that Betsy Ann has learned so young what heartache is like—knowing how it feels to lose something dear and precious—she will always feel sympathy for others in a world that has a lot of trouble in it. She can even try to make them happy again. For there are others who have suffered even more terribly—and Betsy Ann can feel with them, which is the meaning of the word "compassion. . . ."

The greatest miracle in the world is compassion for others, rather than grieving for ourselves. In human sympathy, there is healing for ourselves and power to change the world. People who learn that mystery help to make this a better life. If Betsy Ann can know that miracle, little Jigger will not have died in vain.

Anonymous

And yet these days of dreariness are sent us from above;
They do not come in anger, but in faithfulness and love;
They come to teach us lessons which bright ones could not yield,
And to leave us blest and thankful when their purpose is fulfilled.

Author unknown

Sorrow is the blackboard upon which God writes His promises.

SORROW CAN ENLARGE THE DOMAIN OF OUR LIFE
Morris Adler

Our sorrow can bring understanding as well as pain, breadth as well as the contraction that comes with pain. Out of love and sorrow can come a compassion that endures. The needs of others hitherto unnoticed, the anxieties of neighbors never before realized, now come into the ken of our experience, for our sorrow has opened our life to the needs of others. A bereavement that brings us into the lives of our fellow-men writes a fitting epilogue to a love that had taught us kindliness, and forbearance and had given us so much joy.

Sorrow can enlarge the domain of our life, so that we may now understand the triviality of the things many pursue. We have in our hands a noble and refined measure for judging the events and objects we daily see. What is important is not luxury but love; not wealth but wisdom; not gold but goodness.

And our sorrow may so clear our vision that we may, more brightly, see the God, of Whom it was said, "The Lord is nigh unto them, that are of a broken heart." Beyond the hurry and turmoil of life rises the Eternal. There is God in a world in which love like ours could bloom. There is God in a world in which human beings could experience tenderness. There is God in a world in which two lives can be bound together by a tie stronger than death.

Out of that vision will come a sense of obligation. A duty, solemn, sacred and significant, rests upon us. To spread the love we have known to others. To share the joy which has been ours. To ease the pains which man's thoughtlessness or malice inflicts. We have a task to perform. There is work to be done and in work there is consolation.

Out of love may come sorrow. But out of sorrow can come light for others who dwell in darkness. And out of the light we bring to others will come light for ourselves—the light of solace, of strength, of transfiguring and consecrating purpose.

SUFFERING IS A HOLY THING
Richard C. Trench

O Life! O Death! O World! O Time!
  O Grave, where all things flow!
'Tis yours to make our lot sublime,
  With your great weight of woe.

Though sharpest anguish hearts may wring,
  Though bosoms torn may be,
Yet suffering is a holy thing:
  Without it, what were we?

STARS MAY BE SEEN FROM THE BOTTOM OF A DEEP WELL
Joseph Krauskopf

The precious diamond must be cut in order to show its lustre. The sweet incense must be burned in order to exhale its fragrance. Adversity is like the periods of the former and the later rain—cold, comfortless, unfriendly, yet from such seasons the flower and the fruit have their birth. Stars may be seen from the bottom of a deep well when they cannot be discerned from the top of a mountain. So in adversity are learned many things which the prosperous man dreams of. We ought as fervently to pray for a blessing upon our daily rod as upon our daily bread. Adversity has the effect of eliciting talents which prosperity would permit to lie dormant. Prosperity is a great teacher; adversity is a greater. Possession pampers the mind; privation trains and strengthens it.

E. B. Pusey

God does not take away trials or carry us over them, but strengthens us through them.

TEMPESTS AND TRIALS MAKE THE MAN
Joseph Krauskopf

A smooth sea never made a skilful mariner; neither do uninterrupted prosperity and success qualify us for usefulness and happiness. Shallow and loose-rooted is the tree that has known only sunshine, that has never felt the wrench and shock of the gale. The storms of adversity, like those of the ocean, rouse the faculties—excite the invention, prudence, skill, and fortitude of the voyager. The martyrs of all times, in bracing their minds to outward calamities, acquired a loftiness of purpose and a moral heroism worth a lifetime of ease and security.

It is not the so-called blessings of life—its sunshine and calm, its comfort and ease—that make man, but its rugged experiences, its storms and tempest and trials. Early adversity is often a blessing in disguise. Wherever souls are being tried, there God is hewing out the pillars for His temple.

Alphonse Lamartine

Grief knits two hearts in closer bonds than happiness ever can; and common sufferings are far stronger links than common joys.

PASSING THROUGH THE VALLEY
Rufus Jones

Nobody enjoys by preference going through tunnels, or what the beloved Psalmist called "valleys of shadow." And yet all the greatest guides of the soul have known that there are no detours which go around these "valleys of weeping." They must be travelled through. The great achievement is to so pass through them that one makes them "places of springs of water" for others who come there afterwards.

THERE IS COMPENSATION FOR SUFFERING
Charles Louis Slattery

I have . . . known intimately those who have passed through the various experiences of life, from serene safety in the quiet harbours out into the raging storms of suffering and sorrow and death. It has been my duty to observe the changes and the growth of the human soul through these vicissitudes. Again and again I have seen, in the hour of woe, the souls of men and women arise from a life of selfishness and complacency and worldliness into a life of self-sacrifice, the giving of the whole self for others. A beauty and a radiance have come into faces which had not been there before. Below the kindness and the unselfishness there was always the lingering, unforgetting sorrow, but it was sorrow transcended, transmuted into something "rich and strange."

People in trouble, and particularly youth in trouble, turned to these deep natures made kind and beautiful, and invariably found the help they longed for and feared they could not find. And so there was compensation for the suffering, a new sort of joy which was foreign to anything known in the gay past, a joy which was bought at the heavy price of sorrow.

Perhaps the power to help in the hard places was worth the suffering which they had gone through; for nothing lighter or easier would have fitted them for this final and greatest ministry to the human heart and the human soul. When love reaches its goal, it counts everything that contributes to that achievement an asset in life, and the man who loves to the end is ready to thank God for the power, however that power is given. The man who knows that he has the power looks down with a fierce contempt upon the easy years when his barns were bursting with plenty, when he had every luxury at his door, when all he loved were seated around his heavily laden table.

The ease, the freedom from worry, the exemption from human sorrow, now seem cheap. He was then in the lower grades of the school of life. He really did not know life at all. Now he has been burned as by fire; his soul is branded with hot irons; he has lived through sorrow, and he knows. Henceforth he is as the shadow of the great rock in a weary land. Men shall flee to him for peace. And in his understanding and his love they shall find it. . . .

THE LESSON OF THE ROSE
Harriet Beecher Stowe

It is said that gardeners sometimes, when they would bring a rose to richer flowering, deprive it for a season of light and moisture. Silent and dark it stands, dropping one faded leaf after another, and seeming to go down patiently to death. But when every leaf is dropped, and the plant stands stripped to the uttermost, a new life is even then working in the buds, from which shall spring a tender foliage and a brighter wealth of flowers. So, often, in celestial gardening every leaf of earthly joy must drop before a new and divine bloom visits the soul.

Fulton Oursler

True and strange it is, that often, if we do not run away from our trials but face them and conquer them, the prize is ours.

SORROW—A STIMULANT, NOT A NARCOTIC
H. Adye Prichard

Our tears are often strengthening; they often fit us for higher aims and nobler aspirations; they often send us out more intent upon the work in hand; and the dead, it may be, know that, in the tears that are shed for them, there is something of that same great refining power which will make the mourner stronger, in the future, for his mourning. Perhaps they do not grieve as much as we are warned they do for the sorrow they leave behind them, provided they see that sorrow is being used as a stimulant and not a narcotic.

WHAT HAVE I TO LIVE FOR?

Grace Perkins Oursler and April Armstrong

The Rev. Margaret Blair Johnstone, Congregational minister of Groton, Connecticut, tells of a young widow who determined upon self-destruction because, she said, "I cannot go on without him. What have I to live for? This is the greatest blow in the world."

"Then," said Mrs. Johnstone, "why do you want to inflict it on your mother and your children?"

"But what have I to live for?" the woman moaned.

"You might turn to God and ask. He has a purpose. He is not aimless, I assure you. If you seek Him, he'll show you why He wants you to live."

Fourteen years later that same widow hurried to her nineteen-year-old daughter's bedside.

"I don't want to live," the girl moaned in her first shock of knowledge that her husband had been killed in a highway accident which terminated their honeymoon. "I can't take it," she repeated. "What have I to live for without him, tell me, Mother?"

It was then, and only then, that the older widow knew she had found her own answer.

PSALMS

It is good for me that I have been afflicted, in order that I might learn Thy laws.

I WEPT AND THEN BELIEVED

B. A. Levinson

When the mind is clear of trouble and the body free of pain, most of us feel no call for superhuman comfort and support. The daily round, the common tasks and customary distractions appear to suffice. It is when pain and anguish wring the brow that the yearning comes for help beyond human providence. That yearning becomes with suffering so urgent that its answer follows. . . . As it is said in the Psalms, "They cry out unto the Lord in their trouble and He bringeth them out of their distresses."

So we often read in biographies of a newborn faith coming as a solace to a sufferer. Browning's succinct words are apt: "Knowledge by suffering entereth." One example, quoted because it is as simple as it is poignant, is that of Chateaubriand.—Till then an avowed unbeliever, yet when intense sorrow fell to him upon the death of a beloved sister, he wrote in deep sincerity, "I wept and then believed."

Belief that comes thus to a sufferer, whether it be a wounded heart or a tormented body, is as an "awakening from the dream of life." Is it not truly a revelation?

Henry Ward Beecher

Sorrows are often like clouds, which though black when they are passing over us, when they are past become as if they were the garments of God, thrown off in purple and gold along the sky.

USING TROUBLE CREATIVELY

Harry Emerson Fosdick

Here ... is the real tragedy with us, not that we suffer but that in a world where suffering is the common human lot, sure to come in one form or another to every son and daughter of man, we take toward it merely a negative and defensive attitude, get out of it such habits as resentfulness and self-pity, do not hear it calling with creative voice for those faculties and attributes which ease never asks for and no comfortable happiness ever can produce. If our vocabulary did not have in it words like "trouble," "adversity," "calamity," "grief," our vocabulary by no possibility could have in it words like "bravery," "fortitude," "patience," "self-sacrifice." He who knows no hardship will know no hardihood. He who faces no calamity will need no courage. Mysterious though it is, the characteristics in human nature which we love best grow in a soil with a strong admixture of trouble.

Do not misunderstand me in this. I am not saying that trouble alone brings out our best. ... Trouble by itself is neutral. It can do almost anything to a man. It can make him bitter and resentful. It can make him hard and cruel. It can plunge his life into despair and wreck his faith on futility. But trouble does that only to people who take a negative attitude toward it and let it do that to them.

There are others . . . upon whom trouble fell as cruelly as on other men, yet who had in them something so creative that their calamity became their opportunity. Those who knew them best looked on them in amazement, saying, "We never guessed they had *that* in them until trouble called for it."

THE CHASTISEMENTS OF LOVE
Claude G. Montefiore

. . . If the good suffer, we may say that this suffering tends to make goodness more independent. It helps us to care for goodness for its own sake, to love it, and to love its Source, for themselves and only for themselves. But there is something more. Suffering brings out and develops character. It supplies a field for all sorts of virtues, for resignation, faith, courage, resource, endurance. It stimulates; it purifies. This is an old and familiar and never-to-be-forgotten truth. "The chastisements of love," of which the old rabbis spoke, are very real. The discipline of sorrow, the purification of adversity; preachers often preach about these, and they are right.

Ian Maclaren

What Absalom, in his impulsive way, did with Joab is like what God sometimes does with His sons. Joab would not come to Absalom's palace; so Absalom set his corn on fire and then Joab came. So God sometimes burns our harvests that we may go to Him.

Sir Philip Sidney

A noble heart, like the sun, showeth its greatest countenance in its lowest estate.

A MEDITATION ON AFFLICTION
From "Blessings and Praise"

The Psalmist recalls the somber days of his affliction, the sudden disaster, the dazed heart heavy with grief, then the gradual healing of the wounded spirit, the chastened soul, the deepened understanding, and the blessed sense of God's comfort and mercy. All this he recalls and praises the Lord: "It is good that Thou hast afflicted me, for thus have I learned Thy statutes."

When we live at ease we sail carelessly over the surface of life unaware of its deeper undercurrents. Then calamity overtakes us, and, in the struggle with the waves, we learn how precious is life, how deep is pain, how boundless our gratitude to our Deliverer and Preserver. God brings us to the very gates of death, in order that we may learn, manfully, how to choose life.

It is not only our own affliction which brings us blessing. Our fellowmen suffer for our benefit. From their tragedies we learn how to avoid misfortune. Even the material comforts of our life are largely due to the suffering of those who lived before us. The houses in which we live, the fuel we burn, the streets we traverse, all have a history of toil, suffering, danger, and even death. The musician who delights us with his art, the teacher who brings light to our minds, the physician who rescues us from pain, all have endured years of self-denial, toil and trouble. We live by the sufferings of the mother who bore us and the parents who reared us. The beautiful lives which inspire us have been wrought in the furnace of affliction. The call comes to all of us to bless as we have been blessed; to accept our share of this interblend of pain and benefit. We who profit by the vast linkage of human woe and weal cannot refuse the burden of pain. We must patiently accept the daily restraints of conscience, and walk the arduous way of virtue. Perhaps others may profit by our strivings and find in our humble lives a blessing.

Ian Maclaren

The crushing sorrow is often the key that opens the door of God's treasure-house.

SORROWS RIGHTLY USED
Charles Lewis Slattery

. . . We may accept it (sorrow) as gold accepts the fire which refines it . . . if rightly used, it will mean much to us. We observe what it may mean when we examine certain of our friends. Here is a man who was harsh in his judgments, cynical concerning the virtue of humanity, often cutting and unkind in his wit. One day news was brought that the son he loved best had been killed in a drunken brawl. The old man almost died of the grief. But gradually he came back to life; and when he had made a full return to normal living he was altogether a changed man. None was so generous as he before human failure; none so ready to believe in the ultimate good of questionable character; and henceforth his humour only healed wounds, it never again made them. I knew that man.

Here, again, is a woman who was clever, with charm, limiting her friendship to a few, self-indulgent, just missing being selfish. One day her baby died—a child full of promise. It seemed as if she would never smile again; but for her, too, life came back in its normal phases, and when it came she was a changed character. Her old friends had difficulty in finding her, for she was busied over lonely and desolate people, particularly mothers of little children. Her old self-sufficiency had gone, and in its place appeared a beauty of unselfishness, which shone through her face, especially when she was moved to sympathy. The old charm was still one of her characteristics, but it was lifted into a rare graciousness which made people forget to admire her, because instinctively they gave her their love. That person, too, I knew.

Not all sorrow, you will object, has such effects. You will say that you know how it has turned a blithe man into a crabbed misanthropist; how it has turned a pleasant woman into a moping, dismal hag whom no one willingly sees. No doubt you have seen sorrow which thus disfigured its victims. No doubt, too, the story could be repeated through many examples. But the difficulty is that sorrow with this diabolic power to maim the human soul has been received not as a gift of God, but as a curse from the devil. It has been resented, and fought against, and hated as the final ill in life. It is bathed in darkness, and it remains dark; no light can shine through it. When, on the other hand, sorrow is accepted as an inevitable part of God's order ... I am confident that it can have only one effect, transforming the spirit which dutifully receives it into a new life, and that life beautiful, radiating the deeper joys.

TALMUD

As the drug gives out its perfume when it is crushed,
So the soul yields its fragrance when it is chastened.

LIFE WOULD BE WORTH LITTLE WITHOUT SUFFERING

Maltie Babcock

Present suffering is not enjoyable, but life would be worth little without it. The difference between iron and steel is fire, but steel is worth all it costs. Iron ore may think itself senselessly tortured in the furnace, but when the watch-spring looks back, it knows better. David enjoyed pain and trouble no more than we do, but the time came when he admitted that they had been good for him. Though the aspect of suffering is hard, the prospect is hopeful, and the retrospect will start a song. . . .

James Somerville

Adversity, sage useful guest,
Severe instructor, but the best,
It is from thee alone we know
Justly to value things below.

Washington Irving

Great minds have purposes, others have wishes. Little minds are tamed and subdued by misfortune; but great minds rise above it.

SORROW

Lawrence Binyon

Woe to him that has not known the woe of man
Who has not felt within him burning all the want
Of desolated bosoms, since the world began;
Felt, as his own, the burden of the fears that daunt;
Who has not eaten failure's bitter bread, and been
Among those ghosts of hope that haunt the day, unseen.

Only when we are hurt with all the hurt untold
In us the thirst, the hunger, and ours the helpless hands,

The palsied effort vain, the darkness and the cold—
Then, only then, the Spirit knows and understands,
And finds in every sigh breathed out beneath the sun
The human heart that makes us infinitely one.

Honoré de Balzac

The winter's frost must rend the burr of the nut before the fruit
is seen. So adversity tempers the human heart, to discover its real
worth.

SUFFERING IS THE CORNERSTONE OF LIFE
Anatole France

It is on the parched granite of pain that man has firmly established love and courage, heroism and pity. Suffering is the corner-
stone of life. On it humanity is founded as on a firm rock. If it
should disappear, it would take with it all that makes the worth of
life, it would despoil the earth of its splendor and of its glory. It
would tear from it the tremulous love of mothers and the piety of
sons, it would banish knowledge along with study and would extinguish the lights of the mind.

Deuteronomy

That He might afflict thee, and that He might prove thee, to do
thee good at thy latter end. . . .

HOW WE LEARN
Horatius Bonar

Great truths are greatly won. Not found by chance,
    Nor wafted on the breath of summer dream,
But grasped in the great struggle of the soul,
    Hard buffeting with adverse wind and stream,

Not in the general mart, 'mid corn and wine,
    Not in the merchandise of gold and gems,

Not in the world's gay halls of midnight mirth,
   Not 'mid the blaze of regal diadems,

But in the day of conflict, fear, and grief,
   When the strong hand of God, put forth in might,
Plows up the subsoil of the stagnant heart,
   And brings the imprisoned truth-seed to the light.

Wrung from the troubled spirit in hard hours
   Of weakness, solitude, perchance of pain,
Truth springs, like harvest, from the well-plowed field,
   And the soul feels it has not wept in vain.

Epictetus

Difficulties are the things that show what men are.

Leo Tolstoy

It is by those who have suffered that the world has been advanced.

RISING ON THE STAIRS OF PAIN
S. Alfred Adler

Heaven is not to be won by rest and ease and quiet. Only those who have suffered and endured greatly have achieved greatly. The world's greatest workers, thinkers, and teachers have only reached the pinnacle of fame by surmounting obstacles which to ordinary men, content with the lower slopes, would have seemed insuperable. Man has ever risen nearer to God by the altar stairs of pain and sorrow—those altar-stairs which lead through darkness, forever upwards, towards the very Throne of God.

A. Gordon

Sorrow is only one of the bass notes in the oratorio of our blessedness.

HOW SUFFERING SHOULD BE MET
Harry Emerson Fosdick

However much in doubt a man may be about the theory of suffering, he knows infallibly how suffering practically should be met. To be rebellious, cursing fate and hating life; to pity oneself, nursing one's hurts in morbid self-commiseration—the ignobility of such dealing with calamity we indubitably know. Even where we fall feebly short of the ideal, we have no question what the ideal is. When in biography or among our friends we see folk face crushing trouble, not embittered by it, made cynical, or thrust into despair, but hallowed, sweetened, illumined, and empowered, we are aware that noble characters do not alone bear trouble; they use it. As men at first faced electricity in dread, conceiving toward it no attitude beyond building lightning-rods to ward away its stroke, but now with greater understanding harness it to do their will, so men, as they grow wise and strong, deal with their suffering. They make it the minister of character; they set it to build in them what nothing save adversity can ever build—patience, courage, sympathy, and power. They even choose it in vicarious sacrifice for the good of others, and by it save the world from evils that nothing save someone's suffering could cure.

Aughey

God's corrections are our instructions; His lashes our lessons, and His scourges our schoolmasters.

Midrash

One thing acquired through pain is better for man than one hundred things easily achieved.

Confucius

The gem cannot be polished without friction, nor man perfected without trials.

EVIL CAN BE CONVERTED INTO GOOD
Louis Binstock

Sorrow is as much a part of life as is joy. To live is to suffer as well as to rejoice. Sorrow cannot be avoided; it can only be conquered.

. . . One of the great teachers of Israel, recognizing the inevitability of sorrow and reconciling himself to it, adopted as the maxim of his life the famous phrase, "This also for good." His maxim has become a vital, necessary part of the religious philosophy and program of Israel throughout the ages—yea, of every Jew; sometimes it is his only source of salvation. It teaches that every experience of man may be of value, that even as the darkness eventually changes into light, so evil may be converted ultimately into good.

STARS IN DARKNESS
Peter A. Lea

Darkness makes us aware of the stars,
And so when dark hours arise,
They may hold a bright and lovely thing,
We might never have known otherwise.

Horace

Adversity has the effect of eliciting talents which, in prosperous circumstances, would have lain dormant.

Midrash

God's word recorded in Scripture, "Behold it is very good," refers to the suffering which occurs in the world. But how can the words "behold it is very good" be applied to suffering? Because through it men attain immortality. For go forth in life and see which path leads man to eternity. Surely it is the path of sorrow.

Talmud

As salt sweetened the sacrifices of old, so tribulation purifies the devout soul.

SORROW CREATES SYMPATHY
James M. Barrie

James M. Barrie, the author, tells how his mother returned home after the death of her eldest son. He describes her reaction to the sorrow:

"She came back to her desolate home and bowed herself before God. But she never recovered from the blow. From that time she sat in the chair by the window, tended by her noble daughter Jess. That is how my mother got her soft face," says Barrie, "and her pathetic ways, and her large charities; and how other mothers ran to her when they had lost a child."

HIGH SORROWING
Richard Monckton Milnes

A grace within his soul hath reigned
Which nothing else can bring;
Thank God for all that I have gained
By that high sorrowing.

David Mallet

Affliction is the wholesome soil of virtue, where patience, honor, sweet humanity and calm fortitude take root and strongly flourish.

Goethe

Who ne'er his bread in sorrow ate,
Who ne'er the mournful midnight hours
Weeping upon his bed has sate,
He knows you not, ye Heavenly Powers.

Henri Frédéric Amiel

Those who have not suffered are still wanting in depth.

Alphonse de Lamartine

Thou makest the man, O Sorrow!—yes, the whole man—as the crucible gold.

A PRAYER
Morris Joseph

O God, who healest the broken-hearted and bindest up their wounds, to Thee I turn in trust and submission in this dark hour....

O teach me so that I may get insight, and knowledge, and healing from Thy correction. . . . Send forth Thy light so that amid this shadow of death . . . I may see the path to Thee, to a better use of my powers, to a better understanding of life. I do not ask Thee to take this sorrow from me altogether, but to aid me in purging it from all taint of selfishness. . . . May my own pain make me more heedful of human woe, more responsive to it, more resolute in my endeavour to assuage it!

Fix my thoughts not only on this lower life, but on life with Thee; not only on the things of Time, but on the joyous promise of Eternity. . . . Strengthen my faith in my higher self . . . in my soul which . . . will unite me to Thee hereafter in blissful and endless communion. Then will all things be made plain. Then will the veil that hides Thee from me be torn away, and I shall see Thee clearly. . . . Then shall love come by its own—my dear one's which has been my joy in the bygone years, Thine which has blessed me all my life long. *Amen.*

Arabian Proverb

All sunshine makes the desert.

Author unknown

God sometimes puts us on our back so that we may look upward.

Robert Browning Hamilton

I walked a mile with Pleasure
She chattered all the way
But left me none the wiser
For all she had to say.

I walked a mile with Sorrow
And ne'er a word said she
But oh the things I learned from her
When Sorrow walked with me.

> It is for us, the living, rather, to
> be dedicated here to the unfin-
> ished work they have thus far so
> nobly advanced ... that we here
> highly resolve that the dead
> shall not have died in vain.
>
> —Abraham Lincoln

IT IS FOR US THE LIVING . . .

In describing the death of David, the Bible says: "And David slept with his fathers." This expression induced a Talmudic sage to ask why the Bible employed the word "slept" rather than "died," which the Bible used elsewhere. The answer he gave to his own question was that since David was survived by a son who cherished the same high ideals and values which were dear to him, David did not really die. He lived on in his progeny. Therefore David "slept."

Rabbi Phineas bar Hama, the Sage in question, was not alone in calling attention to the power of the survivors to confer a meas-ure of immortality upon the departed. Men have always felt that they perpetuate the pulsating influence of their beloved dead when they identify themselves with their pursuits and reach out for their goals. By extending the impact of the remembered personalities be-yond the span of their days, the survivors attest to the deathlessness of their loved ones. In a very real sense, it is the living who deter-mine whether or not the departed live on.

In our own war-filled years, this interdependence of the genera-tions has become more pronounced. Our liberty, our security, our very right to exist have been dearly purchased. On far-flung battle-fields young men have died in unprecedented numbers in the cause of Freedom and Democracy. To them we feel an obligation too sacred to be discharged by mere rituals of remembrance. To them we owe the fulfilment of the vision which lured them on to their premature deaths. To them we owe a world united in peace and brotherhood, a society in which diverse political systems, religious orientations and racial groups live and work together for the common good. To the extent that we strive to achieve these difficult yet attainable goals, do we redeem their deaths from futility and we invest our lives with high purpose.

Whether we mourn the honored dead who fell in the cause of peace or grieve over the loss of someone who stood near to us, we would do well to hear and heed the wise words the poet spoke on behalf of the dead to the living:

> "Complete these dear unfinished tasks of mine
> And I, perchance, may therein comfort you."

ADDRESS AT GETTYSBURG
Abraham Lincoln

Four score and seven years ago our fathers brought forth upon this continent a new nation, conceived in liberty, and dedicated to the proposition that all men are created equal.

Now we are engaged in a great civil war testing whether that nation, or any nation so conceived and so dedicated, can long endure. We are met on a great battlefield of that war. We have come to dedicate a portion of that field as a final resting place of those who here gave their lives that that nation might live.

It is altogether fitting and proper that we should do this. But in a larger sense we cannot dedicate, we cannot consecrate, we cannot hallow this ground. The brave men, living and dead, who struggled here, have consecrated it far above our power to add or detract.

The world will little note, nor long remember what we say here, but it can never forget what they did here. It is for us, the living, rather, to be dedicated here to the unfinished work they have thus far so nobly advanced. It is rather for us to be here dedicated to the great task remaining before us, that from these honored dead we take increased devotion to that cause for which they here gave the last full measure of devotion; that we here highly resolve that the dead shall not have died in vain, that this nation, under God, shall have a new birth of freedom; and that government of the people, by the people and for the people shall not perish from the earth.

WEEP NOT FOR THEM

Daniel A. Poling, father of one of the chaplains

In the Chapel of the Four Chaplains which stands in the city of Philadelphia, there is a Book of Remembrance. Its first page tells us that the chapel "is a memorial to John P. Washington, George L. Fox, Alexander D. Goode and Clark V. Poling, the four young clergymen of three faiths—Catholic, Jewish and Protestant—who gave their life-belts and their lives that others might live when the *S. S. Dorchester* was sunk by enemy action in the North Atlantic just after midnight on February 3, 1943. . . ." After these words of dedication, there are the last two stanzas of the following poem:

> On coral isles, on desert sands,
> Beneath the swelling tides,
> They sleep their long, untroubled sleep—
> Their hard won rest abides.

> They do not rise to meet the dawn,
> Nor heed the battle call;
> For they have finished with the fight,
> These who have given all.

> They lived and loved, their time was youth,
> And youth they gave to time—
> Now they have won eternity,
> These warriors, yours and mine.

> Weep not for them, nor for their cause,
> Our sons who faltered not;
> Weep only for ourselves who failed,
> Who vowed the vow—forgot.

> Weep for ourselves, but vow again,
> Pledge in our children's blood,
> To keep the faith, to win the peace
> To make the world a Brotherhood.

PLANTING TREES
Talmud

A rabbi was once passing through a field where he saw a very old man planting an oak-tree. "Why are you planting that tree?" he asked. "Surely you do not expect to live long enough to see the acorn grow into an oak-tree?"

"Ah!" replied the old man. "My ancestors planted trees not for themselves, but for us, in order that we might enjoy their shade or their fruit. I am doing likewise for those who will come after me."

MIND THE LIGHT
Author unknown

In New York Harbor, between Manhattan Island and Staten Island, is a sunken shoal called Robbins Reef. A small lighthouse stands there, and for many years the keeper was an elderly widow, Mrs. Jacob Walker. One day she told her story to a reporter, who gave it to the world.

"I was a young girl living at Sandy Hook, New Jersey," she said, "when I first met my husband. He was keeper of the Sandy Hook Light, and took me there as his bride. I was happy there, for the lighthouse was on land and I could have a garden and raise flowers. Then one day we were transferred here—to Robbins Reef. As soon as we arrived I said to my husband, 'I can't stay here! The sight of water wherever I look makes me too lonesome. I won't unpack. . . .' But somehow all the trunks and boxes got unpacked.

"Four years later my husband caught cold while tending the light. The cold turned to pneumonia, and they took him to the infirmary on Staten Island.

"I stayed behind to tend the light. A few nights later I saw a rowboat coming through the darkness. Something told me the message it was bringing. The man in the boat said, 'We're sorry, Mrs. Walker, but your husband's worse.' 'You mean he's dead,' I answered; and there was no reply.

"We buried my husband on a hillside on Staten Island. Every morning when the sun comes up I stand at a porthole and look across the water toward his grave. Sometimes the hill is green, sometimes it is brown, sometimes it is white with snow. But it always brings a message from him—something I heard him say more often than anything else. Just three words—'Mind the light!' "

LET US NOW PRAISE FAMOUS MEN
Ecclesiasticus

Let us now praise famous men,
And our fathers that begot us.
The Lord hath wrought great glory by them
Through his great power from the beginning . . .
But these were merciful men,
Whose righteousness hath not been forgotten.
With their seed shall continually remain a good
    inheritance,
And their children are within the covenant.
Their seed standeth fast,
And their children for their sakes.
Their seed shall remain for ever,
And their glory shall not be blotted out.
Their bodies are buried in peace;
But their name liveth forevermore.
The people will tell of their wisdom,
And the congregation will show forth their praise.

TURN AGAIN TO LIFE
Mary Lee Hall

If I should die and leave you here awhile,
Be not like others, sore undone, who keep
Long vigil by the silent dust and weep.
For my sake turn again to life and smile,
Nerving thy heart and trembling hand to do
That which will comfort other souls than thine;
Complete these dear unfinished tasks of mine,
And I, perchance, may therein comfort you.

WE CAN GRANT RENEWED LIFE
Jacob J. Weinstein

Whatever science or reason may ever say about the nature and persistence of matter, the profounder wisdom of the heart will guarantee the immortal life of our dear ones. But how they live—the quality of the influence they radiate—depends not alone on the kind of life they lived. It depends as much on us. We, the living, can determine the kind of immortality our beloved shall have. We can be more selective than they were when they lived among us. They had to compromise with the needs of the flesh and of the hour. Their good was mingled with the bad; the fine with the gross. We can sift the dross. We can recreate them as the fury and heat of their earthly life would not permit. We can grant renewed life to their nobler insights and their finest visions. We can act as their personal representatives to the living. Where they lifted the burden of worry from a fellow man, we can give encouragement and help; where they brought cheer and care and loyalty, we can be instead. That is how we can bind them into the bundle of eternal life, and build for them a memorial more enduring than stone, sweeter than the rose.

VALLEY OF THE SHADOW
John Galsworthy

God, I am travelling out to death's sea,
    I, who exulted in sunshine and laughter,
Dreamed not of dying—death is such waste of me!
    Grant me one prayer: Doom not the hereafter
Of mankind to war, as though I had died not—
    I, who in battle, my comrade's arm linking,
Shouted and sang, life in my pulses hot,
    Throbbing and dancing! Let not my sinking
In dark be for naught, my death a vain thing!
    God, let me know it the end of man's fever!
Make my last breath a bugle call, carrying
    Peace o'er the valleys and cold hills forever!

THE LEGACY OF INFLUENCE
Joseph I. Weiss

There is no death when one is held fast in the imagery of the mind. The sharp, stunning blow of sudden loss is relieved through time, as soft and fond memories begin to take their shape out of the bewildered haze of bereavement. Let our memories be full. They will make us strong if from them we can gain the inspiration to ennoble our own lives. What greater tribute can we pay to the dead, and what greater good can come to us than to activate their memories into living deeds of worth? Let our legacy of influence, through our own conduct in life, become increasingly great, that they may walk the earth again through us, and we and all of them through the years that are yet to be.

A PLEDGE FROM THE LIVING
Leo Jung

The father's heart beat no more. The kindly eye was closed forever. . . . The son had stepped into the parent's shoes. He had undertaken the responsibilities for the honor of his house. And there at the open grave . . . he stood in the presence of the whole congregation of friends and strangers, before those of the age passing and those who were to lead in the age after him, and there at the saddest moment of his life he recalled neither sorrow nor his loss, but his duty. As a real Jew he knew the holiness of the moment, and he framed his resolution in the words holiest to Jewish hearts; there he opened his lips and made a pledge, a holy promise: "Yissgadal Veyisskadash Sh'meh Rabbah, Lord God, I do not murmur against Thy decree, I am a child of Jewry. Lord God, hear my voice at this moment. As my father lived for Thee, as his life was dedicated to Thy glory and Thy name, so do I declare Yissgadal Veyisskadash, 'that Thy great Name may be magnified and sanctified' as the promise for my future. So do I undertake to remember his fidelity, and never to forget my own duty."

That was the meaning of Kaddish in the times when Jews were Jewish. That is the meaning of the words today when said for mother and father. Not a prayer for the dead, but a pledge from the living; not a superstitious phrase, but a man's motto of life.

IN FLANDERS FIELDS
John McCrae

In Flanders fields the poppies blow
Between the crosses, row on row,
That mark our place; and in the sky
The larks still bravely singing fly
Scarce heard amid the guns below.

We are the Dead. Short days ago
We lived, felt dawn, saw sunset glow
Loved and were loved; and now we lie
In Flanders fields.

Take up our quarrel with the foe:
To you from failing hands we throw
The torch; be yours to hold it high.
If ye break faith with us who die
We shall not sleep, though poppies grow
In Flanders fields.

DEEDS OF LOVE TO THE DEAD
Talmud

The rabbis taught: In three things are deeds of love greater than charity. Charity is done at the mere sacrifice of money, deeds of love are performed with one's money and with one's person. Charity is only for the poor, deeds of love are for the poor and the rich, Charity is only for the living, deeds of love are for the living and the dead.

WATER SPILT ON THE GROUND
Beryl D. Cohon

"For we must needs die, and our lives are as water spilt on the ground, which cannot be gathered up again; neither doth God respect any person" (II Samuel 14:14).

It is an ancient truth ever new. It has been voiced by saint and cynic alike, by the wisest of men and by the simple-minded. Life is like water spilt upon the thirsty ground. It sinks into the sands and is no more. Never may it be recalled; never may it be enjoyed again. . . .

Granted that this is true. Are our lives futile therefore? Is water spilt upon the ground lost? Is it not true that it is precisely this submerged water that makes life possible? It is the rain and the dew that fall on the ground and cease to be that make for life. Without it we perish.

Even so, is it with the life of the spirit. Our fathers and the many generations that went before them have poured out the red, sweet wine of their dreams and ideals and high hopes, and have been absorbed by the hungry earth of life; you and I are the harvest. They have given us not only our bodies; they have given us our minds, our appreciation of the good and the true, our will to live and achieve. We have absorbed into our personalities the spilt waters of their lives, just as we in turn, will be absorbed in the lives of our children and children's children. Teachers will be absorbed in the lives of their students and disciples; poets will be absorbed in the lives of the sensitive who appreciate their writings; the heroes and the martyrs of our social life will be absorbed in the lives of those who fight for the right. Thus the cycle runs its course.

Withhold this water from being spilt on the ground—if we can— and the world perishes; withhold the influences of parents, teachers, preachers, artists, and the life of the spirit is parched. A menacing dust bowl will develop in one generation. It is precisely in this absorption that we realize ourselves and achieve immortality. Alas for those who are not absorbed in someone's else life!

Is there nobility in our lives? Do we cherish high hopes? Is there strength, dignity, loyalty, capacity for whatever the cup of life may hold for us? That, largely, is the harvest with which our fathers have endowed us; it is the submerged water of their lives transformed within our souls.

Are we continuing the cycle? Are we bringing nobility, high hope, courage, loyalty into the lives of those dear to us? Are we pouring out fresh, sweet water that yields a harvest of goodness?

Wisdom of Ben Sira

A man shall be known through his children.

THE CHALLENGE TO FULFILL
THE PLEDGES

Joshua Loth Leibman

All over the world today there are fathers, mothers, and young wives who remember the songs of youths whose lives were brief in duration—songs of freedom defended and of humanity guarded. While we can never minimize the sadness of young melodies cut off in the first stanza, we are also quite certain that the singers of those songs, young aviators and sailors and brave young soldiers at their posts of freedom, would wish the living not to weep too long, but would remind us that there was a kind of fulfillment in their fleeting days of courageous and sacrificial living better than the futility of cowardly decades, and at the same time would challenge us to fulfill the pledges for which they have been called upon to die.

MONUMENTS MORE BEAUTIFUL
THAN THE TAJ MAHAL

Louis I. Newman

Let me tell you of one family, which, in the wilderness of its grief, was helped to discover a secret spring of healing and consolation. When her father died in the very prime of his years, a young girl received a letter from her high-school companions which I am privileged to impart to you in all its eloquent simplicity and beauty:

"Once there was an Indian Maharajah who had a beautiful and loving wife, Mehal. All his dreams and ambitions were wrapped up in her. When she died, he was bewildered and lost. He felt that his soul had died, too. One day an aged wise man came to him, saying: 'Oh, great Rajah, if you would keep the memory of your wife alive, build to her a monument of jewels, marble and ivory; a monument that would make all men remember Mehal, the beautiful.'

"The Maharajah took the wise man's advice and built a monument lovelier than any other. Mehal's memory was preserved forever in the exquisite beauty of the Taj Mahal.

"You, our friend, can make your life an everlasting monument to those who gave it to you. The monument can be made of materials more beautiful and precious than those of the Taj Mahal. Materials such as courage, faith, honor and work are infinitely more beautiful than any precious jewel. As you build this monument slowly and tediously, remember that we are always at your side, in your struggle against sorrow."

AT YOUR GRAVE, MY BROTHER EPHRAIM

Tsvi Guber (Translated from the Hebrew by the editor)

Ephraim died on the battlefield in Israel's War for Independence. He had not quite reached his twenty-first birthday.

Good brother, I still cannot believe that you whom I followed constantly are gone. You were better and stronger than I, so why didn't I fall instead? . . . I stifle the cry of my pain with gritted teeth and restrain my tears with clenched fists. . . .

Mother, do not weep! Our dear one is still alive! He lives in the youthful joy of his friends and comrades in our homeland; he lives in the clear eyes of children, in the buds of this land which was soaked with his blood; he lives in the merry blossoms of spring and in the green growth of our fields; he lives and breathes in everything that throbs and grows under these skies! . . .

Can a leaden bullet destroy courage and purity of soul, an impish smile overflowing with jokes, longings, hopes and the love of a twenty-year-old heart? No! The soul does not die! Who knows—perhaps it flies like a summer butterfly or like a bee thirsty for the honeycomb? Or perhaps, Mother, the earth which swallows the soul returns to its bosom, sends it forth again in the blades of grass and in the roots of trees. And the soul which once sprouted forth from the depths of sparkling eyes now laughs from the cups of flowers. . . .

Mother, do not cry! If he has fallen, I have remained to carry his burdens on my shoulders as much as is humanly possible. And if I, too, shall fall on the battlefield—you still have many sons left. Know this, Mother: Every lad who goes out at night to stand guard in the darkness where terror lurks; every youth who seals with his body the breach in the wall which the enemy made; every boy who rides among the horrors of the road of death; and everyone who fights on the battlefield against the jaws of danger and death with a youthful song which is gay and filled with faith—he is your son, Mother! . . .

My brother, I vow to you: My heart will be the candle of your soul and I shall cherish your memory within me like a priceless treasure! In the very path where you met your death I shall go, even though it be filled with pain and anguish, even if I knew for certain that it is my last road! . . .

By the holiness of the pain and by the holiness of my love for you I swear to you; by the sacredness of everything worth living for and the sanctity of everything worth dying for! . . .

He fulfilled this promise which he made to his brother at the age of sixteen-and-a-half. He enlisted immediately in the Palmach and was killed a little while later after some heroic exploits. A year went by before his remains were discovered and brought to the military cemetery in the village of Warburg where he was born. He was buried in the same grave with his brother Ephraim, according to his own request in one of his letters. In honor of the two brothers the village was named "The Village of The Brothers."

Zohar

"A son honoreth his father." This is true during his lifetime. Is he exempted from honoring him after his death? No! Although he is dead, the son is duty-bound to honor him still more. If the son walks in the proper path, and improves his deeds. this certainly gives the father honor in the other world before the Holy One, praised be He.

A PRAYER

From "Rabbinical Assembly Manual"

Almighty God, whose mercies are from everlasting to everlasting, to Thee alone do Thy children turn for refuge in their affliction, for comfort from the grief that burdens the spirit, for peace from the sense of solitude and loss, and for strength of the soul in trouble.

O Thou, divine Comforter, Who lovest us with an everlasting love and Who turnest the shadows of night into the cloudless day that dawns, help these mourners wait upon Thee with reverent and submissive hearts. As we read the words of promise of eternal life, let them be filled with hope that love dies not, that righteousness is mightier than the grave and that the legacy of a good name is the most enduring memorial we can leave behind.

Let them return to their tasks with new cheerfulness and hope, gladly to accept whatever Thou dost give us to do or to endure, that neither sorrow nor death shall have dominion over us. Let this hour be for them a time of consecration, to resolve so to act that through their conduct and behavior, they may reflect honor upon him who was so dear to them in life. *Amen.*

MY KID BROTHER LOSES A HEROIC FIGHT
Bob Considine

Just before midnight Saturday, My Kid Brother, name of George, got a better offer. He took it, leaving this world for what surely can't be a worse one.

I have not seen many people die, and none as close to me as was this quiet, abundantly witty fellow I had known for so much of my life—and had presumed would outlive me by many years.

George didn't have much hair left when he finally tired of battling his cancer. The long hard pull had taken so terribly much out of him in other ways, too. But I kept thinking of him as I remembered him on his second birthday—a July 2, by the way—when we lived in the swamp-poodle section of Washington and he had long yellow curls. On that birthday, I remembered, he was happy with an apple pie with two little American flags stuck in it. George never asked for much.

My brother lay there at the Washington Sanitarium, a place as gentle as he himself was, and fought for his life with majestic determination. At times his pulse became imperceptible and he barely breathed. And holding his hand, when his wonderful girl wasn't, I thought of the hilarious and semi-violent tournament tennis we once had played in the stifling Washington heat. And I marveled at the hidden springs of strength in so shattered a vessel. And, by turn, I was proud—and wishful that his ordeal would end. . . .

My brother lived as cleanly as anybody I ever met. His appetite for the fleshpots was all but nil. But one morning he woke up with a pain in the stomach. No warning. No alarm. No reason. Just a pain in the stomach. And in a few swift and awful months it was to kill him as only cancer can kill. Almost everything else takes you. Cancer is just plain killer, unless met militantly.

I write about my brother not only because my mind is filled with the memory of his inherent goodness but because I watched him play a fearsome role in the great tragedy of our time, the appalling incidence of cancer. I write, too, because of the mountains that were moved by the staff of Memorial Hospital in New York. In vain, as it turned out. Yet what prodigious efforts and ever-inching progress!

Some day a man in a white coat will speed down the hall from Sloan-Kettering Institute or some such place in the world, and he will bear triumphantly in his hand that for which the world has searched since man became a thinking animal—a cure for this horrid thing that now attacks one in five. My brother and many others could not wait for him. But he will come, this man, if we give him the tools with which to fashion this cure. There is always a heart-lifting, searching, praying chance that he has already taken his first step down the hall, and if the stricken can hang on a bit longer, well, maybe. . . .

THE PUREST DEMOCRACY
Roland B. Gittelsohn

Sermon on the Dedication of 5th Marine Division Cemetery on Iwo Jima.

This is perhaps the grimmest and surely the holiest task we have faced since D-Day. Here before us lie the bodies of comrades and friends. Men who until yesterday or last week laughed with us, joked with us, trained with us. Men who were on the same ships with us, and went over the sides with us as we prepared to hit the beaches of this island. Men who fought with us and feared with us. Somewhere in this plot of ground there may lie the man who could have discovered the cure for cancer. Under one of these Christian crosses, or beneath a Jewish Star of David, there may rest now a man who was destined to be a great prophet . . . to find the way, perhaps, for all to live in plenty, with poverty and hardship for none. Now they lie here silently in this sacred soil, and we gather to consecrate this earth in their memory.

It is not easy to do so. Some of us have buried our closest friends here. We saw these men killed before our very eyes. Any one of us might have died in their places. Indeed, some of us are alive and breathing at this very moment only because men who lie here beneath us had the courage and strength to give their lives for ours. To speak in memory of such men as these is not easy. Of them, too, can it be said with utter truth: "The world will little note nor remember what we say here. It can never forget what they did here."

No, our poor power of speech can add nothing to what these men and the other dead of our division who are not here have already done. All that we even hope to do is follow their example. To show the same selfless courage in peace that they did in war. To swear that, by the grace of God and the stubborn strength and power of human will, their sons and ours shall never suffer these pains again. These men have done their job well. They have paid the ghastly price of freedom. If that freedom be once again lost, as it was after the last war, the unforgivable blame will be ours, not theirs. So it is we "the living" who are here to be dedicated and consecrated.

We dedicate ourselves, first, to live together in peace the way they fought and are buried in this war. Here lie men who loved America because their ancestors generations ago helped in her founding, and other men who loved her with equal passion because they themselves or their own fathers escaped from oppression to her blessed shores. Here lie officers and men, Negroes and whites, rich men and poor . . . together. Here are Protestants, Catholics, and Jews . . . together. Here no man prefers another because of his faith or despises him because of his color. Here there are no quotas of how many from each group are admitted or allowed. Among these men there is no discrimination. No prejudices. No hatred. Theirs is the highest and purest democracy.

Any man among us "the living" who fails to understand that will thereby betray those who lie here dead. Whoever of us lifts his hand in hate against a brother, or thinks himself superior to those who happen to be in the minority, makes of this ceremony and of the bloody sacrifices it commemorates, an empty, hollow mockery. To this, then, as our solemn, sacred duty, do we the living now dedicate ourselves: to the right of Protestants, Catholics, and Jews, of white men and Negroes alike, to enjoy the democracy for which all of them have here paid the price.

To one thing more do we consecrate ourselves in memory of those who sleep beneath these crosses and stars. We shall not foolishly suppose, as did the last generation of America's fighting men, that victory on the battlefield will automatically guarantee the triumph of democracy at home. This war, with all its frightful heartache and suffering, is but the beginning of our generation's struggle for democracy. When the last battle has been won, there will be those at home, as there were last time, who will want us to turn our backs in selfish isolation on the rest of organized humanity, and thus to sabotage the very peace for which we fight. We promise you who lie here: we will not do that! We will join hands with Britain,

China, Russia—in peace, even as we have in war, to build the kind of world for which you died.

When the last shot has been fired, there will still be those whose eyes are turned backward, not forward, who will be satisfied with those wide extremes of poverty and wealth in which the seeds of another war can breed. We promise you, our departed comrades: this, too, we will not permit. This war has been fought by the common man; its fruits of peace must be enjoyed by the common man! We promise, by all that is sacred and holy, that your sons—the sons of miners and millers, the sons of farmers and workers, will inherit from your death the right to a living that is decent and secure.

When the final cross has been placed in the last cemetery, once again there will be those to whom profit is more important than peace, who will insist with the voice of sweet reasonableness and appeasement that it is better to trade with the enemies of mankind than, by crushing them, to lose their profit. To you who sleep here silently, we give our promise: we will not listen! We will not forget that some of you were burnt with oil that came from American wells, that many of you were killed by shells fashioned from American steel. We promise that when once again men seek profit at your expense, we shall remember how you looked when we placed you reverently, lovingly, in the ground.

Thus do we memorialize those who, having ceased living with us, now live within us. Thus do we consecrate ourselves, the living, to carry on the struggle they began. Too much blood has gone into this soil for us to let it lie barren. Too much pain and heartache have fertilized the earth on which we stand. We here solemnly swear: this shall not be in vain! Out of this, and from the suffering and sorrow of those who mourn, this will come—we promise—the birth of a new freedom for the sons of men everywhere. *Amen.*

> The tomb is not a blind alley. It is an open thoroughfare. It closes in the twilight to open with the dawn.
>
> —Victor Hugo

DEATH IS NOT THE END

Ours is an age in which theological matters do not occupy too prominent a role in our thinking. We are nonchalant about beliefs and doctrines over which former generations speculated abundantly and in which they believed passionately. The belief in immortality is one such doctrine towards which we display conspicuous indifference. Our emphasis has been largely humanistic, underscoring the importance of leading worthy lives here and now and letting the hereafter take care of itself. We normally presume that it makes little difference one way or another whether the soul survives death or not.

In the time of bereavement, however, it matters profoundly whether we believe that death is "a period which brings the sentence of life to a full stop" or whether we believe that "it is only a comma which punctuates it to loftier significance." It makes an enormous difference whether we believe that the essence of our loved ones has been totally erased from the slate of life or whether it survives with the Author of Life, Himself. Our personal indifference departs when sorrow enters. Thus even so confirmed an agnostic as Robert G. Ingersoll, speaking at the funeral services for his brother, felt constrained to add this comforting assurance: "But in the night of death Hope sees a star, and listening Love can hear the rustle of a wing."

It is not without significance that this section is among the largest in the book. It contains but a fraction of the abundant literary harvest which is available on this theme in mankind's library. From ancient man with his naïve beliefs down through the long corridors

236

of time reaching into the present most sophisticated faiths, men have persistently and in decisive numbers held the human soul indestructible. Nor has this belief been limited to religious thinkers alone. Philosophers, poets, scientists, physicians are all included in the throng who answer "present" when the roll is called among the believers that death is not the end. The more we have learned about the universe in which we live, the more persuasive have grown the intimations of our immortality. Robert Millikan spoke for a host of his scientific colleagues when he declared: "The Divine Architect of the Universe has not built a stairway that leads to nowhere."

When death separates us from a loved one, the pain of parting can be assuaged in no small measure through our faith that the essence of our beloved lives on not only in our hearts and in our memories but more especially with the inexhaustible source of all life. We can be sustained by what the philosopher Santayana called "the Soul's invincible surmise." It is this faith which burst forth out of Emerson after the passing of his little son. "What is excellent," he wrote, "as God lives is permanent."

This was the conviction that welled up in the heart of Charlotte Brontë as she lay dying. "God will not separate us now; we have been so happy." Our craving for eternity in a world which responds to our every other fundamental yearning and need points to a God who, in the words of the Hebrew prayer-book, "implanted within us everlasting life."

Simple parables illustrate great truths. Little David found a bird nest near his home which contained some speckled eggs. He visited it for a few days and then had to leave on a trip to the city. Upon his return he rushed to the nest to look at the eggs. To his deep dismay he found that the beautiful eggs were no longer there. Indeed, there were only broken, empty shells. With tears in his eyes he ran to his father and cried: "Father, they were such beautiful eggs. Now they are all spoiled and broken." "No, son," his father reassured him, "they are not spoiled. The best part of them has taken wings and flown away."

THERE IS NO DEATH—THERE'S IMMORTALITY
Anonymous

There is a plan far greater than the plan you know;
There is a landscape broader than the one you see.
There is a haven where storm-tossed souls may go—
You call it death—we, immortality.

You call it death—the seeming endless sleep;
We call it birth—the soul at last set free.
'Tis hampered not by time or space—you weep.
Why weep at death? 'Tis immortality.

Farewell, dear voyageur—'twill not be long.
Your work is done—now may peace rest with thee.
Your kindly thoughts and deeds—they will live on.
This is not death—'tis immortality.

Farewell, dear voyageur—the river winds and turns;
The cadence of your song wafts near to me,
And now you know the thing that all men learn:
There is no death—there's immortality.

Henry Wadsworth Longfellow

The grave itself is but a covered bridge leading from light to light, through a brief darkness.

OUR HOPES ARE NOT DELUSIONS
From "Blessings and Praise"

The hope of immortality is the strength of our life on earth. Whenever we yield to the fear that our earthly labor will some day cease forever, we lose the courage to overcome circumstance, and lack the will to resist failure. If our toil is but for a day, we cannot build. But if, as our sages assure us, we may labor on beyond the accident of death into eternity, then no failure is irreparable, no task is too great. When we may include infinity in our plans then no aim is unattainable, no vision is too exalted.

We tend to doubt our immortality whenever life defeats us. When our plans go awry and our efforts fail, when friends disappoint and solitude grows bitter, then our strength seems to vanish, a sense of our frailty overpowers us and there comes the dread that all our hopes will soon be quenched in an eternal darkness. Our disappointments and our discouragements engender the fear that our life will end in a final defeat and the grave will win its ultimate victory. The terror of death grows from our failures in life.

Yet when each morning dawns and our strength is renewed, when our efforts succeed and the spirit of God, calling to our souls, reveals our innate divinity, then our life again seems triumphant and indestructible. Hope revives and we see our spirit entering, beyond the grave, into the gateway of greater life. Death loses its sting and the grave its victory. When life is strong we foresee our immortality.

We are poised between despair and hope. Each day our failures bring the terror of the grave and our victories bring intimations of immortality. We have ever before us both life and death. It is for us to choose the hope of life eternal; to depart from fear and to be strong in faith; to assert to our failing hearts that we shall not die, but live, and declare forever the wonders of God.

Our hopes are not delusions, for God is just and merciful. He would not bid us toil in His name, and then deny us the joy of completing our work. He would not bid us prepare in this antechamber of eternity, and then close against us the doors of His eternals halls. Since His mercies endure forever, He would not bid us sow in tears, without permitting us to reap in joy. We may trust in His love. We have known bereavement and the pain of death. He will comfort us. He will destroy death forever and wipe the tears from every face. Though the cords of death encompass us, we will yet walk before Him in "the land of the living."

Sir Walter Scott

Is death the last sleep? No, it is the last and final awakening.

BOOK OF LIFE
John Donne

All mankind is of one Author, and is one volume; when one Man dies, one chapter is not torn of the book, but translated into a better language; and every chapter must be so translated; God employs several translators; some pieces are translated by age, some by sickness, some by war, some by justice; but God's hand is in every translation; and His hand shall bind up all our scattered leaves again, for that Library where every book shall lie open to one another.

Psalms

Into Thy hand I commit my spirit;
Thou hast redeemed me, O Lord, Thou God of Truth.

DEATH MAY GIVE US MORE
Sir Edwin Arnold

Birth gave to each of us much; death may give very much more, in the way of subtler senses to behold colors we cannot here see, to catch sounds we do not now hear, and to be aware of bodies and objects impalpable at present to us, but perfectly real, intelligibly constructed, and constituting an organized society and a governed, multiform State.

A COMRADE RIDES AHEAD
Douglas Malloch

Time brings not death, it brings but changes.
I know he rides, but rides afar,
To-day some other planet ranges
And camps to-night upon a star
Where all his other comrades are.

IMMORTALITY
Solomon Solis-Cohen

I dreamed my spirit broke the bars of sense
That hold the gates of consciousness shut fast,
Threw off the prison-garb of Self, and passed
Into the wonder of Omniscience.

I saw mists rise from ocean and condense
In clouds; in million raindrops melt, and at last,
Through brooks and rivers join again the vast
Primeval sea. And thus I read the Whence
And Whither of the soul.
When stream meets sea,

Is the swift river wave forever gone?
When souls rejoin All-soul, cease they to be?
Nay, there where All is Thought and Thought is One,
Within the Infinite All, eternally,
The thought once bound in me, lives boundless on.

FROM "CONTEMPLATIONS"
Anne Bradstreet

When I behold the heavens as in their prime,
   And then the earth, though old, still clad in green,
The stones and trees insensible of time,
   Nor age nor wrinkly on their front are seen;
If winter come, and greenness then do fade,
A spring returns, and they more youthful made;
But man grows old, lies down, remains where once
    he's laid.

By birth more noble than those creatures all,
   Yet seems by nature and by custom cursed—
No sooner born but grief and care makes fall
   That state obliterate he had at first;
Nor youth, nor strength, nor wisdom spring again
Nor habitations long their names retain,
But in oblivion to the final day remain.

Shall I then praise the heavens, the trees, the earth,
  Because their beauty and their strength last longer?
Shall I wish therefore never to had birth,
  Because they're bigger and their bodies stronger,
Nay, they shall darken, perish, fade, and die,
And when unmade so ever shall they lie;
But man was made for endless immortality.

I Samuel

The Lord killeth, and maketh alive;
He bringeth down to the grave, and bringeth up.

A UNIVERSAL AND PERSISTENT LONGING
Ralph W. Sockman

Just as science postulates a gas to explain the phenomena of the laboratory, or a new planet to explain the movement of the stars, or a body of water to explain the existence of fish, why is it not the part of wisdom to believe that there must be a land which "eye hath not seen and ear hath not heard" in order to explain the presence in man of the persistent and universal inclination towards it? For "this longing after immortality" is a normal appetite of the human soul, felt by the best minds in their healthiest moments. It is universal, being found among all races. It is persistent, haunting the twentieth-century sage as well as the primitive savage. Can it be that the universe which keeps faith with the instincts of the bird by providing air in which to fly, and with the instincts of the fish by furnishing water in which to swim, has played most cruelly false to man by endowing him with this craving for eternity only to deny its gratification? A heavenless universe would seem to be as deceptive and dishonest as a foodless one. And if this is a nonmoral world order, how can we explain the rise of moral aspiration in man? It needs a moral universe and immortal life to explain man.

FROM "SNOW-BOUND"

James Greenleaf Whittier

Henceforward, listen as we will,
The voices of that hearth are still;
Look where we may, the wide earth o'er
Those lighted faces smile no more. . . .
Yet Love will dream, and Faith will trust
(Since He who knows our need is just)
That somehow, somewhere, meet we must.

WHENCE THIS LONGING AFTER IMMORTALITY?

Joseph Addison

It must be so. . . .
Else—whence this pleasing hope, that fond desire,
This longing after immortality?
Or whence this secret dread and inward horror
Of falling into naught? Why shrinks the soul
Back on itself, and startles at destruction?
'Tis the Divinity that stirs within us:
'Tis Heaven itself that points out an hereafter
And intimates Eternity to Man.

FROM "ODE TO THE SETTING SUN"

Francis Thompson

For birth hath in itself the germ of death,
But death hath in itself the germ of birth.
It is the falling acorn buds the tree,
The falling rain that bears the greenery,
The fern-plants moulder when the ferns arise.
For there is nothing lives but something dies,
And there is nothing dies but something lives.
Till skies be fugitives,
And Time, the hidden root of change, updries,
Are Birth and Death inseparable on earth;
For they are twain yet one, and Death is Birth.

Benjamin Franklin's Own Epitaph

The body of
B. Franklin Printer,
(Like the cover of an old Book
Its Contents torn out
And stript of its Lettering and Gilding)
Lies here, Food for Worms,
But the Work shall not be lost;
For it will (as he believ'd) appear once more
In a new and more elegant Edition
Revised and corrected,
By the Author.

EPITAPH

Composed by Dorothy Kahan Bar-Adon (1907–1950) and engraved on her tombstone in Merhavia, Israel.

I, Dorothy Ruth, am in this ground,
Roots and rich soil close around,
Growth, creation, taking and giving
So life was death and death is living.

DEATH IS NOT SEVERANCE

Sir Oliver Lodge

I tell you, it pains them to be thought dead. They have passed through the physiological process we call death; they have shuffled off the mortal body; but they themselves have more life than ever. If the bereaved and sorrowful could only realize that, the pain of parting would be greatly alleviated. I believe one of the outcomes of the war will be to make people realize the fact, much more vividly than before, that death is not severance, it is a change of condition but not of personality. Bullets and shells injure the body, but they are not amongst those things which assault and hurt the soul. The soul continues after death, and, by our love and affection, we can give some joy to those on the other side who have their lives before them, a different life from ours, but as helpful and as useful and more happy.

Cicero

I consider this world as a place which Nature never designed for my permanent abode; and I look upon my departure out of it, not as being driven from my habitation, but as leaving my inn.

MY SUN SETS TO RISE AGAIN
Robert Browning

From "At the Mermaid"

Have you found your life distasteful?
   My life did, and does, smack sweet.
Was your youth of pleasure wasteful?
   Mine I save and hold complete.
Do your joys with age diminish?
   When mine fail me, I'll complain.
Must in Death your daylight finish?
   My sun sets to rise again.

THE SEA HAS ANOTHER SHORE
Harry Emerson Fosdick

Death is a great adventure, but none need go unconvinced that there is an issue to it. The man of faith may face it as Columbus faced his first voyage from the shores of Spain. What lies across the sea, he cannot tell; his special expectations all may be mistaken; but his insight into the clear meanings of present facts may persuade him beyond doubt that the sea has another shore. Such confident faith, so founded upon reasonable grounds, shall be turned to sight, when for all the dismay of the unbelieving, the hope of the seers is rewarded by the vision of a new continent.

IMMORTALITY
Cicero

There is, I know not how, in the minds of men, a certain presage, as it were, of a future existence; and this takes the deepest root, and is most discoverable, in the greatest geniuses and most exalted souls.

James D. Burns

I have been dying for years: now I shall begin to live.

IT CANNOT BE

David Banks Sickels

It cannot be that He who made
This wondrous world for our delight,
Designed that all its charms should fade
And pass forever from our sight;
That all shall wither and decay,
And know on earth no life but this,
With only one finite survey
Of all its beauty and its bliss.

It cannot be that all the years
Of toil and care and grief we live
Shall find no recompense but tears,
No sweet return that earth can give;
That all that leads us to aspire,
And struggle onward to achieve,
And every unattained desire
Were given only to deceive.

It cannot be that, after all
The mighty conquests of the mind,
Our thoughts shall pass beyond recall
And leave no record here behind;
That all our dreams of love and fame,
And hopes that time has swept away,
All that enthralled this mortal frame,
Shall not return some other day.

It cannot be that all the ties
Of kindred souls and loving hearts
Are broken when this body dies,
And the immortal mind departs;
That no serener light shall break
At last upon our mortal eyes,
To guide us as our footsteps make
The pilgrimage to Paradise.

FROM "THRENODY"
Ralph Waldo Emerson

When Emerson lost his young son, he wrote to Carlyle: "My son, a perfect little boy of five years and three months, has ended his earthly life. You can never sympathize with me; you can never know how much of me such a young child can take away."

His grief found creative expression in that poetic masterpiece, "Threnody," from which the following lines are taken.

> Wilt thou not ope thy heart to know
> What rainbows teach, and sunsets show?
> Verdict which accumulates
> From lengthening scroll of human fates,
> Voice of earth to earth returned,
> Prayers of saints that only burned,
> Saying, What is excellent,
> As God lives, is permanent;
> Hearts are dust; hearts' loves remain;
> Hearts' love will meet thee again.

AWAY
James Whitcomb Riley

> I cannot say, and I will not say
> That he is dead! He is just away!
> With a cheery smile, and a wave of the hand,
> He has wandered into an unknown land.
> And left us dreaming how very fair
> It must be, since he lingers there.
> And you—O you, who the wildest yearn
> For the old-time step and the glad return.
> Think of him faring on, as dear
> In the love of There as the love of Here.
> Think of him still as the same, I say;
> He is not dead—he is just away!

Sir Rabindranath Tagore

Death is not extinguishing the light; it is putting out the lamp because the dawn has come.

COMFORT
William Morris

From out the throng and stress of lies,
From out the painful noise of sighs,
One voice of comfort seems to rise:
"It is the meaner part that dies."

THE SPIRITUAL SELF CANNOT PERISH
Felix Adler

Vast possibilities suggest themselves to us of an order of existence wholly different from all that we have ever known; what may be the nature of that other life it is impossible to know and it is useless to speculate. . . . Only this I feel warranted in holding fast to—that the root of my selfhood, the best that is in me, my true and only being, cannot perish. In regard to that the notion of death seems to me to be irrelevant. . . . I let go my hold on the empirical, transient self. I see it perish with the same indifference which the materialist asserts, for whom man is but a compound of physical matter and physical force. It is the real self, the eternal self, upon which I tighten my hold. I affirm the real, the irreducible existence of the essential self, though I know not the how or where of its survival. I affirm that there verily is an eternal divine life, a best beyond the best I can think or imagine. What I retain is the conviction that the spiritual self is an eternal self, and cannot perish.

TIS LIFE BEYOND
Anonymous

I watched a sail until it dropped from sight
Over the rounding sea. A gleam of white,
A last far-flashed farewell, and, like a thought
Slipt out of mind, it vanished and was not.
Yet to the helmsman standing at the wheel
Broad seas still stretched beneath the gliding keel.
Disaster? Change? He felt no slightest sign,

Nor dreamed he of that far horizon line.
So may it be, perchance, when down the tide
Our dear ones vanish. Peacefully they glide
On level seas, nor mark the unknown bound.
We call it death—to them 'tis life beyond.

Robert Browning

And I shall thereupon
Take rest, ere I be gone
Once more on my adventure brave and new.

ON THE DEATH OF AN AGED FRIEND

Roselle Mercier Montgomery

You are not dead—Life has but set you free!
   Your years of life were like a lovely song,
   The last sweet poignant notes of which, held long,
Passed into silence while we listened, we, who loved
     you listened still expectantly!
And we about you whom you moved among would
     feel that grief for you were surely wrong—
You have but passed beyond where we can see.

For us who knew you, dread of age is past!
You took life, tiptoe: to the very last:
It never lost for you its lovely look;
You kept your interest in its thrilling book;
To you Death came no conqueror; in the end
You merely smiled to greet another friend!

Joseph Addison

How can it enter into the thoughts of man, that the soul, which
is capable of such immense perfections and of receiving new im-
provements to all eternity, shall fall away into nothing almost as
soon as it is created?

Robert Louis Stevenson

He is not dead, this friend; not dead,
But, in the path we mortals tread,
Got some few, trifling steps ahead,
  And nearer to the end;
So that you, too, once past the bend
Shall meet again, as face to face this friend
You fancy dead.

DEATH CANNOT BE THE END OF LIFE
Milton Steinberg

Death cannot be and is not the end of life. Man transcends death in many altogether naturalistic fashions. He may be immortal biologically, through his children, in thought through the survival of his memory; in influence, by virtue of the continuance of his personality as a force among those who come after him, and, ideally, through his identification with the timeless things of the spirit.

When Judaism speaks of immortality it has in mind all these. But its primary meaning is that man contains something independent of the flesh and surviving it; his consciousness and moral capacity; his essential personality; a soul.

HE IS A PORTION OF THE LOVELINESS
Percy Bysshe Shelley
From "Adonais"

He is made one with nature; there is heard
His voice in all music, from the moan
Of thunder, to the song of night's sweet bird,
He is a presence to be felt and known
In darkness and in light, from herb and stone
Spreading itself where'er that Power may move
Which has withdrawn His being to its own;
Which wields the world with never wearied love
Sustains it from beneath, and kindles it above.
He is a portion of the loveliness
Which once he made more lovely.

Charles Darwin

Believing as I do that man in the distant future will be a far more perfect creature than he now is, it is an intolerable thought that he and all other sentient beings are doomed to complete annihilation after such long-continued slow progress.

EVOLUTION

John Banister Tabb

Out of the dusk a shadow,
    Then a spark;
Out of the cloud a silence,
    Then a lark;

Out of the heart a rapture,
    Then a pain;
Out of the dead, cold ashes,
    Life again.

DEATH, BE NOT PROUD

John Donne

Death, be not proud, though some have called thee
Mighty and dreadful, for thou art not so;
For those whom thou think'st thou dost overthrow
Die not, poor Death; nor yet canst thou kill me. . . .

  One short sleep past, we wake eternally,
  And Death shall be no more: Death, thou shalt die!

TRIUMPH OF THE DEFEATED

Lord Byron

They never fail who die
In a great cause. The block may soak their gore;
Their heads may sodden in the sun; their limbs
Be strung to city gates and castle walls;

But still their spirit walks abroad.
Though years
Elapse and others share as dark a doom,
They but augment the deep and sweeping thoughts
Which overpower all others and conduct
The world, at last, to freedom.

THE OVERWHELMING MAJORITY
SAYS "AYE"

Sir James Frazer

The question whether our conscious personality survives after death has been answered by almost all races of men in the affirmative. On this point sceptical or agnostic peoples are nearly, if not wholly, unknown. Accordingly, if abstract truth could be determined, like the gravest issues of national policy, by a show of hands or a counting of heads, the doctrine of human immortality, or at least of a life after death, would deserve to rank among the most firmly established of truths; for were the question put to the vote of the whole mankind there can be no doubt that the "ayes" would have it by an overwhelming majority. The few dissenters would be overborne; their voices would be drowned in the general roar.

A REASONABLE FAITH

Julian Huxley

We do not know all. For instance, I have studiously avoided ever mentioning the word *immortality*, since I believe that Science cannot yet profitably discuss that question. But the discovery of unity in all that has so far been studied gives me reasonable faith that its wings will reach out to cover all that we shall still be enabled to learn, while the unbroken continuity of evolutionary direction gives us the same sort of right to believe that it will continue tomorrow and on into time as we have to believe that apples will continue to fall to the earth.

GOD GRATIFIES OUR CRAVINGS
F. W. Robertson

We wish for immortality. The thought of annihilation is horrible; even to conceive it is almost impossible. The wish is a kind of argument: it is not likely that God would have given all men such a feeling, if he had not meant to gratify it. Every natural longing has its natural satisfaction. If we thirst, God has created liquids to gratify thirst. If we are susceptible of attachment, there are beings to gratify that love. If we thirst for life and love eternal, it is likely that there are an eternal life and an eternal love to satisfy that craving.

Edward Young

Still seems it strange, that thou shouldst live forever?
Is it less strange, that thou shouldst live at all?
This is a miracle; and that no more.

SOLO
Corporal Harold Applebaum

You cannot hear me now, my voice is lost
In thunder. The song of me is drowned
In the earth's grim symphony like the sound
Of violins all beaten flat and tossed
Against a cliff of brass. You cannot hear me,
But I am singing still beneath the clash,
Below the metal chorus and the lash
Of trumpets at the sky. I will be
But a tiny voice, saying there is yet a dawn,
Stars to dream at and the world beyond.
I will hold my keening note until the wand
Waves back the brasses and the drums are gone,
And brave against the stillness sing my part—
The deathlessness of beauty in the heart.

Leigh Hunt

Doth this soul within me, this spirit of thought, and love, and infinite desire, dissolve as well as the body? Has nature, who quenches our bodily thirst, who rests our weariness, and perpetually encourages us to endeavor onwards, prepared no food for this appetite of immortality?

THE REASONABLENESS OF GOD'S WORK
John Fiske

I believe in the immortality of the soul, not in the sense in which I accept the demonstrable truths of science, but as a supreme act of faith in the reasonableness of God's work.

THE BUTTERFLY
Alice Freeman Palmer

I hold you at last in my hand,
Exquisite child of the air.
Can I ever understand
How you grew to be so fair?
You came to my linden tree
To taste its delicious sweet,
I sitting here in the shadow and shine
Playing around its feet.
Now I hold you fast in my hand,
You marvelous butterfly,
Till you help me to understand
The eternal mystery.
From that creeping thing in the dust
To this shining bliss in the blue!
God give me courage to trust
I can break my chrysalis, too!

Henry van Dyke

The cry of the human for a life beyond the grave comes from that which is noblest in the soul of man.

THE GIFT OF NEW LIFE
Grace Perkins Oursler and April Armstrong

. . . We know the horrors of birth in similar manner. The pain, responsibility, possible loss of health, of looks, and of a measure of youth, even the risk of death. We know the forfeit of time, comfort, money, calling for selfless sacrifice. There are some who avoid parenthood and all it entails, many who cannot rise to it, even more who cannot live up to the full contract. But those who do know the beauty and the rewards, the joy and the glory, are in the millions, and the rewards far overshadow the losses. Everyone recognizes that the agony of labor is discounted in the gift of new life. The pain and goriness are soon gone, and what remains is joy in the product of union. That we experience and understand and welcome.

How do we dare to guess the same is not with death?

THOU WILT RESTORE IT TO ME
Hebrew Prayer Book

O my God, the soul with which Thou didst endow me is pure. Thou didst create it and fashion it; Thou didst breathe it into me and Thou preservest it within me. Thou wilt reclaim it from me but Thou wilt restore it to me in the life to come. So long as the breath of life is within me, I will give thanks unto Thee, O Lord my God and God of my fathers, Master of all works, Lord of all souls. Blessed art Thou, O Lord, who restorest life to mortal creatures.

FOREVER
John Boyle O'Reilly

Those we love truly never die,
Though year by year the sad memorial wreath,
A ring and flowers, types of life and death,
Are laid upon their graves.

For death the pure life saves,
And life all pure is love; and *love can reach*
From heaven to earth, and nobler lessons teach
Than those by mortals read.

Well blest is he who has a dear one dead;
A friend he has whose face will never change—
A dear communion that will not grow strange;
The anchor of a love is death.

THERE IS SOMETHING . . . THAT CANNOT WHOLLY PERISH

George D. Prentice

. . . In the beautiful drama of Ion, the hope of immortality . . . finds deep response in every thoughtful soul. When about to yield his young existence as a sacrifice to fate, his Clemantha asks if they should meet again, to which he replies: "I have asked that dreadful question of the hills that look eternal—of the clear streams that flow forever—of the stars among whose fields of azure my raised spirit has walked in glory. All were dumb: but as I gaze upon thy living face I feel that there is something in the love that mantles through its beauty that cannot wholly perish. We shall meet again Clemantha."

A FORCE THAT CANNOT DIE

Louis Pasteur

There are two men in each one of us: the scientist, he who starts with a clear field and desires to rise to the knowledge of Nature through observation, experimentation and reasoning; and the man of sentiment, the man of faith, the man who mourns his dead children and who cannot, alas, prove at all that he will see them again, but who believes that he will, and lives in that hope, . . . the man who feels that force that is within him cannot die.

Robert Browning

Fool! All that is, at all,
Lasts ever, past recall;

Earth changes, but thy soul and God stand sure:
What entered into thee,
That was, is, and shall be:
    Time's wheel runs back or stops; Potter and clay endure.

CAN HE HAVE BECOME NOTHING?
Charles Lewis Slattery

Our first intimation of the necessary idea of a future life comes
in the presence of the death of a truly great man at the height of
his power and influence. Again and again, through the centuries,
a man to whom thousands look for inspiration falls by the wayside. An hour ago his eye flashed hope, his smile cheered, his word
gave knowledge, his love gave confidence. He was like a dynamo,
giving force to his whole wide environment as it lay about him.
Then, a moment ago, without warning, he died.

What has become of him? Can he have become nothing? If we
talk calmly of the conservation of energy in the physical world,
can we fail to go one step farther and say a word of belief in the
conservation of energy in the spiritual world? Is not such abound-
ing life living somewhere, though its manifestation in this world
has ceased? The wide-eyed disciples of Socrates, who knew the
wisdom and love and strength of their master in that room in
Athens where he drank the hemlock, and then saw him die, could
not possibly believe that such wisdom and love and strength as his
had stopped. A nation exulting in the great heart of Abraham
Lincoln, which had by sheer strength and love and pity brought a
warring people together and had won peace, received the sudden
news that Abraham Lincoln had been fatally shot. Could anyone
who had entered fully into the emotions of that hour believe for
one instant that so mighty a personality could thus suddenly stop
living? Somewhere, all thinking men said to themselves, that heart
of love and pity and infinite patience must be living still.

A PARABLE OF SOME GRUBS
Walter Dudley Cavert

In the bottom of an old pond lived some grubs who could not
understand why none of their groups ever came back after crawling
up the lily stems to the top of the water. They promised each other

that the next one who was called to make the upward climb would return and tell what had happened to him. Soon one of them felt an urgent impulse to seek the surface; he rested himself on the top of a lily pad and went through a glorious transformation which made him a dragon fly with beautiful wings. In vain he tried to keep his promise. Flying back and forth over the pond, he peered down at his friends below. Then he realized that even if they could see him they would not recognize such a radiant creature as one of their number.

The fact that we cannot see our friends or communicate with them after the transformation which we call death is no proof that they cease to exist.

Edwin Markham

The few little years we spend on earth are only the first scene in a Divine Drama that extends on into Eternity.

William Wordsworth

> Our birth is but a sleep, and a forgetting;
> The Soul that rises with us, our life's Star,
> Hath had elsewhere its setting,
> And cometh from afar;
> Not in entire forgetfulness,
> And not in utter nakedness,
> But trailing clouds of glory do we come
> From God, who is our home.

TIME AND ETERNITY
Yedaya Penini

God, the source of life, has placed in our nature the blessed hope of immortality, by which we may console ourselves for the vanity of life, and overcome the dread of death. Use thy time as thou wouldst a doubtful companion: extract the good and avoid the evil. Avail thyself of the few opportunities of improvement in his company, and use thy discretion so that thou mayest suffer no injury from thy association with him. And remember that the companionship of time is but of short duration. It flies more quickly than the shades of evening. We are like a child that grasps in his hand a sunbeam. He opens his hand soon again, but, to his amazement, finds it empty and the brightness gone.

HE IS NOT DEAD
Percy Bysshe Shelley
From "Adonais"

Peace, peace! he is not dead, he doth not sleep—
He hath awakened from the dream of life—
'Tis we who, lost in stormy visions, keep
With phantoms an unprofitable strife. . . .
He has outsoared the shadow of our night;
Envy and calumny, and hate and pain,
And that unrest which men miscall delight
Can touch him not, and torture not again. . . .
The One remains, the many change and pass;
Heaven's light forever shines, Earth's shadows fly;
Life, like a dome of many-colored glass,
Stains the white radiance of Eternity.

HEAR THE IMMORTAL SYMPHONIES
Victor Hugo

You say the soul is nothing but the resultant of bodily powers. Why, then, is my soul more luminous when my bodily powers begin to fail? . . . The nearer I approach the end, the plainer I hear around me the immortal symphonies of the worlds which invite me. It is marvelous yet simple. It is a fairy tale and it is a fact.

Charles Mackay

There is no such thing as death.
In nature nothing dies.
From each sad remnant of decay
Some forms of life arise.

THIS EARTH IS BUT THE PROLOGUE
Joshua Loth Liebman

. . . The very reasonableness of the world demands immortality. . . . Nature could not have placed mind in man like a candle to be gutted in a passing wind. The human soul is not a bit player, condemned to say one brief line upon the stage of time and then make a final exit. The Divine Playwright surely could not have written His drama so poorly—prepared all the resplendent scenery of the earth as a prelude to the appearance of the hero, Man, only to permit him the stammering sentence of a brief moment of time— this life—and then make both him and the drama of existence ludicrous by eternal silence. . . .

. . . This earth is but the prologue and many a rich act has been prepared for Man in other worlds. Reason demands it, and morality cries out that our human strivings, for justice, for love, for peace, require some eternal denouement, some immortal stage upon which all the perplexities and inequities of the prologue shall be solved and human destiny find both reconciliation and fulfillment. . . .

George MacDonald

I came from God and I'm going back to God, and I won't have any gaps of death in the middle of my life.

PRAYER IN APRIL
Sarah Henderson Hay

God grant that I may never be
A scoffer at Eternity—
As long as every April brings
The sweet rebirth of growing things;
As long as grass is green anew,
I shall believe that God looks down
Upon his wide earth, cold and brown,
To bless its unborn mystery
Of leaf, and bud, and flower to be;
To smile on it from tender skies—

How could I think it otherwise?
Had I been dust for many a year,
I still would know when Spring was near,
For the good earth that pillowed me
Would whisper immortality,
And I, in part, would rise and sing
Amid the grasses murmuring.
When looking on the mother sod,
Can I doubt that this be God?
Or when a primrose smiles at me,
Can I distrust Eternity?

HIS PROVIDENCE WILL FOLLOW ME
Moses Mendelssohn
From "Phaedon"

As for myself, I am content with the conviction that God's eyes are ever upon me, that His providence and justice will follow me into the future life as it has protected me in this, and that my true happiness consists in the development of the powers of my soul. It is such felicity that awaits me in the life to come. More I do not desire to know.

Cawdray

As he that is to pass over some broad and deep river must not look downward to the current of the stream, but must set his foot sure, and keep his eye on the bank, on the farther shore; so he that draws near death must look over the waves of death, and fix his eye of faith on eternal life.

Max Muller

Without a belief in personal immortality, religion surely is like an arch resting on one pillar, like a bridge ending in an abyss.

TO POETS ALL
Thomas Curtis Clark

We shall not wholly die.
Perhaps some truth

That we have sung
Shall linger on,
And from some tongue
More eloquent
Shall hail the dawn
That we have glimpsed.
Though we be spent,
We shall be well content.

Helen Hunt Jackson

Oh, write of me not "Died in bitter pains"
But "Emigrated to another star!"

LIFE IS EVER LORD OF DEATH

James Greenleaf Whittier
From "Snow-Bound"

Alas for him who never sees
The stars shine through his cypress trees!
Who, hopeless, lays his dead away,
Nor looks to see the breaking day
Across the mournful marbles play!
Who hath not learned, in hours of faith,
The truth to flesh and sense unknown,
That Life is ever lord of Death,
And Love can never lose its own!

Abba Hillel Silver

Death is the peak of a life-wave, and so is birth. Death and birth
are one.

MIND CANNOT BE MORTAL

Cicero

When I consider the wonderful activity of the mind, so great a
memory of what is past, and such a capacity of penetrating into
the future; when I behold such a number of arts and sciences and

such a multitude of discoveries thence arising; I believe and am firmly persuaded that a nature which contains so many things within itself cannot be mortal. . . . But if I err in believing that the souls of men are immortal, I willingly err; nor while I live would I wish to have this delightful error extorted from me; and if after death I shall feel nothing, as some minute philosophers think, I am not afraid lest dead philosophers should laugh at me for the error.

Sir Thomas Browne

There is surely a piece of divinity in us, something that was before the elements, and that owes no homage to the sun.

DEATH, OR LIFE ETERNAL?
Arthur H. Compton

. . . Though it is true that science presents no weighty evidence for life eternal, it is only fair to point out also that science has found no cogent reason for supposing that what is of importance in a man can be buried in a grave. The truth is that science cannot supply a definite answer to this question. Immortality relates to an aspect of life which is not physical, that is, which cannot be detected and measured by any instrument, and to which the application of the laws of science can at best be only a well-considered guess.

If one is to have either a positive faith in a future life or a conviction that death is the end, such beliefs must, it seems to me, be based upon religious, moral, or philosophical grounds rather than upon scientific reasoning. It is primarily to clear the way for such metaphysical thinking that it seems desirable to consider certain scientific aspects of death. Few of us living in the present age would accept a doctrine which is demonstrably contrary to scientific fact or to the spirit of scientific thought. On the other hand, our lives would be exceedingly narrow if we based our thoughts and actions solely on facts that can be subjected to scientific test. Science, that is, erects a foundation on which our emotional and religious life, if it is to be stable, must be built. The strength and form of the foundation, however, by no means determines the architectural merit of the structure that is to be erected. If a belief in immortality is found to be of value to man, it will not be because of any scientific basis on which the belief rests, but because certain important ideals toward which men are striving can be attained only by a more complete life than is possible in the flesh.

Howard Lee McBain

There is no more mystery or miracle or supernaturalness . . . in the wholly unproved fact of immortality than there is in the wholly unexplainable fact of life or in the unimaginable fact of the universe.

'TIS LIFE BEYOND

John Bowring

If in the material world
No atom ever perished—though
In multitudinous changes hurl'd
Upwards and downwards, to and fro;
And all that in the present orb'd,
From silent growth and sudden storms,
Is but a former past absorb'd
In ever-shifting frames and forms—
If He who made the worlds that were,
And makes the worlds that are to be,
Has with all-wise, all-potent care
Preserved the smallest entity
Imperishable—though it pass
From shape to shape, by heat or cold
Dispersed, attracted, monad, mass—
A wind-blown sand, a solid mass—
Shall He not save those nobler things,
Those elements of mind and thought,
Whose marvellous imaginings
Have the great deeds of progress wrought?
Those instincts, be they what they may,
Of which the soul of man is made,
By which he works his wondrous way
Up to the light's very fountain head? . . .
If in the cycle of the earth
No atom of that earth can die—
The soul, which is of nobler birth,
Must live—and live eternally.

LIFE HAS AN OUTLET
Charles Lewis Slattery

The vigor of life on earth is such that we must find ourselves convinced that it has an outlet. If it had no outlet, life here would become choked and heavy. It is no forced analogy to compare such a possible picture of life with the Dead Sea. The Dead Sea receives the waters of the Jordan, but it keeps those waters in its dreary basin, and only the sun takes them away by evaporation. And so that body is sterile, lifeless.

I think, by way of contrast, of the five inland seas of North America. From the enormous Superior, the living water is poured and the falls of Niagara, down through the rapids of the St. Lawrence, through a broadening stream till it reaches the wide Atlantic.

You know the destiny of the waters of Superior and Huron and Michigan and Erie and Ontario because their waters are alive. You know the hopelessness and limitation of the waters of that sea in Palestine because it is dead. When I see the sparkle and the endless hope, in spite of all adversity and calamity, in the countless generation of earth, I know that the waters of our life are not hemmed in by the earthly banks of time, but flow out through that narrow stream, between the rocks on either side, called death, through whatever course I know not, at last into the wide, sunlit sea, called eternal life.

Wisdom of Ben Sira

Have regard to thy name;
For it continueth with thee longer than a thousand great treasures
    of gold.
A good life hath its number of days;
But a good name continueth forever.

THE UNBELIEVABLE
Edwin Markham

Impossible, you say, that man survives
The grave—that there are other lives?
More strange, O friend, that we should ever rise

Out of the dark to walk below these skies.
Once having risen into life and light,
We need not wonder at our deathless flight.
Life is the unbelievable; but now
That this Incredible has taught us how,
We can believe the all-imagining Power
That breathed the Cosmos forth as a golden flower,
Had potence in his breath
To plan us new surprises beyond death—
New spaces and new goals
For the adventure of ascending souls.
Be brave, O heart, be brave:
It is not strange that man survives the grave:
'Twould be a stranger thing were he destroyed
Than that he ever vaulted from the void.

Proverbs

In the way of righteousness is life, and in the pathway thereof
there is no death.

DIVINE RHYTHM

Henry Meade Bland

Clouds, then the glory of sunset;
Darkness, then burst of the morn;
Dearth, then the gentle shower;
Sacrifice—Truth is born!
The earth-throe, then comes the harvest;
Silence, and then the word;
Mist, before the full starlight;
Discord, ere music is heard!
Erring, and then the forgiveness;
Heart's-ease after the strife;
Passion, and then the refining—
Death, then the wonder of life!

I WILL BE AS MUCH ALIVE
Israel Davidson

To those who will study my books a hundred years hence, I will be as much alive then as I was to those who studied them yesterday. So please do not mourn. . . . Glorified be the spirit—the pure spirit.

KINGSLEY'S EPITAPH

The epitaph over Charles Kingsley's grave consists of three Latin words which he chose: "Amavimus. Amamus. Amabimus." (We have loved. We love. We shall love.)

THERE IS NO REAL DEATH
Wilfred Thomason Grenfell

It has been my lot in life to have to stand by many deathbeds, and to be called in to dying men and women almost as a routine in my profession. Yet I am increasingly convinced their spirits never die at all. I am sure that there is no real death. Death is no argument against, but rather for, life. Eternal life is the complement of all my unsatisfied ideals; and experience teaches me that the belief in it is a greater incentive to be useful and good than any other I know. . . .

Immortality may be the complement of mortality as water becomes steam and steam becomes power, and power becomes heat and heat becomes light. The conclusion that life beyond is the conservation of energy of life here may be as scientific as the great natural laws for material things. I see Knowledge become Service, Service become Joy. . . . (I have seen) hope bring back color to the face and tone to the blood. . . . I have seen love do physical things which mere intellectual convictions cannot. . . . I prefer to stand with Moses in his belief in the Promised Land and that we can reach it. . . .

Herman Melville
Life is a voyage that's homeward bound.

I CANNOT SUSPECT THE ANNIHILATION OF SOULS

Benjamin Franklin

. . . When I see nothing annihilated and not even a drop of water wasted, I cannot suspect the annihilation of souls, or believe that He will suffer the daily waste of millions of minds ready made that now exist and put Himself to the continual trouble of making new ones. Thus finding myself to exist in the world, I believe I shall, in some shape or other, always exist; and, with all the inconveniences human life is liable to, I shall not object to a new edition of mine; hoping, however, that the errata of the last may be corrected.

Ralph Waldo Emerson

The blazing evidence of immortality is our dissatisfaction with any other conclusion.

DEATH IS ONLY A NEW BEGINNING

J. H. Jowett

Death is not the end; it is only a new beginning. Death is not the master of the house; he is only the porter at the King's lodge, appointed to open the gate and let the King's guests into the realm of eternal day. And so shall we ever be with the Lord. The range of our threescore years and ten is not the limit of our life. Our life is not a land-locked lake enclosed within the shore lines of seventy years. It is an arm of the sea. And so we must build for those larger waters. We are immortal!

Ecclesiastes

Before the silver cord is snapped asunder,
And the golden bowl is shattered,
And the pitcher is broken at the fountain,
And the wheel falleth shattered into the pit;
And the dust returneth to the earth as it was,
And the spirit returneth unto God who gave it.

FROM "THERE IS NO DEATH"

John Luckey McCreery

There is no death! The stars go down
To rise upon some fairer shore;
And bright, in heaven's jeweled crown,
They shine for evermore.

There is no death! The dust we tread
Shall change beneath the summer showers
To golden grain or mellow fruit,
Of rainbow-tinted flowers.

There is no death! The leaves may fall,
And flowers may fade and pass away;
They only wait through wintry hours
The coming of May-day

There is no death! An angel-form
Walks o'er the earth with silent tread;
And bears our best-beloved things away,
And then we call them "dead."

He leaves our hearts all desolate,
He plucks our fairest, sweetest flowers;
Transplanted into bliss, they now
Adorn immortal bowers.

And ever near us, though unseen,
The dear immortal spirits tread;
For all the boundless universe
Is life—there are no dead!

THE ROSE STILL GROWS BEYOND
THE WALL

A. L. Frank

Near a shady wall a rose once grew,
Budded and blossomed in God's free light,

Watered and fed by morning dew,
   Shedding its sweetness day and night.

As it grew and blossomed fair and tall,
   Slowly rising to loftier height,
It came to a crevice in the wall,
   Through which there shone a beam of light.

Onward it crept with added strength,
   With never a thought of fear or pride.
It followed the light through the crevice's length
   And unfolded itself on the other side.

The light, the dew, the broadening view
   Were found the same as they were before;
And it lost itself in beauties new,
   Breathing its fragrance more and more.

Shall claims of death cause us to grieve,
   And make our courage faint or fail?
Nay! Let us faith and hope receive:
   The rose still grows beyond the wall.

Scattering fragrance far and wide,
   Just as it did in days of yore,
Just as it did on the other side,
   Just as it will forevermore.

The Kotzker Zaddik

Death is merely moving from one home to another. If we are wise, we seek to regard the latter as the abode of beauty.

CONCERNING IMMORTALITY
Adelaide Love

Freely He lets us look upon some pages,
Bidding us read as best we can the preface.
Over and over we ponder words and phrases,
Slow to interpret.

Just as the meanings grow a little clearer
And the eager mind would turn to the coming chapters,

Would any God exclaim: "Here endeth the lesson!"
Closing the volume?

BACK HOME

May Williams Ward

To live is to go on a journey,
To die is to come back home.
My shoe-soles are thin with wandering,
Sticky with clay and loam;
There are marks of stones and of brambles,
The leather is scuffed and torn,
And I must not have walked quite straight, I think,
For the heels are unevenly worn.
I shall take off my shoes, and sleep, and rest . . .
If I dream, shall I dream that I roam?
To live is to go on a journey.
To die is to come back home.

TURNING THE CORNER

Arthur B. Rhinow

I often saw you
When I turned the corner
Into your street.

A while ago I followed you
As you bent to meet the storm
Along the one-way street.
And then you turned the corner
Where the shadows lie,
And I lost sight of you.

And I must still go on,
But when I turn the corner
I hope to see you again.

Proverbs

A good man leaveth an inheritance to his children's children

'Tis well to learn that sunny hours
May quickly change to mournful shade;
'Tis well to prize life's scattered flowers
Yet be prepared to see them fade.

—Eliza Cook

TO HOLD WITH OPEN ARMS

The closing chapter of this book represents a departure from the pattern followed by all the preceding ones. It does not contain brief excerpts from a variety of sources on a central theme. Instead it presents a slightly condensed version of a single, sustained development of a basic thought by one author—Milton Steinberg. This is not a chance occurrence.

In the opinion of the editor, Steinberg's inexhaustible human compassion has combined with his penetrating brilliance to frame a message of abiding worth. As a prescription for a mature appreciation of life and a courageous acceptance of death it is unexcelled. Here out of the stubborn substance of his own tribulation he has chiseled a work of uncommon spiritual art and literary beauty. Like Job, he saw God out of his own flesh.

The message was first spoken as a sermon to his congregation at the Park Avenue Synagogue in New York City. Too soon thereafter it was to become a source of solace and comfort to a bereaved family and an impoverished Jewish community when Milton Steinberg's noble heart stopped beating at the untimely age of forty-six.

TO HOLD WITH OPEN ARMS

Milton Steinberg

There are texts in us, in our commonplace experiences, if only we are wise enough to discern them.

272

One such experience fell to my lot not so long ago. There was nothing dramatic about its setting nor unusual in its circumstances. And yet to me it was moment of discovery, almost of revelation.

Let me recount it very briefly, as befits a text. After a long illness, I was permitted for the first time to step out of doors. And, as I crossed the threshold, sunlight greeted me. This is my experience—all there is to it. And yet, so long as I live, I shall never forget that moment. It was mid-January—a time of cold and storm up north, but in Texas, where I happened to be, a season much like our spring. The sky overhead was very blue, very clear, and very, very high. A faint wind blew from off the western plains, cool and yet somehow tinged with warmth—like a dry, chilled wine. And everywhere in the firmament above me, in the great vault between earth and sky, on the pavements, the buildings—the golden glow of the sunlight. It touched me, too, with friendship, with warmth, with blessing. And as I basked in its glory, there ran through my mind those wonder words of the prophet about the sun which some day shall rise with healing on its wings.

In that instant I looked about me to see whether anyone else showed on his face the joy, almost the beatitude, I felt. But no, there they walked—men and women and children, in the glory of a golden flood, and so far as I could detect, there was none to give it heed. And then I remembered how often I, too, had been indifferent to sunlight, how often, preoccupied with petty and sometimes mean concerns, I had disregarded it. And I said to myself—how precious is the sunlight but, alas, how careless of it are men. How precious—how careless. This has been a refrain sounding in me ever since.

It rang in my spirit when I entered my own home again after months of absence, when I heard from a nearby room the excited voices of my children at play; when I looked once more on the dear faces of some of my friends; when I was able for the first time to speak again from my pulpit in the name of our faith and tradition, to join in worship of the God who gives us so much of which we are so careless.

And a resolution crystallized within me. I said to myself that at the very first opportunity I would speak of this. I knew full well that it is a commonplace truth, that there is nothing clever about my private rediscovery of it, nothing ingenious about my way of putting it. But I was not interested in being original or clever or ingenious. I wanted only to remind my listeners, as I was reminded, to spend life wisely, not to squander it.

I wanted to say to the husbands and wives who love one another: "How precious is your lot in that it is one of love. Do not be, even for a moment, casual with your good fortune. Love one another while yet you may."

And to parents: "How precious is the gift of your children. Never, never be too busy for the wonder and miracle of them. They will be grown up soon enough and grown away, too."

We human beings, we frail reeds who are yet, as Pascal said, thinking reeds, feeling reeds, how precious are our endowments—minds to know, eyes to see, ears to listen, hearts to stir with pity, and to dream of justice and of a perfected world. How often are we indifferent to all these!

And we who are Jews and Americans, heirs of two great traditions, how fortunate our lot in both, and how blind we are to our double good fortune.

This is what struggled in me for utterance—as it struggled in Edna St. Vincent Millay when she cried out:

"O world I cannot hold thee close enough."

I want to urge myself and all others to hold the world tight—to embrace life with all our hearts and all our souls and all our might. For it is precious, ineffably precious, and we are careless, wantonly careless of it.

And yet, when I first resolved to express all this, I knew that it was only a half-truth.

Could I have retained the sunlight no matter how hard I tried? Could I have prevented the sun from setting? Could I have kept even my own eyes from becoming satiated and bored with the glory of the day? That moment had to slip away. And had I tried to hold on to it, what would I have achieved? It would have gone from me in any case. And I would have been left disconsolate, embittered, convinced that I had been cheated.

But it is not only the sunlight that must slip away—our youth goes also, our years, our children, our senses, our lives. This is the nature of things, an inevitability. And the sooner we make our peace with it the better. Did I urge myself a moment ago to hold on? I would have done better, it now begins to appear, to have preached the opposite doctrine of letting go—the doctrine of Socrates who called life a "peisithanatos"—a persuader of death, a teacher of the art of relinquishing. It was the doctrine of Goethe who said: *Entsagen sollst, du sollst entsagen*"—"Thou shalt renounce." And it was the doctrine of the ancient rabbis who despite their love of life said: He who would die let him hold on to life.

It is a sound doctrine.

First, because, as we have just seen, it makes peace with inevitability. And the inevitable is something with which everyone should be at peace. Second, because nothing can be more grotesque and more undignified than a futile attempt to hold on.

Let us think of the men and women who cannot grow old gracefully because they cling too hard to a youth that is escaping them; of the parents who cannot let their children go free to live their own lives; of the people who in times of general calamity have only themselves in mind.

What is it that drives people to such unseemly conduct, to such flagrant selfishness except the attitude which I have just commended—a vigorous holding on to life? Besides, are there not times when one ought to hold life cheap, as something to be lightly surrendered? In defense of one's country, for example, in the service of truth, justice, and mercy, in the advancement of mankind?

This, then, is the great truth of human existence. One must not hold life too precious. One must always be prepared to let it go.

And now we are indeed confused. First we learn that life is a privilege—cling to it! Then we are instructed: Thou shalt renounce!

A paradox, and self-contradiction! But neither the paradox nor the contradiction are of my making. They are a law written into the scheme of things—that a man must hold his existence dear and cheap at the same time.

Is it not, then, an impossible assignment to which destiny has set us? It does not ask of us that we hold life dear at one moment, and cheap at the next, but that we do both simultaneously. Now I can grasp something in my fist or let my hand lie open. I can clasp it to my breast or hold it at arm's length. I can embrace it, enfolding it in my arms, or let my arms hang loose. But how can I be expected to do both at once?

To which the answer is: With your body, of course not. But with your spirit, why not?

Is one not forever doing paradoxical and mutually contradictory things in his soul?

One wears his mind out in study, and yet has more mind with which to study. One gives away his heart in love and yet has more heart to give away. One perishes out of pity for a suffering world, and is the stronger therefor.

So, too, it is possible at one and the same time to hold on to life and let it go, provided—well, let me put it this way:

We are involved in a tug of war: Here, on the left, is the necessity to renounce life and all it contains. Here, on the right, the yearning to affirm it and its experiences. And between these two is a terrible tension, for they pull in opposite directions.

But suppose that here in the center I introduce a third force, one that lifts upward. My two irreconcilables now swing together, both pulling down against the new element. And the harder they pull, the closer together they come.

God is the third element, that new force that resolves the terrible contradiction, the intolerable tension of life.

And for this purpose it does not especially matter how we conceive God. I have been a great zealot for a mature idea of God. I have urged again and again that we think through our theology, not limping along on a child's notion of God as an old man in the sky. But for my immediate purpose, all of this is irrelevant. What is relevant is this: that so soon as a man believes in God, so soon indeed as he wills to believe in Him, the terrible strain is eased; nay, it disappears, and that for two reasons.

In the first place, because a new and higher purpose is introduced into life, the purpose of doing the will of God, to put it in Jewish terms, of performing the "Mitzvoth." This now becomes the reason for our existence. We are soldiers whose commander has stationed them at a post. How we like our assignment, whether we feel inclined to cling to it, or to let it go, is an irrelevant issue. Our hands are too busy with our duties to be either embracing the world or pushing it away.

That is why it is written: "Make thy will conform to His, then His will be thine, and all things will be as thou desirest."

But that, it might be urged, only evades the problem. By concentrating on duty we forget the conflicting drives within ourselves. The truth is, however, that, given God, the problem is solved not only by evasion but directly; that it is solved, curiously enough, by being made more intense. For, given God, everything becomes more precious, more to be loved and clung to, more embraceable; and yet at the same time easier to give up.

Given God, everything becomes more precious.

That sunshine in Dallas was not a chance effect, a lucky accident. It was an effect created by a great Artist, the Master Painter of Eternity. And because it came from God's brush it is more valuable even than I had at first conceived.

And the laughter of children, precious in itself, becomes infinitely more precious because the joy of the cosmos is in it.

And the sweetness of our friends' faces is dearer because these are fragments of an infinite sweetness.

All of life is the more treasurable because a great and Holy Spirit is in it.

And yet, it is easier for me to let go.

For these things are not and never have been mine. They belong to the Universe and the God who stands behind it. True, I have been privileged to enjoy them for an hour but they were always a loan due to be recalled.

And I let go of them the more easily because I know that as parts of the divine economy they will not be lost. The sunset, the bird's song, the baby's smile, the thunder of music, the surge of great poetry, the dreams of the heart, and my own being, dear to me as every man's is to him, all these I can well trust to Him who made them. There is poignancy and regret about giving them up, but no anxiety. When they slip from my hands they will pass to hands better, stronger, and wiser than mine.

This then is the insight which came to me as I stood some months ago in a blaze of sunlight: Life is dear, let us then hold it tight while we yet may; but we must hold it loosely also!

And only with God can we ease the intolerable tension of our existence. For only when He is given, can we hold life at once infinitely precious and yet as a thing lightly to be surrendered. Only because of Him is it made possible for us to clasp the world, but with relaxed hands; to embrace it, but with open arms.

A TREASURY OF THE ART OF LIVING

by Rabbi Sidney Greenberg
foreword by Harry Golden

A TREASURY OF THE ART OF LIVING is divided into 86 themes and the quotations have each been artfully woven into a basic theme of life so that they each appeal like so many sparkling jewels set into a crown.

Living as an Art
Reflection on Age
The Art of Using Time

The Quest for Happiness
The Art of Contentment
The Measure of Wealth

The Art of Aspiration
The Goals of Life
The Art of Building Character
The Art of Discontent

The Art of Succeeding
In Praise of Humility
The Art of Speaking Gently
The Greatness of Little Things
The Art of Seeing
The Blessing of Work

The Grandeur of Man
The Art of Looking Within
The Art of Self-Control
The Art of Independence

The Art of Building a Home
The Art of Being Parents

The Art of Living Together
A Touch of Kindness
The Art of Caring
A Touch of Courtesy
The Blessing of Friendship
In Praise of Praise
Pathways to Peace

Art and Beauty
Treasures in Books
The Light of Learning
The Art of Teaching
The Art of Progress

My Country 'Tis of Thee
Freedom's Holy Light

The Uses of Adversity
The Blessing of Hope
Patience and Perseverance
Death and Beyond

What Is Religion?
Pathways to God
Words and Deeds
Conscience — The Still Small Voice
The Grateful Mood

The Measure of a Man
The Art of Remembering and Forgetting
The Marks of Greatness

The Joy of Living
The Art of Laughter
The Perils of Wealth and Poverty

Dreams and the Dreamer
The Art of Growing Up
As a Man Thinketh
Creeds to Live By

The Art of Mastering Fate
The Power of the Spirit
The Eloquent Silence
The Art of Performing Our Duty
The High Cost of Worrying

The Art of Choosing
To Thine Own Self Be True
The Art of Judging Ourselves
The Power of Truth

The Gifts of Love
Mothers of Men

The Art of Giving
The Quality of Mercy
The Art of Forgiving
The Art of Judging Others
Justice, Justice Shall Thou Pursue
The Curse of War

Music Hath Charms
The Book of Books
The Art of Using the Past
What Is Wisdom?

The Idea of Democracy
In Praise of Tolerance

The Art of Facing Sorrow
The Meaning of Courage
The Art of Failing

The Art of Believing
Man and God
Reward and Punishment
The Reverent Mood
The Search for Meaning

384 Pages . . . $6.00 postpaid
Available from Wilshire Book Company
12015 Sherman Road, No. Hollywood, California 91605